INDEPENDENT
FILM
PRODUCING

INDEPENDENT
FILM
PRODUCING

HOW TO PRODUCE A LOW-BUDGET FEATURE FILM

PAUL BATTISTA

ALLWORTH PRESS
NEW YORK

Allworth Press books may be purchased in bulk at special discounts for sales promotion, corporate gifts, fund-raising, or educational purposes. Special editions can also be created to specifications. For details, contact the Special Sales Department, Allworth Press, 307 West 36th Street, 11th Floor, New York, NY 10018 or info@skyhorsepublishing.com.

17 16 15 14 13 5 4 3 2

Published by Allworth Press, an imprint of Skyhorse Publishing, Inc.
307 West 36th Street, 11th Floor, New York, NY 10018.

Allworth Press® is a registered trademark of Skyhorse Publishing, Inc.®, a Delaware corporation.

www.allworth.com

Cover and interior design by Mary Belibasakis
Cover based on a design by George Foster

Library of Congress Cataloging-in-Publication Data is available on file
ISBN: 978-1-62153-264-4

Printed in the United States of America

Praise for
Independent Film Producing:
How to Produce a Low-Budget Feature Film

"Pick a page, any page, Paul Battista's book is more than just 'Hollywood for Dummies.' If ever there was a book where all the possible answers are given away, this invaluable manual is like having a good lawyer, Yoda, and a .44 magnum guiding you through the jungle known as the Movie Business."
—Adam Novak / William Morris Endeavor

"Although it's nearly impossible even trying to get an independent film made, you must read this book, it's that good!"
—Joe Boucher, Emmy Award-Winning Producer, *King of the Hill* and the *Simpsons*; writer of the well-regarded feature scripts *King of Spring* and *Dude: The Legend*; aspiring filmmaker

"Without Paul Battista's book, I'd still be an 'outsider' sitting on the sidelines with a script and a pipe dream of making a film. Paul's instructive, straightforward language and well-organized content simplifies the process and outlines the steps necessary to produce an independent film. Step #1: Buy this book and hire a knowledgeable entertainment attorney!"
—Bob Heske, Writer/Producer of the film *Blessid*; writer/creator of the comic horror anthology *Cold Blooded Chillers* and the graphic novel *The Night Projectionist*

"When producing your first indie film, you are only as good as your resources. As his client, Paul provided me clarity on the ever-shifting business of film. A straight shooter, he poured his experience and perspective into this guide. No matter how limited or extensive your knowledge base is, this book will fill in the blanks."
—Dennis Dortch, Writer, Director, Producer, *A Good Day to Be Black & Sexy*, 2008 Sundance Film Festival, Official Selection, 2008 IFP Gotham Independent Film Awards Nominee for *Breakthrough Director*

"Perhaps the most practical resource available for first time producers who desire to tackle independent film's most challenging business elements. Like a canteen to the hiker, this book is a practical empowerment guide that belongs in every prudent producer's backpack."

—Steven C. Beer, Film Attorney and Producer's Representative

"As graduates of the Peter Stark Producing Program, we have read just about every book there is on filmmaking and producing. While most of them have fabulous anecdotes from established producers, few give such a comprehensive overview as well as specifics about what it actually takes to make your first independent film. This book provides thorough and precise advice and is a must read for all aspiring and established indie producers."

—Oscar Eugenio Guido and Rebecca L. Brown, Producers Stylopik, LLC

"This book is a must for filmmakers on all levels—beginners and veterans. It is a thorough look at the complete process from a practical perspective with real world experiences."

—Doug Deluca, Co-Executive Producer, *Jimmy Kimmel Live*

"One of the most lucid and entertaining books out there. Paul knows his stuff, and he wants you to, also. Anecdotes, hard core info—the whole shot. His new sections on crowdfunding are timely and brilliant."

—Eric Sherman, Author, Filmmaker, Educator, Private Filmmaking Consultant, Film and Entertainment Industry Consultant

"This is a terrific book for anyone with any level of experience in the film business—very practical, realistic and authoritative."

—Jeffrey Schwarz, Producer, *Spine Tingler! The William Castle Story* **and** *Wrangler: Anatomy of an Icon*

"In the book Paul digs into the details essential to getting a sellable film done and to the marketplace. Only an experienced entertainment attorney currently in the fray of the indie production wars can write with such authority, and Paul has ten years on the front lines, which he brings to the book. In the book he breaks down the producing process step by step and explains from experience the problems that will be faced and how to do things the right way."

—Ted Betz, Writer, Director, Producer, *The Unbreakable Sword*

"This book will open the eyes of filmmakers to the minefield of legal issues and production decisions that can create liability for the production or destroy the profitability of their films. I will carry this book in my computer bag from start to finish on our next project."

—Tom Lockridge, Producer and Co-Writer, *Unrequited*; **President and Co-Founder of Lucky Day Studios, LLC**

"As a client of Paul's for many years, I know that he gives you the facts in an industry that's made a business of selling the fiction. I recommend any person thinking about making a feature film to read this book before they begin."
—Nicholas Tana, Writer, Director, Producer, *Sticky: A Documentary on Masturbation*

"As a filmmaker it's so important to be able to merge art with business. Your project has less of a chance to succeed without the understanding that there is more to your film than the creative aspects. Any first, second, or even third time filmmaker should have this book at their disposal so they can have a real solid framework of what to do from raising money to signing a distribution deal."
—Carl T. Evans, Writer, Director, Producer, *Criticsized, Frame of Mind,* **and** *Walking on the Sky*

"This book has been instrumental to me as a producer and a director, providing much needed guidance in a business that lacks a clear path to success. Paul's experience on the legal and business end of independent film producing sheds light on the common mistakes that many beginning filmmakers tend to make. Thereby, allowing you the reader to eliminate such common issues and to enjoy a much smoother production process!"
—Chris Sheng, Writer, Director, Producer, *Knock Knock 2*

"Paul Battista, attorney extraordinaire and author of this invaluable handbook, knows more about indie filmmaking than anyone I know. Every quarter when I teach 'Low-Budget Filmmaking' at UCLA Extension, I beg Paul to be a guest speaker because he's incredibly generous with his extensive knowledge."
—Kim Adelman, Writer, *Making it Big in Shorts: The Ultimate Filmmakers Guide To Short Films***; Instructor, Low-Budget Filmmaking, UCLA Extension**

"As an attorney, Paul has consistently helped filmmakers understand the nuanced relationship between creativity and practicality. His book exudes this spirit of guidance on every page, and should be required reading for anyone hoping to not only make independent films, but make them the right way."
—Stu Pollard, Producer, *Nice Guys Sleep Alone, Keep Your Distance, Ira & Abby, True Adolescents,* **and** *Dirty Country*

"Paul's book is a clear and practical map to build a strong foundation to a film production, on which a filmmaker can comfortably focus his efforts on the many creative challenges, confidently knowing his back is covered legally."
—Sam Bozzo, Writer/Director/Producer, *Blue Gold: World Water Wars***; Writer/Producer,** *Sweet & Sour*

Acknowledgments

I would like to acknowledge and thank my wife, Leah, without whose support and encouragement this book would not exist. I would also like to acknowledge and thank my parents, Carmine and Antoinette, for their support and encouragement. I would especially like to thank my father who provided thoughtful editing of the numerous drafts of the manuscript. His humor, focus, and talent made the tedious editing process an enjoyable experience in addition to making the final manuscript much better than the original.

Contents

PART II: PRODUCING THE FILM

PART III: DISTRIBUTING THE FILM

Introduction

There is much to learn about the process of making a low-budget film, but let me begin by dispelling the prevailing sentiment that seems to be drummed into the head of the novice feature filmmaker in most books written on making an independent film, that is, that *filmmaking is a business*. Filmmaking is not a business; it is an art form. It is no less an art form than painting, sculpting, or writing poetry or a novel. If you approach the making of your low-budget film solely from a business perspective you will fail for the simple reason that you will not be able to compete for an audience on an economic level. Your only chance for success is to compete on an artistic level because there really is little competition on this level at present. After saying this let me also say that whereas filmmaking is an art form, distribution is definitely a business and it behooves a feature filmmaker never to forget that. The major, minor, and "independent" studios are first and foremost distribution companies with filmmaking as an afterthought. It is also wise to think of domestic and international distributors as "studios" as well since they function more or less on the same model as studios. That *is* the "business," and there is nothing *independent* about any aspect of it. If you are looking to play in their schoolyard, then this book is probably not for you.

But, if you feel a compulsion to express something, which you believe has value, and have chosen film as your medium, then this book may be useful in helping you achieve that goal. And if you are successful in achieving that goal you may indeed find yourself in the position to enter the "business" on your own terms. A feature film of between eighty and one hundred and twenty minutes can be created for several hundred thousand dollars or for as little as thirty thousand dollars and receive critical acclaim. It is not easy, but it was my intention, after dealing with many aspiring independent filmmakers, to write this book to help filmmakers in that process. We are entering a new age in filmmaking in both technological and institutional innovation. The emerging digital age—and I use the word emerging advisedly, since the greatest breakthroughs are still on the horizon—will offer unique opportunities for the truly "independent" filmmaker. Even in the distribution business where the "independent" filmmaker is presently locked out, new channels will emerge. For example, there is no reason why websites might not emerge with unique facilities for the submission of films for view in a category promoted as "made for under $100,000" or something like that. The goal of this book is to help guide a relatively inexperienced, low-budget independent filmmaker through the technical and legal maze which has the potential to stymie his or her creative effort.

In the course of my practice as an entertainment and tax attorney I have had the pleasure of interviewing and working with many film clients striving to produce their first feature film, including writers, actors and directors of both commercials and short films. They have all had two things in common—enthusiasm and a basic lack of knowledge of the process of producing a low-budget feature film. This book is a concise digest of those hundreds of hours of counsel and advice, and is designed to give the independent filmmaker the best chance to bring a low-budget feature film project to a successful conclusion.

The projects that my clients have made range from a $65,000 film screened at a top United States film festival to a $6 million film distributed by a major studio, and everywhere in between. In the context of my relationships with my clients, especially those making their first film, I found myself consistently going over the same issues; I naturally address the legal issues in this context, but I rarely have had the chance to provide information regarding nonlegal aspects of the process. By nonlegal I mean the knowledge that I have garnered while working with my clients during their filmmaking process, as well as from my personal experience as a low-budget independent filmmaker in making the feature film *Crooks*. This book will explore the major legal, business, and creative issues in the independent filmmaking process with the aim of educating filmmakers so they will be able to approach their low-budget project with a sound and realistic understanding of the process, and be better able to interact with the professionals upon whom they will need to depend to achieve a successful outcome.

A first principle in making a film is the recruitment of a team. It has been said often, but worth repeating now, that the presence or absence of an effective team will determine whether or not a film project will be brought to a successful completion. This principle is the same whether the film is a low-budget first time effort or a $100 million project. The only difference is that the $100 million producer has sufficient funds to purchase any and all talent necessary for the project, whereas the low-budget producer does not. However, the low-budget filmmaker always has some money, so the key questions to be answered are: 1) How should the limited money be expended to maximize potential success?; and 2) When should it be spent? But the first principle of team building is still the critical one. The core of the filmmaking team, upon which all future members will rely, consists of the filmmaker/director, the producer, and the attorney. Without three separate people acting in each of these capacities it will be difficult to complete the film, and even if it is completed there will be technical and legal problems that will effectively preclude the film's distribution, unless the filmmaker obtains more money to overcome those obstacles. Even having the right core team is not a guarantee that a completed film will find distribution. There is no accounting for which films will find market acceptance. It is wise to remember that a majority of Hollywood films are not successful. Hollywood approaches the process by simply spending as much money as needed when a problem arises. The major film companies spend an average of $106 million to make and market *each* movie that they theatrically release. Their business model is to spend so much money so as to capture the lion's share of the movie going audience, and to create a cultural milieu which makes such films the only product worth the ten to fifteen dollar price tag for admission, and, thereby, effectively driving out any competition. To a large degree their model has worked. These developments have had important implications for the low-budget feature filmmaker. The most important implication, which will be a common thread running through each of the topics contained in this book, is that whereas the major studios no longer seem concerned about the costs of making their movies, the low-budget filmmaker must be obsessed with it. There are hundreds of items necessary in making a film, and not having millions of dollars at his or her disposal, the low-budget filmmaker must be obsessed with knowing what things should cost and when money should be spent for those things. Most importantly, it is critical to know which things in the original plan are essential to the film's success and which things are expendable—in other words, what to hold and what to fold. There is, however, no escaping the fact that it does cost money to bring off even a low-cost feature film. From my experience in counseling low-budget filmmaker clients, and my own personal experience in making a feature film, I can say that for a film to be competitive in the marketplace it will take between fifty and two hundred and fifty thousand dollars. There are distributors who will distribute a low-budget film, but there is a certain threshold of expected quality which will make it acceptable to this highly competitive market, and the key is money. Maximizing the quality of the film will come from spending the small amount of money available to the average low-budget filmmaker where it will absolutely do the most good. The object is to make the money spent on the screen appear as three to five times what was actually spent. Each chapter in this book will have this as its underlying theme.

There are times when the low-budget filmmaker can successfully parlay the elements gathered at the beginning of the process of producing the film into a larger budgeted project. Such good fortune as attaching a "name" talent to the film or securing product placement commitments or obtaining increased financial backing is always possible. However, this process would require established film companies such as foreign sales agents, major or mini-major distributors, talent agents, talent managers, and lending institutions to become committed to the project. Throughout the book I will address the issues and guidelines for working with these established players as they relate to the low-budget filmmaking process. Further, the overall process and some of the issues involved when financing an independent film with players "inside the system" are addressed by attorney Michael Blaha in Chapter 6. Obviously, a bigger budget film can be a better opportunity for the low-budget filmmaker because of the experience gained by working on a larger canvas and the prestige acquired by working with established film entities. However, it must always be kept in mind that this process involves many more moving parts and generally requires the filmmaker to relinquish control over creative and business decision making in order for the film to move forward. Although the stated goal of this book is primarily aimed at examining the issues involved in making a $50,000 to $1 million film, I have included, as appropriate, information relating to larger budgeted films, since even a low-budget filmmaker should be prepared to make carefully calculated decisions in the event he or she is presented with this opportunity.

Legal information is provided and discussed throughout the book in order to help educate the reader regarding the issues involved in the process of producing a low-budget feature film. It should be noted that the facts specific to any situation in which the reader will find himself or herself will be unique and different from the facts presented in this book, thereby making any parallel conclusions to the reader's specific circumstances inaccurate. Legal information presented in the book is generally based on federal law, California state law and New York state law. Many of the nuances of the legal issues and processes are omitted for sake of clarity and brevity. Further, the reader may be subject to laws different from the federal and state laws presented in this book. In addition, the law is dynamic and is changing daily, and the legal information presented at the date of publication of this book will not be updated until a subsequent edition is published. **THEREFORE, I MUST POINT OUT THAT THE READER SHOULD NOT RELY ON THE LEGAL INFORMATION PRESENTED IN THIS BOOK TO ANSWER HIS OR HER SPECIFIC LEGAL QUESTIONS NOR RELY ON THE ACCURACY OF SUCH INFORMATION; RATHER THE**

READER SHOULD ENGAGE THE SERVICES OF QUALIFIED, EXPERIENCED LEGAL COUNSEL.

It should also be noted that technological developments have empowered the low-budget feature filmmaker and are changing the means of distribution almost on a daily basis. My hope is that this book will provide the low-budget feature filmmaker information that translates into more efficient, effective decision making in the process of making his or her film. As someone who has made a low-budget feature film, I can confidently say that in spite of the daunting challenges there are few endeavors that are as rewarding as making your first feature film. I wish you all the best in your journey.

PART I

Developing the Film

1

Overview

"Remember, there's always work at the post office."
—Hollywood Shuffle

FEATURE FILMS

From the perspective of the low-budget filmmaker, it is important to differentiate between a feature film and a short film. A feature film is defined by its length; generally, films of eighty minutes or longer are considered feature films. Over the years the major studios have released a number of films that have had a running time of less than eighty minutes which were, nevertheless, still considered feature films. The point is that the market expects a feature film to be at least eighty minutes long, so, once it has been decided to make a feature film, based on audience expectations, a decision to make an eighty minute film has also been reached. Many low-budget filmmakers try to avoid allowing business aspects to affect their creative decision-making process, and this is how it should be, but choosing to make a feature film is also an economic choice, and the length that the market has determined for a feature film is between eighty and one hundred and twenty minutes. This is purely a market driven fact, and not an artistic one. If a film is less than eighty minutes, the audience will tend to feel it is not

3

receiving fair value for their purchase. A running time of over two hours, on the other hand, pushes the audience's attention span beyond its comfort zone, and can be as much of a negative for the distribution of a film as is a film of less than eighty minutes.

These are guidelines and not absolute rules, but successful films that have deviated from these norms are the exceptions to the rule. Furthermore, the norms for film length can be further classified according to genre. Comedies tend to run between eighty and ninety-five minutes. For example, *Thirty Minutes or Less* runs eighty-three minutes, *Our Idiot Brother* runs ninety minutes, *Due Date* runs ninety-five minutes and *The Dictator* runs eighty-three minutes. On the other end of the spectrum, dramas and epics can run more than two hours. *The Pirates of the Caribbean: On Stranger Tides* runs one hundred and thirty-six minutes, *A Beautiful Mind* runs one hundred and thirty-five minutes, *The Tree of Life* runs one hundred and thirty-nine minutes and *Star Wars III: Revenge of the Sith* runs one hundred and forty minutes. Other aspects of the importance of genre in filmmaking will be discussed in detail in Chapter 3. At this point it is important to take note of how Hollywood follows (and establishes) the rules regarding the running time of movies. Even if not making a Hollywood film, it is important to be mindful of the fact that a potential audience has been conditioned to believe that certain films are going to be of a predictable length, and that over time audiences have tended to have an attention span based on the genre of the movie. A filmmaker, and especially a low-budget filmmaker, had better have very sound reasons for violating these norms, and should carefully weigh the perils of such a decision, preferably with objective third party consultation.

HOLLYWOOD

Of the 677 new films released theatrically in 2012, 128 were released by companies that are members of the Motion Picture Association of America (MPAA), and 549 by non-MPAA-affiliated independent companies. Over one billion, three hundred million tickets were sold at the US/Canada box office generating over $10 billion, $800 million in revenue. The MPAA has discontinued reporting the average costs of producing and distributing movies, but its last report of these costs stated that in 2007 the average cost of making a movie for companies that are members of the MPAA was over $106 million. It cost an average of $70 million to make the movie and $36 million to advertise it and make prints for the theaters. The philosophy of the Hollywood system is to make larger films with bigger stars and cutting-edge special effects and then spend large amounts on advertising to make movie-going a spectacle event.

In an address at ShowWest in 2002, then MPAA president Jack Valenti pointed out that "theatrical admissions were more than professional baseball, football, basketball and hockey combined in 2002." The MPAA enlarged on this point in 2012 when it stated that "movie theaters continue to draw more people than all theme parks and major US sports combined." Mr. Valenti and the MPAA were more than simply making the point that going to a movie is more popular than theme parks and athletic events. The clear implication to be taken from identifying theme parks and athletic events as movies' competition is that films are supposed to match up with the thrill of Disneyland, or watching LeBron James, Kobe Bryant, Kevin Durant, and Dwyane Wade compete for the NBA championship, or watching the Superbowl. It behooves the low-budget feature filmmaker seeking distribution for his or her product to take this observation very seriously.

The escalating cost of making films also reflects this belief, as witnessed by Hollywood's propensity to spend increasing amounts of money on stars and special effects in order to satisfy audiences' increasing appetite for a "thrill" ride. The low-budget feature filmmaker can never compete on this level; however, there are a few relevant lessons that can be learned from these facts. Although Hollywood is spending more money to make movies, they are not generating greater profits—ignoring cost comes with a price. Whether someone is making their first film or the next Hollywood blockbuster, the amount spent to create the film is the key element. With few exceptions, blockbuster movies do not generate more than they cost to produce, market, and distribute. The trials and tribulations of Hollywood efforts to create "spectacle" films have been meticulously reported by numerous entertainment news outlets. The low-budget filmmaker has to adopt a mindset at the opposite end of the spectrum from Hollywood's. Simply stated, monitoring and controlling the cost of every single item in the process is the most crucial element in the successful completion of an independent film project. Recognizing that there is no way to compete on the same field with Hollywood compels low-budget filmmakers to focus even more intently on the resources they do have available to them which can make a difference in the quality of the final product. Keeping a close eye on how the major studios operate can offer many clues to the low-budget filmmaker. He or she should watch carefully and ask: "Where are the weaknesses in the system that could spell opportunity for me?" For example, although there are many US outlets that report US box-office revenue to Hollywood, the fact is that less than half of a typical film's costs are recouped from these sources. In fact, in 2012 over 70 percent of the costs incurred in the making of the average major studio movie were recovered from other media and territories. DVD, Blu-ray, free and subscription television and foreign outlets have become the main source of revenue for major studio movies. The massive advertising dollars spent on major studio releases are designed to generate that 70 percent from these other sources. These facts provide an environment pregnant with possibilities for a healthy market for all manner of feature films, not just those manufactured by the major studios—especially within the ancillary markets, i.e., home video, video-on-demand, viewing films via the Internet, etc. The implications of these developments should be deeply ingrained in the consciousness of the independent filmmaker, and most especially the low-budget filmmaker.

DEAL MAKING VERSUS FILMMAKING

It is not necessary to know everything about the history or current state of Hollywood or the independent film industry in order to make an independent feature film. Skipping the next two sections would not preclude the possibility of making a film, but if there is any desire to have people other than one's friends and family view the film, then it would be wiser for the filmmaker to seek out as much knowledge as possible about Hollywood and the independent industry that has evolved around it. An independent film can be categorized by the source of financing, by the sources of distribution, and by the people involved in making the film. Each January the *Hollywood Reporter* publishes its annual box office report with the latest being "2012 Box Office: By the Numbers"; another source for statistics is BoxOfficeMojo.com which reports daily, weekly, and yearly statistics regarding theatrical releases. In 2012, BoxOfficeMojo.com listed approximately one hundred and twenty-five different companies that released feature films theatrically that year. The *Hollywood Distributor Directory* (nineteenth edition, since discontinued) listed over four hundred domestic distributors (for all media), and over one hundred and seventy-five international film companies. In addition, the *Hollywood Creative Directory* for 2011 listed over thirteen hundred production companies. If any of these companies, or anyone associated with them, become involved with a film, a film is no longer an independent film. The project will have become part of the "system." This is not necessarily a bad thing. There are many advantages that can accrue from making films within the system. However, most independent filmmakers have a specific vision for their film and want to maintain control over its creation. Most only want to become a part of the "system" when they have the desire to have their completed film distributed; although it should be noted that the distribution process is slowly changing to allow filmmakers the choice of distribution outside of the "system" (see Chapter 13, "Self Distribution").

Hollywood filmmaking (within the "system") is really about deal making. The film itself is an ancillary aspect of the process, and, in fact, is very close to last on anyone's list of priorities at any given moment. A film is more of a by-product of what is really important to Hollywood people—making deals. The emphasis of this book is on the priority of making a low-budget film of the highest quality and at the most efficient cost possible, as well as the deals necessary to be struck in order to produce it. There have been a number of books written on deal making in Hollywood and many of them are excellent. However, they are geared toward a different game and a different result. They are oriented toward those who are already operating within the Hollywood system and those who dream to be. There are many assumptions with the approaches in these types of books that have nothing to do with the reality of someone trying to make a low-budget feature film. The reality is that a person who has never sold a screenplay or made a feature film will most likely not be "deal making" in Hollywood in their immediate future. That is not to say that it will never happen, it can and it does. It is just being pointed out here that there are two completely different paradigms at work: those wishing to catch the eye of a Hollywood insider so as to get inside to make his or her film, and those who wish to make their own film independently. Within the system the objective is to "package" certain elements together, namely, the script, the financing, and the name talent. To illustrate just how competitive that process is, consider the fact that even established writers and actors who already have agents, managers, and entertainment attorneys have a difficult time getting their own projects produced within the "system." It is possible at some point in the filmmaking process that an independent filmmaker may find people within the system who may become interested in the elements developed to a certain point. If this does occur, then the independent may decide to enter the system, which will most likely necessitate relinquishing control over the process and direction of the film. At that point it will become primarily about deal making and not filmmaking. One encounters many individuals on the independent filmmaking pilgrimage; however, the object is to find the people who will best fit the filmmaker's needs, and, to put it bluntly, to avoid being ripped off. In this regard, there may be people who will promise that they have a doorway into the Hollywood system. They might, but it is just as likely that they are saying whatever is necessary to get hired or attached to the film. The best strategy for handling this situation is to put that person's proverbial feet to the fire. When one hears someone say, "my cousin's uncle's brother is a development executive at Lionsgate," the best response is "great, then set up a meeting for next week." If by some miracle the meeting takes place, make sure their cousin's uncle's brother pays for lunch, and never, under any circumstances, sign anything. On the other hand, there may be someone who can sincerely open an access to the "system." If that is the case, it is crucial to understand the parameters that surround the choice to team up with established "system" players. The point of this discussion is to highlight the different paths a filmmaker can take, and to recognize that each decision being made will affect the control of the creative process.

Michael Blaha's chapter on financing independent films "inside the system" (Chapter 6) explores some of the "control" issues, but perhaps the story of filmmaker Kenneth Lonergan's ordeal in the making of his film *Margaret* best highlights the risks. Kenneth Lonergan had developed into an award-winning playwright when he wrote and directed his first film, *You Can Count on Me.* The film achieved Sundance success, critical success, relative financial success, and was an Oscar nominee for the screenplay. Mr. Lonergan's second film, *Margaret,* was a natural "step-up" from his first film and he entered into its production having already acquired a production-finance-distribution deal with Fox Searchlight that included financing with a third party to partially cover the film's $12 million budget. However, it took seven years from the wrap of production in September 2005 to the film's release, and involved numerous disagreements with the distributors/financiers and three lawsuits before the film was finally "released" in two theaters. Reportedly, the basic problem was that Mr. Lonergan could not deliver a film within the contractually obligated length of 150 minutes or less, and the financiers and distributor would not agree to release Mr. Lonergan's delivered film of a reported length of approximately three hours (180 minutes). It is interesting to note that the approved shooting script was reported to have been approximately 168 pages and the rule of thumb is that each script page will yield one minute of screen time. The point of mentioning this story is not to determine which of the parties was "right" or "wrong," but to illustrate the fact that relinquishment of control over the filmmaking process is an absolute prerequisite when making films within the "system," even if the participant is a writer-director coming off a successful, Oscar-nominated screenplay and film.

FILMMAKER'S CONTROL OVER THE FILMMAKING PROCESS

Two things are of crucial importance regarding the filmmaker's control over his or her film. First, any money spent that cannot be directly attributed to the completion of the film can lead to fatal consequences. Second, in making a feature film many people will be needed to work on the project. It is common to find the names of fifty to one hundred people in the credits of low-budget films, and even a bare-bones film with a budget under fifty thousand dollars requires at least twenty to twenty-five people to participate in some capacity in making the film. Naturally, the latter will mean the relinquishment of the day-to-day control of much of the process to others. Once again it comes down to a question of timing and understanding what is needed from each person and what it should cost. One could maintain personal control over every aspect of the film but the reality is that there are too many aspects of making a film for any one person to maintain total control. It is also not cost effective to approach filmmaking in this manner. There are individuals in the industry who are skilled at what they do, take pride in doing it, and will add to the quality of the film. Again, one of the objectives of this book is to help identify who the filmmaker will have to rely upon, when to rely on them, and roughly how much their reliability and talents are worth in dollars.

It is a further objective of this book to explore various strategies to avoid being painted into any corners. The process of making a movie is an exercise in power. Within the "system," there are very few who have the power to effectuate their will, and even in those who believe they can, it is, in most instances, illusory. In making a film, the filmmaker has the power to make the decisions. Wise delegation of that decision-making power will seriously impact whether or not the film will reach completion and whether it will appear to have cost three to five times actual cost. This book will also assist the low-budget independent filmmaker, especially a first-time filmmaker, to know how to effectively and efficiently delegate authority. The aim is also to create a degree of comfort with the process, so that control will be delegated with confidence. These are rather abstract concepts usually not addressed by low-budget filmmakers; however, they are critical elements, and will impact every other aspect of the process required for a successful completion of the film project. As the captain of the ship, at the very least the filmmaker wants to avoid a mutiny and optimally wants to be on course, under budget, and at the final port ahead of schedule.

VERY BRIEF HISTORY OF THE INDEPENDENT FILM

How much should a low-budget feature filmmaker know about the history of independent film before making his or her low-budget feature film? The answer is nothing. A low-budget filmmaker could make a film without any appreciation at all of the evolution of filmography which made such a thing as "independent film" a viable option in the first place. The important issues for the filmmaker to know, however, are what types of films are being distributed in the market and what types of films are being screened at film festivals. Of course, the history of independent film has shaped the answer to these questions and to some degree dictates the direction of independent cinema. On a practical level, a careful study of the films that do achieve distribution and those that achieve screening at major festivals is arguably more important to know than the history of independent cinema.

With that said, what follows are some general observations regarding how the history of American independents affects the low-budget filmmaking process. Currently, the highest profile American independent film festival is The Sundance Film Festival. From its beginning with Robert Redford in 1981 (when he took over the fledgling USA Film Festival in Utah) until the screening of Steven Soderbergh's film *sex, lies, and videotape* in 1989, this festival was a small-time, low-key, non-Hollywood industry festival. So how did it evolve into the "mecca" for independent filmmakers? Put simply, because a few unknown filmmakers, including Soderbergh in 1989, have "sold" films at the festival, becoming rich and famous in the process. To keep the shine on this image as *the* mecca for independent film, every few years or so at the festival a few more rags-to-riches stories of unknown filmmakers who strike it rich and famous are promoted: Tarantino, Edward Burns, Kevin Smith, The Blair Witch group, and Craig Brewer being standout examples. It is interesting to note that even though there have been relatively few newly minted rags-to-riches filmmakers crowned at Sundance, it has not diminished the popularity of the festival (it was reported that more than 4,000 feature films were submitted for acceptance to the 2013 festival). In fact, two of the foregoing filmmakers, Kevin Smith and Edward Burns, have decided to self-release their recent pictures, only partnering with certain distributors to assist in releasing certain rights to those films.

However, American independent cinema started much earlier than 1989. Technically, it could be argued that *Birth of A Nation* was the first independent movie because none of the established studios wanted to be involved with the film. What got that movie made was D. W. Griffith's personal drive to get it off the ground by convincing investors to give him money and by taking on great personal debt (which remains a common aspect of making an independent film). But perhaps the most important American independent feature film that created a paradigm for the modern indie feature was *Little Fugitive* by Ruth Orkin, Ray Ashley, and Morris Engel. This film was made in 1953 by the use of jerry-rigged, light-weight cameras, actual New York locations, and nonactors, techniques borrowed from post-war Italian neo-realism filmmaking. Orkin, Ashley, and Engel served as producers, writers, directors, cinematographers, and editors of the film which screened at international film festivals, won the top honor at the Venice International Film Festival, and was nominated for an Academy Award for writing. Upon release, the film went on to be very profitable mainly because of its very small budget. It was a watershed moment for American independent filmmakers because it demonstrated that it was possible to make films without stars (or even professional actors), with small budgets, and without studio participation. It must be noted that in spite of the success of *Little Fugitive*, Orkin, Ashley, and Engel found it hard to get money for a second film. In fact, it was Ashley's only filmmaking endeavor and Orkin and Engel completed only three films together after their initial success.

From 1953 until 1989, indie filmmakers often followed the paradigm forged by Orkin, Ashley, and Engel; these subsequent filmmakers, however, struggled to get their films made in relative obscurity and without financial rewards. Although it is a generalization, it is safe to say that most filmmakers during that time pursued independent filmmaking as a means of artistic expression and not as a lottery ticket to achieve wealth and fame. The paradigm shifted with *sex, lies, and videotape* because the budget for that film was over $1 million and it featured three "known" names: James Spader, who had been featured in *Diner, Pretty in Pink*, and *Wall Street*; Andie MacDowell, who was a well-known model; and Peter Gallagher, who was a working television actor. Most importantly, the writer/director, Steven Soderbergh, became rich and internationally famous from the success of the film which launched his Hollywood career.

Although all of the low-budget filmmakers with whom I have worked have been very aware of Sundance and the "lottery" potential, for the most part they were motivated by the desire to make their feature film a building block as a writer and director or simply from a drive to create a personal expression. Not that they would find a showing at Sundance and the sale of their film for a million dollars a bad outcome, but rather that they were very aware of the realities of finding a large audience for their low-budget feature film. They are ultimately driven by a burning desire to make their film. Most low-budget feature filmmakers are still working from the paradigm created by Orkin, Ashley, and Engel (and carried forward more recently by Dogme95 filmmakers and the DIY/Mumblecore filmmakers); they are working in more than two capacities on their film (writer, director, producer, cinematographer, editor, etc.), they have a very low-budget (from $30,000 to less than $1 million), are utilizing existing locations as sets, and are working with actors who have not yet, by and large, become working professionals.

Although, as previously stated, a low-budget feature filmmaker need not know anything about the history of independent cinema in order to make his or her film, the fact is that a knowledge of which films have worked utilizing established paradigms will give the filmmaker a better basis from which to work, eliminating the necessity of reinventing the wheel. It will also provide clues for new directions from the films already made. The combination of a knowledge of the history of independent film with the knowledge of what will interest distributors and programmers of festivals, together with the filmmaker's knowledge of genres is what will give the filmmaker a better chance of reaching an audience with his or her low-budget film. A recommendation for a filmmaker regarding low-budget cinema is to watch the films listed in Appendix A (and if accessible, read the screenplays of the films) for a starting point in this process.

2

The Initial Stages in Making an Independent Film

"Joel, let me tell you something. Every now and then, you gotta say, 'What the f*#&.'" —Risky Business

"You gotta be nuts…And you're gonna need a crew as nuts as you are." —Ocean's 11

WHEN IS A FILMMAKER READY TO MAKE A LOW-BUDGET FEATURE FILM?

Of course, it must be acknowledged that the point at which a low-budget feature can be made is when a sufficient amount of money has been raised. Recognizing this fact, this book is designed to guide an individual in preparing months or even years in advance of actually making his or her film. One of the questions an aspiring feature filmmaker must answer is, when is the right time to make a low-budget feature film? The answer depends on the individual. Some want the making of a feature film to be their first creative effort, while others want to make many short films in different genres and write a number of different feature-length scripts before they decide to risk the investment of money, time, and energy necessary in making a feature film. Although there is no "right" answer as to when the plunge should be taken, my observations have revealed certain elements that successful low-budget filmmakers have in common.

My experience has shown that there are three predominant elements shared by successful low-budget feature filmmakers: 1) they have a clear vision of what the film should be; 2) they have pre-existing relationships with other creative people; and 3) they have developed a confidence in their abilities as filmmakers. To be successful in a feature filmmaking effort, at least two of the three attributes must be present. In circumstances where there may be special challenges, for example, insubstantial finances, the filmmaker must possess all three attributes. So how can a filmmaker obtain these attributes? The most common paths to their attainment are attending film school, making short films, working in other capacities in all types of filmmaking, and reading books like this one. However, a filmmaker can go to the number one ranked film school in the country, make award-winning short films, and study all of the best books on filmmaking and still fail miserably at a low-budget filmmaking effort. On the other hand, very successful efforts have come from filmmakers who have taken less traditional paths leading to their film. Watching many movies, or writing stories, or developing an artistic talent in a different medium are just some examples. There is nothing dogmatic regarding creative ability in a medium. There is a certain aspect of mystery in understanding the roots of creativity; nevertheless, regardless of how attained, a close study of successful low-budget filmmakers will reveal the presence of these three common attributes, or in the context of very favorable conditions, at least two of them.

BUILDING THE CORE TEAM

Usually a low-budget feature film gets made because in the beginning there is a very motivated person who bonds with two or three other very motivated people who will do whatever it takes to get a film made. The key players in a low-budget feature film effort are the writer, the director, the producer, and the attorney. Most likely the low-budget feature filmmaker will fill one or more of these key positions. The particular dynamic that will arise in any particular situation will depend on who fills each of those positions, with the success or failure of the project hinging on who fills them. Once again, I am defining success as having achieved a completed film that looks like it cost three, four, or five times the actual cost. Some hard questions will have to be asked, for example, should you choose the script written by your best friend which may not be as good as another script written by a stranger? How well do you get along with each of these people? Does that matter? Does the producer have access to money? Is he or she power hungry? Does he or she like movies? Does any of this matter?

Just getting the film made is an accomplishment in and of itself. Make no mistake about it, making a film with little or no money defies basic logic, which is a fact worth dwelling upon. There aren't too many other endeavors where so many people expend so much time and effort for so little guarantees as to the outcome. Imagine if someone with little money was very motivated to build their dream house, and they attempted to convince an architect, a builder, an attorney, suppliers, and other necessary people to join in with them in exchange for little or no money. How far do you think they would get? Yet that is exactly what a low-budget filmmaker is trying to accomplish. Individuals who decide to take this path are really defying basic logic. In filmmaking, however, logic rarely represents a deterrent. People decide to pursue this path for as many different reasons as there are people, and we will not stop here to try to analyze why that is, or to recommend that this should be something the filmmaker needs to particularly dwell upon. However, it is important to recognize and embrace the fact that even though one may be engaging in something that is, by all accounts in American society, illogical, one should not therefore engage the process in an illogical or cavalier manner—quite the opposite. This discussion is included to emphasize that the core group of the writer/director, producer, and attorney must be approached in a logical, hard-headed manner. Yet more often than not, the group of people who come together to expend such enormous amounts of time and energy do not explore the synergy between the individuals who will play those roles. An important point to keep in mind is that changing any of the four horses in midstream will more than likely lead to the failure of the project.

SYNERGY AND THE CORE TEAM

Any "successful" film (that is, appearing on the screen to have cost three to five times more than actually spent) will have a core group who are crystal clear as to their individual responsibilities, and are on the same page as the other core people as to what "type" of film they are all striving to make. There are a myriad of combinations of personas which can emerge as a core group representing every imaginable group personality. It is not possible here to discuss each and every type or category. The goals of this chapter are to outline what aspects of team building are necessary, what are the ideal types of situations to look for and which are not worth getting involved in at any price. With that said, the core group of people who have successfully created their low-budget feature film in the past are most often a group of people who: 1) can perform the function they're being hired to perform; 2) have worked hard on previous projects; 3) have similar tastes as to movies in general; and 4) have similar perspectives on the film they plan to make together. Completing a film that looks like it cost three to five times more than it actually did entails a great deal of hard work and sacrifice on the part of the main participants of the film (the writer, director, and producer), so making sure the "right" core people have been assembled is of primary importance.

WORKING WITH A WRITER

What is a writer? A writer is a person who writes. An obvious statement, one might think, but it is critically important to examine the person whose script is being chosen to be the basis of the film. If the primary moving force behind the desire to make the film is the writer, then obviously this person usually does not want to engage another writer. However, this writer should take steps to ensure that he or she is being critically objective as to whether his or her script is suitable to be the basis of a low-budget independent film.

In any case, experience has shown me that, with few exceptions, adding a screenwriter markedly enhances a project. The reasons for believing that the project will be enhanced by the addition of a screenwriter are based firstly on the observation that in the process of making an independent film an added creative participant (i.e., the writer) is needed to address revisions, especially if the writer is also the director and the producer who will not have the time or focus to properly address the revisions; secondly, it is rare for anyone to be a good writer and a good director, and thirdly it is easier for a director or producer to be more objective regarding a script written by someone else.

If a screenwriter is engaged in the process, the latter obstacles can be avoided, but as might be expected new obstacles will emerge. One of the greatest challenges facing the director and producer is to find a writer who is willing to relinquish control over how the script should be translated into a film. The reality is that the writer will be needed all the way through the end of principal photography since there will be developments that will necessitate rewriting the story, and usually the original writer is in the best position to do any of the additional writing. It is true that another writer could be used, but new people bring different perspectives and may inject a point of view at odds with what has already been created, thereby creating the potential of producing a disjointed film. To work, there would have to be a seamless integration of the new perspectives into the aesthetics of the existing script—a daunting task for even the most experienced and talented writers. Further, from a practical point of view, it will be difficult to dismiss the writer unless you can give to him or her an amount of money up front in exchange for relinquishment of control over the script—not often an option for a low-budget feature filmmaker.

Some producers and directors argue that since the screenwriter will become someone whose work will actually have been produced it should be enough incentive for the writer to relinquish control over the script without any need for monetary incentive. On a business level, there is merit to this argument. If someone is willing to invest money and time in something a writer has written, it should be a positive step in building that writing career. It is a simple truth that a screenwriter whose work has been produced into a movie has become differentiated from the hundreds of thousands of other screenwriters who have not had their work produced. On an artistic level, the knowledge a writer gains from watching the words he or she has written become an actual movie is of incalculable benefit in honing screenwriting skills. It is unfortunate, however, that experience has shown that most writers would rather have their script sit on a shelf forever than give up control without some form of monetary compensation.

For a producer or director looking to build their team, they cannot give in to any demands by the writer on the team regarding large advances of money. The writer will argue that he or she should get twenty thousand dollars or thirty thousand dollars of the one hundred thousand or two hundred thousand dollar budget of the film. After all, the typical writer might argue, that is only 17 percent to 25 percent of the whole budget in exchange for all of the work, time, effort, and intellectual creativity the writer has expended in creating the script! Without a script, the writer's argument goes, there is no film. If that is not enough, the writer will strengthen his or her claims by bringing up the comments about the script made by the other team members. Wasn't it a "wonderful," "brilliant," and "great" script? A writer may then, at the very least, ask for ten thousand dollars deferred payment, or the right to direct the film, or upgrades to their laptop computer or whatever else happens to pop into their mind at that moment. If the goal is the successful completion of a low-budget feature film, then the answer to these demands should be "no," and "it was nice working with you, good-bye and best of luck in the future."

The key to successfully making a low-budget feature film is to recognize that in the beginning of the process, everyone is replaceable (and possibly by someone better than the person who is being replaced). Once the right person is found (writer, director, producer, etc.), there must be an up-front discussion of what that person is giving and what they will receive in return. The best course is for a writer to receive between three and five percent of the budget. If they are not happy with this exchange, then you must move on. If they are happy and are going to join the team, then they must transfer the rights to the script to the producer and sign an employment contract for their services. Once both parties sign the contracts, renegotiating in the future is limited to mutually agreed upon exigencies. This is a hard-line position to take, but it is absolutely essential if the project is to come to a successful conclusion.

As a practical matter, it will be found that most people who come together to make an independent low-budget feature film understand the realities of the situation, and are more than willing to be reasonable about making the project work, so usually the interaction does not unfold in an acrimonious or cold manner. If it does then you are dealing with a person who *is not* going to be of help in completing a successful low-budget feature film. Do not be seduced into giving in to demands based on the initial excitement over a particular writer or script. There are many other scripts and writers waiting in the wings. Keep searching. It will definitely be worth it in the end. It should be noted that too many times a low-budget filmmaker, especially a first-time filmmaker, is reluctant to move on once involved in negotiations with someone who they at first believed they wanted to be attached to their film. However, if there is any money involved in making the film, then common sense dictates that it must be handled in a business-like manner if it is to succeed. Good business involves exploring all available options before making a decision, without compromising the filmmaker's vision.

There are many, many great scripts available. To put this discussion into perspective let us look at one screenwriting competition. The Don & Gee Nicholl Screenwriting Fellowship Competition is one of the most prestigious screenwriting competitions in the world (actually considered by many to be the most prestigious). The number of scripts entered has steadily increased since its inception in 1986. There have been approximately 116,197 total number of scripts entered with 7,197 having been entered in 2012. Every year since 1989, roughly 100 semifinalists and 10 finalists have been chosen. Over the last twenty-three years less than 10 percent of the *finalists'* scripts have been made into feature films. According to the information provided by the Nicholl's Fellowship In Screenwriting website, only 16 of the 121 scripts that were chosen for fellowships from among the finalists' scripts have been produced since 1986. This is one competition, and arguably the one that has produced the "best" scripts in the country and still over 90 percent of the finalist scripts and 87 percent of the "winning" scripts have yet to be made into feature films.

In making decisions regarding each and every person, good, or service that you will need in making the film, look at the realities of the supply and demand for the particular item or service that you are considering. This does not mean that writers should never be paid or scripts that wash out at Nicholl are no good, but simply, to drive the lesson home, that the little money available to a low-budget independent feature filmmaker should be reserved for the items for which there is little or no alternative for replacement and/or will provide you with the greatest return. For example, the ten thousand dollars you might pay a writer could rent the best High Definition camera available for a three week shoot *and* buy the tape stock, while one thousand dollars could buy you a full day of gun special effects or better catering for the cast and crew. Remember, a successful film is one that will look like it cost three to five times what was actually spent.

Assuming it is the right script, what the filmmaker wants to hear from the writer before closing the deal is: "I will, right now, sign any contract giving you all of the rights in all mediums and I don't want to direct the film, and I will be available to do rewrites that are reasonably needed with no monetary demands." That is the ideal. However, the reality of any particular situation is that there will be some negotiating. Normally the producer and/or director will like something in particular that they find in a certain writer or script, and the writer, recognizing that the producer and/or director feel that way, will hold out for some demands to be met. What deal should be agreed to will depend on the facts and circumstances of any particular situation, and situations can run from one extreme to another. If the producer and/or director have ten scripts that they think are "wonderful" and "brilliant," and they then have all ten writers show up together waiting in the lobby for their turn to be interviewed, the negotiating will be much easier. But if at the other extreme the producer and/or director tell one writer that they want only that writer's script, will not make a movie unless they get that script, and will do anything to secure the rights, well then negotiations will be markedly different. Of course, most situations fall somewhere in between.

The ideal writer is a person who not only wants to see their script become a film, but also shares the same "vision" for the film as the producer and director, and understands the realities of making an independent film. "Vision" is a word that is tossed around by film people and it seems to have as many definitions as there are people. Very simply put, as used in this context it means that the writer, director, and producer(s) are aiming to make the same "type" of film. For example, if it's a horror film, the writer should not be envisioning a moody, psychological film while the director is envisioning a film shot entirely from the point-of-view of the killer, and the producer is envisioning an explicit, gory, bloody film. These are very different "visions" of the film. Perhaps they could be seamlessly combined into one film, but if it's not clear what the "vision" of the film is, there are bound to be disagreements and tensions which will undermine the project (genres and scripts are discussed in Chapter 3). This is not to say that there won't be disagreements as to how to best reach the stated goals of what the film is going to become, but merely to state that the writer, director, and producer should be headed in the same direction, in other words, have the same "vision."

HIRING A LAWYER

A good number of independent films are undertaken without the services of a lawyer. The fact is that most independent filmmakers don't believe they can retain a knowledgeable, experienced entertainment lawyer for a reasonable price. For the most part, these filmmakers have a point. Entertainment law is a specialized niche within the legal field, and is practiced by only a handful of attorneys. Most of these attorneys reside in the few largest cities in America, primarily Los Angeles and New York. The few attorneys who have developed the expertise in order to maintain a law practice focusing solely on entertainment law charge fees between two hundred and fifty and seven hundred and fifty dollars an hour… yes, *per hour*. These attorneys cannot afford to devote the necessary time and attention to independent filmmakers because it is just not cost effective for them to do so. At the other end of the spectrum, there are affordable attorneys available, but generally they have little or no experience in the entertainment field in general or independent filmmaking in particular. Surveying these choices, many independent filmmakers have decided to proceed without an attorney; instead they most often purchase a "kit" consisting of the contracts necessary to make an independent film. In many cases they simply grab contracts off the Internet or from friends or colleagues or from a book, and run from there.

Scores of "horror" stories could be told where the ultimate cost of not securing an independent film attorney at the beginning of the process resulted in a greater, sometimes catastrophic, unexpected cost when things went wrong. Things always go wrong to one degree or another. I could relate stories of filmmakers who have approached me for representation *after* a problem arose only to realize that the cost of fixing the problem so outweighed the amount they could raise, that their completed film was left unacceptable for distribution and sitting on their shelf as an expensive paperweight. It is better to focus on how the services offered by an experienced entertainment attorney outweigh *a reasonable, flat fee* paid for such services—that is, *plan for success*. With that said I would relate one scenario that is not uncommon in the world of independent feature filmmaking.

Three friends make an independent film and the final film turns out very well. The cinematography and acting are extremely professional and there could possibly be a market for the film. One of the friends was an assistant to a casting agent and obtained "inside" information about an unknown actor who had accepted a lead role in a major studio's summer blockbuster film to be shot in the subsequent year, and scheduled to be released the year after. The friends decide to pool their resources (let us say, one hundred and fifty thousand dollars and many outstanding favors), secure the young, unknown actor's services and shoot the feature film. They pay the young, unknown actor twenty-five thousand dollars for two weeks of acting services. He accepts because he needs money until the studio film begins paying him. They find a writer with a script that they like and a producer friend who contributes the vast majority of the money. They cast the film and shoot it in a three-week period. The writer contributed the script to the project for free, the director contributed the equipment (and contributed some money), the casting assistant contributed the actors (and the soon-to-be-famous actor) and the producer friend contributed the money. Unfortunately, the friends signed no paperwork regarding the rights and responsibilities among themselves and used contracts they bought from the Internet to secure releases from the actors and crew. The film gets completed, makes the festival circuit, wins a few awards and has great prospects. As hoped for, two years later the young actor became a "known actor" upon the release of the big summer blockbuster. The road ahead is set regarding their film, right?

To make a complicated story simple, the film never gets released in any medium. The core group of friends in this story made some critical mistakes regarding the Screen Actors Guild-American Federation of Television and Radio Artists (SAG-AFTRA), and also the Writers Guild of America (WGA): the writer didn't volunteer that she was a member and had submitted paperwork on behalf of the film to make the film a WGA signatory. Did she have the authority to legally represent the film to the WGA? It is an open question (i.e., it would need to be decided in court) because the parties did not agree upon the rights and responsibilities in writing. Who was bound to the WGA rules based on the writer's signature? The film? The writer? The other filmmakers? When the smoke clears there are multiple potential claims against the film in addition to thousands of dollars that are potentially owed to various parties. The core group of friends does not have the kind of money in question, and although there are distributors interested in the film, none could be found willing to provide the needed money up front. In addition, the group borrowed about thirty thousand dollars on credit cards to finish the film. The money was borrowed in the name of an unaffiliated corporation that has been utilized for many years by the producer, and the group could not subsequently agree as to the percentage of the debt owed by each person. Apparently the producer incurred the debt after a discussion with the director, but did not discuss it with the writer or the casting director. Although all four of them were aware that the money was borrowed to finish the film, there was no signed paperwork addressing the issue. Another complicating factor is that although the producer created a new C corporation for the film, the writer never transferred to that company the copyright of the final screenplay reflecting the numerous re-writes she did, and she is now refusing to do so until her compensation is decided and the debt issue settled. In the meantime, years have passed since the creation of the California C corporation for the film. No one filed any tax returns and no one addressed the tax bill of over four thousand dollars they eventually received from the California Franchise Tax Board (representing a minimum $800 per year tax, plus penalties and interest). At this point each participant approaches a lawyer to fight on their behalf, but the legal issues are too expensive for the group to solve so the film will remain unreleasable as the participants begin the process of evading creditors.

This scenario illustrates how things can go very wrong without any bad intentions on the part of any of the friends. The reported experiences with the film *Don's Plum* starring then unknown actors Leonardo DeCaprio, Toby McGuire, and Kevin Connelly could also be cited. Even independent films that have production counsel and attain simply a DVD deal often have at least one lawsuit or potential lawsuit that must be addressed. It seems to be the nature of the endeavor.

How can a low-budget independent feature filmmaker secure proper legal advice with the limited funds available? Following are some basic guidelines whereby an independent filmmaker can secure the services of an experienced, accessible entertainment attorney for a cost of about 3 to 5 percent of the total budget of the film. Generally, if a film's budget is $50,000, then the attorney for the film should be secured for approximately $2,500. If the budget is $350,000, then the attorney should cost approximately $10,500. A first principle in the making of an independent film is that the writer, director, and producer(s) should secure the attorney's services at the very beginning of the development phase. Second, the team should be initiated as to what services they should expect. In a word, they should seek and secure the full service of legal work necessary in making a feature film. This should include, but not necessarily be limited to:

a) copyright registration;
b) formation of entities (whether a corporation, S-corporation, limited liability company or other entity);

c) compliance with state and federal securities laws (e.g., drafting a Private Placement Memorandum);

d) full service contracts including: (1) writer collaborations; (2) literary options and sales; (3) above-the-line agreements (writer, director, producer, actors); (4) below-the-line agreements (all other crew members);

e) location releases and permits;

f) music rights: synchronization and master use licenses (and other clearance contracts);

g) union and guild contracts (SAG-AFTRA, WGA, DGA).

Many experienced film production attorneys charge an hourly rate for legal services in connection with the making of a feature film, which generally places their services beyond the reach of most low-budget feature filmmakers. Even if an experienced film production attorney offers a flat fee, most often the amount charged is not within the parameters of the amount of money that a low-budget filmmaker can raise in order to make a film. That does not mean that there are no experienced film production attorneys in major cities that offer reasonable, flat fees in exchange for the legal services necessary to make a feature film that is in compliance with all legal formalities (i.e., a distributable film). However, the filmmaker needs to review precisely what services any attorney will provide for that flat fee rate since each attorney will provide a different menu of services for the fee (i.e., comparing proverbial apples to other apples).

It is always a temptation to hire a lawyer with little or no experience in film production because he or she might be willing to work for little or no money. It is not particularly wise to be the classroom in which the attorney learns the craft and gains his or her experience in the field. In general, the cost to the filmmaker from possible mistakes the neophyte independent film attorney may make will be at least equal to what it would cost to hire an experienced attorney. At worst, I have known of more than one instance where the mistakes were unresolvable without large expenditures of money by the filmmaker—money the filmmaker didn't have in the first place—leaving the low-budget filmmaker with an unreleasable film.

PARTNERING WITH A PRODUCER

It would not be an exaggeration to say that the most critical relationship and the most difficult to develop is the partnership with a producer. Even for films that have budgets above $1 million the role of the producer is far from simple and requires strict attention to detail, but at the million plus level money is usually available to secure the proper person, and the prospects for raising enough money to actually produce the film are reasonably high. For low-budget films it is damn near impossible since there is usually no money at the development stage to hire a producer, and the prospects for raising enough money to actually produce the film are far lower.

Minimally, the issues involved in negotiating a producer agreement includes, but is not limited to, the time the producer is expected to dedicate to producing the film, the services the producer is to provide, the compensation the producer is to receive in exchange for those services, the control over the project the producer has, and the credit the producer is to receive. These issues, of course, have to be settled in the context of the money available for the project, if any. If there is development money available to pay a producer a salary, then the level of control that the producer is granted can be minimized because the producer would be providing certain services for a fee. However, it is more common at this stage of the process that the producer is pooling his or her resources with one or two other parties (a writer and director or a writer/director). So in addition to a producer contract the producer is often named as a "manager" of a limited liability company that will be formed to produce the film. There are other arrangements that can be agreed to by the parties; for example, he or she could be a principal with the other parties in an S corporation that is to be formed, with such S corporation then to be named the "manager" of the limited liability company to be formed to produce the film.

When a producer is also a "manager" of a limited liability company (or a principal in an S corporation formed in order to be the "manager" of the limited liability company), then many of the issues that are addressed in the producer contract become redundant. They are addressed in the operating agreement for a limited liability company or the by-laws of an S corporation. These and other issues will be covered in more detail in Chapters 7 and 8. It is important to create a producer agreement whether or not the producer(s) will become principal(s) in the entity (or entities) to be created because there are issues in the producer contract that are not addressed in the entity documents. Disagreements have emerged between the principals of a company resulting in one of the team members (writer, director, producer) leaving the company. As a result, the producer or writer or director contracts are left to cover the other issues regarding the film, such issues as salary (if any), the person's credit in the final film, ownership of the person's work by the company and other rights and responsibilities.

It is important to discuss the expectations of the parties regarding the services the producer will provide and what he or she will receive in return for providing those services. It is usually expected that the producer will assist in raising money (maybe even contributing his or her own money), work on developing the script, be involved when approaching potential actors and distributors and be involved with all of the other primary aspects of developing and producing a low-budget feature film. A complicating factor is that a producer may faithfully provide all of the required services and at the end of the development process the collaborators may still not have raised the money necessary to make the film. This possibility and its impact on the rights and responsibilities regarding the project must also be discussed and addressed in the paperwork among the parties. An experienced independent film attorney will review the issues and possible paths available to address the rights and responsibilities of the writer, director, and producer who are pooling their resources to produce the independent film and ensure that the terms of the various documents reflect the needs and wants of the parties while not containing conflicting terms. These issues represent only a sampler of the legal issues an experienced lawyer may be called upon to address in the process of producing a low-budget independent film.

3

Selecting the Script and Evaluating Actors

"How far do you want me to take him?
Till he stops. Ok, sounds like a pretty good ride. Hope so."
—Seabiscuit

SELECTION ISSUES

It has been my experience that by the time low-budget filmmakers reach the point of engaging attorney services they have already chosen the script that will be the basis of the film they intend to make. In the beginning of the process a script can range from basic ideas sketched out in three or four pages to a slick, finished version that has been through multiple polishes, possibly over a number of years. Sometimes it will also reflect feedback from professional script consultants. But, regardless of the state of the script, the one thing that seems to be a constant is that the filmmaker is completely committed to the script as *the* project he or she is going to make. There is nothing wrong with this attitude; it is an attitude that is absolutely necessary for committing the years of hard work it takes to make an independent film. Unfortunately, too often the choice of script is based on a gut-instinct the filmmaker has that the script is *the* story he or she must tell, and less often on a more calculated reasoning process. Although a gut connection should be present for the independent filmmaker to successfully complete his or her film, there are a number of considerations that can enhance the process which most often are not considered by the low-budget filmmaker, first-time or otherwise, before settling on the script to be made. The issues to be considered include: 1) the genre; 2) the story; 3) the scale of the script, that is, whether it is realistic to shoot the film because of the big scale of the project, or whether it is not "big" enough and might be perceived as a "boring" and/or noncinematic film; and 4) the source of the script, that is, whether the script is written by the filmmaker or is obtained from another writer.

RESEARCHING DISTRIBUTOR INPUT

Once these issues have been identified and addressed, the filmmaker should take this information and seek out any distributors who may be interested in acquiring/licensing the finished film. It is very frustrating to dedicate years and thousands of dollars to producing an independent film only to find that certain choices regarding the script would have made a world of difference. At the end of this chapter is a listing of thirteen distribution companies and some of the films each company has distributed in the last few years. A review of the films a distribution company distributes usually reveals a pattern as to the type of films that a particular company would be interested in acquiring/licensing, that is to say, the genre, the story, the level of name talent, the budget level, the "quality" of the finished film, whether the films have screened at film festivals (and if so, which festivals), etc. This information will guide the filmmaker in identifying which companies may be interested in distributing the film the filmmaker intends to make. Doing this research at this point in the process will enable the filmmaker to more critically address the script (i.e., whether the script just needs some tweaking or whether a completely new script should be chosen). This research will also assist in the shaping of the business plan for the film and the most appropriate budget, which in turn will maximize the possibility of recovering the costs when (and if) the film is distributed. It should be remarked here that the gathering of this information is ancillary to the creative process and need not compromise the filmmaker's vision at all. Rather, it is the attempt to address these issues later in the filmmaking process when the greatest damage is usually done to the filmmaker's creative vision for the film.

SELECTING A GENRE

One of the first questions anyone will ask about any film is: What kind of film is it? Films are made to reach an audience, and audiences have expectations about what a film experience should be, which is based upon expectations that have been formulated by viewing a myriad of previous films. The popularly recognized genres include comedy, drama, thriller, horror, westerns, science fiction, gangster/crime, musicals, action, and war. While some filmmakers approach the choice of genre from a market perspective, that is, looking at what genre of film is most commercial, it has been my experience that independent filmmakers (and first-time filmmakers especially) commonly choose the genre for their film based primarily on what he or she needs to express in a film. The discussion here is not intended to direct any filmmaker into selecting a genre solely because audiences like a particular genre and/or distributors are seeking a particular genre. Rather, the discussion is intended to point out the need for more rational decision making while simultaneously creating realistic expectations as to likely audience and distributor reactions when the film is presented in exchange for money. Filmmaking, more than any other art, is the fusion of the business and the creative, and the most "successful" films are the ones where the filmmakers followed their creative instincts while balancing the practical aspects in the process. It is very often the case that when the process involves more money these responsibilities are divided between the business-minded individuals on the team and the creative individuals on the team. In a capitalist system that espouses an ever-increasing specialization of work (the proverbial "pin factory") this may work, but in the making of a film, it usually leads to failure. Fox Studios, widely held in the highest regard in the industry, has been lead by two individuals, Jim Gianopulos and

Tom Rothman, who were named co-chairmen in 2000. A recent article in *Variety* expressed their operating relationship as follows:

> And the execs offer a study in contrasts. Gianopulos enjoys studying the latest technology and the inner workings of new systems. He has a mathematical mind. Rothman seems much more comfortable delivering script notes—personally, with his trademark booming baritone—than poring over spreadsheets. "I love that at least once a week I see the chairman of the studio wandering the halls of Building 88 shoeless and untucked," says on-the-lot producer-director Shawn Levy of Rothman. "His head is in the movies. He could give a shit about the rest of it." But it's too easy to say that Gianopulos and Rothman have split the job into money and creativity, since both are involved in both aspects—particularly enforcing budgets. (*Variety*, "Can Fox Stay On Top?," Tatiana Siegel, May 23, 2008).

Similarly an independent filmmaker improves chances of "success" if his or her head is in both the creative and business aspects, and, most importantly, he or she will need to be able to fuse each as called for, which will be different for each project.

A genre is defined by a "set of rules" that the filmmaker and audience recognize and accept. No centralized film committee has ever been commissioned by the government to debate and pass "laws" on what aspects each genre should possess. It is actually quite the opposite in that genres have evolved over time through a process of trial and error. Filmmakers made films without knowing particularly how to make those films, and as audiences responded to certain elements, subsequent films eliminated what the audiences didn't like while repeating the elements to which the audiences reacted favorably. It is actually a very democratic process and in many respects mirrors the positives and negatives of the popular will (i.e., the tyranny of the majority, the inevitable pushback by the minority, and the struggle between the two camps). Over time filmmakers and audiences developed expectations of what "belonged" in each genre and "what didn't belong." Desiring the largest potential income stream from each film, major studios have produced years of genre films that have basically met the audiences' expectations for such film genres. It has been said that "genre films" is one of the few purely American contributions to art in the world; this is, of course, debatable, but how deep a connection film audiences have to genres must be noted. It is true that deviations from the "rules" of any genre have been accepted by audiences but only to the extent such changes do not alter the "fundamental rules" of the genre and merely make minor additions and/or revisions to them. Except for the 1940s (when the studios had a complete monopoly and gave various filmmakers some freedom), and the late 1960s/early–mid 1970s (when the studios were in collapse and the filmmakers were calling the shots) it has been independent filmmakers who have been able to create films that challenge audiences' expectations. Challenging the "rules" of the game entails great risk, because if the film is not accepted by the audience/distributors, there is no "fall back" position of appealing to fans of a particular genre. As stated above, an analysis of the companies listed at the end of this chapter can be very instructive. There are few greater determinates of whether an audience/distributor will be interested in a film than the genre, which is usually locked in at the time the script is chosen.

THE STORY

Although there are examples of very successful nonstory, nonplot driven films, as a general rule, films that successfully reach an audience almost always have a well-developed story that is moved forward by a plot. Well-developed stories typically have defined beginnings, middles, and conclusions. The beginning of the script "tells" the audience what the basic premise of the story is, and this most often ties in with the genre of the film. For example, if it is a "thriller" genre in which a husband and wife go sailing with a man they just met, this would be the "set-up," which is usually between five and fifteen pages of the script (the rule of thumb is that each page of the script is about one minute of screen-time). The middle of the script then develops the opening premise. In the above example, it could turn out the wife and the man the couple just met are actually lovers who planned the boat trip to kill the husband, and so the middle of the script is all of the complications that go with murder and betrayal. As mentioned above, independent film often bends (but does not break) the genre expectations. For example, rather than the wife and the stranger being lovers, it could be that the stranger is the husband's gay lover and they plan to eliminate the wife. When the classic story structure ends, it does not simply "end," but rather it attempts to resolve the relevant "plot" and "story" elements that have been presented in the beginning and middle of the script. A review of the films distributed by nonstudio distributors reveals that they primarily distribute films that follow the model of beginning, middle, and end. Audiences (and hence distributors) still respond to the well-developed classic film structure whether it is made by a studio or independently, yet too often independent filmmakers (and studios) do not consider this aspect of the script. However, unlike studios, independent filmmakers don't have the resources to spend $100 million on special effects and $60 million on prints and advertising in releasing one single film in over four thousand theaters simultaneously in order to compensate for the lack of story.

This discussion regarding genres and classic story structure is not intended to dictate emulation by an independent filmmaker, but rather to merely alert the filmmaker to the reality of what the end-user (the audience, usually via an established distributor) has been conditioned to expect. In the independent arena, if a script ignores these established "rules" or mixes and matches them in a manner not expected by the audience, it increases the chances that the final film will not be distributed by an established distributor and/or will not be accepted by an audience. Pioneering is fine as long as the filmmaker has carefully considered these possibilities and planned accordingly. At the very least, this information should influence the filmmaker's decisions in terms of: a) how much money the film should be made for; b) what the filmmaker will tell potential investors regarding the prospects of recouping their investment; c) the manner in which the film will be "marketed" to distributors, film festivals, and film reviewers; and, perhaps most importantly, d) the filmmaker's expectations and understanding as to the risks involved in making the film, including a) through

c) above. Remember that if a studio script is a mess and the film reflects this messed-up script studios have big stars, special effects, large marketing budgets and a wide theatrical release to fall back on—fail-safes not usually afforded to a low-budget independent filmmaker.

THE SCALE OF A FILM

The scale of a film is determined by the number of locations, the number of actors, the number and type of props, etc., and is another aspect of script to be considered. Scripts can range from one room with two characters to over fifty locations, many special effects, and a cast of the proverbial thousands. Does the script call for actors who are senior citizens or children? Are any stunts and/or special effects involved? Low-budget filmmakers primarily raise between $50,000 and $1,000,000 to make their film. The low end of this budget would represent the purchase of a BMW or Lexus, while the high end would be the equivalent of a purchase of a home near the beach in California. In everyday thinking these amounts seem like a lot of money, but the reality of making low-budget feature films is much different than everyday thinking, meaning that the money never goes as far as the filmmaker would like it to go in pursuing the vision of his or her film, and even if it does fulfill the filmmaker's vision, the film competes for an audience with films that have spent much more money.

The filmmaker can't control the fact that other films are made utilizing more money, but the filmmaker can ensure that the money he or she spends ends up looking like three to five times what was actually spent. An important step in achieving the latter is to evaluate what is possible in terms of the scale of the film in the low-budget range. This can be facilitated by reviewing as many completed low-budget films as possible and then comparing the budget of each film with its final production value. This is easier said than done because obtaining the truth regarding the budget of an independent film is very difficult. When asking "what was the budget?" it seems the number received in answer in no way coincides with what is viewed on the screen. However, a brief look at the experience of some well-known and some lesser-known independent films can be enlightening: well-known films such as: 1) *The Brothers McMullen* (1994); 2) *Pi* (1998); 3) *Napoleon Dynamite* (2004); 4) *Open Water* (2003); 5) *Kissing Jessica Stein* (2001); 6) *The Signal* (2007) and 7) *Winter's Bone* (2010), and some lesser known films such as: 1) *Funny Ha Ha* (2002); 2) *Great Wall of Sound* (2007); 3) *Rhythm Thief* (1994); 4) *Head Trauma* (2006); 5) *Quiet City* (2007); 6) *Rubberneck* (2012); and 7) *Knock Knock 2* (2012).

What becomes immediately apparent when reviewing the above films is that "successful" independent films in this budget range generally limit the number of locations, use very few actors, avoid roles for senior citizens and children, and have little or no stunts and/or special effects. Of course, there are low-budget films that defy these criteria: *Head Trauma* and *The Signal* being examples. The trick is to stay within these parameters and still create a film that doesn't feel like you are in the same location the entire movie, and doesn't feel constrained or boring because of a lack of production value—this is no easy trick. The Motion Picture Association of America reported that in 2007 Hollywood studios spent an average of approximately $70 million to make big-budgeted films and spent on average $36 million to market these films. Hollywood studios, affiliates, and subsidiaries (e.g., Miramax, Fox 2000, Fox Searchlight, Fox Faith, Fox Animation, Focus Features, Rogue Pictures, Paramount Vantage, Sony Pictures Classics, Screen Gems, TriStar Pictures, and Destination Films) really cinched their belts on the budgets for the "independent" movies they made in 2007 spending *only* $49 million to make their "little art house" films and $25 million to market them. This trend has been on the upswing over the years and the result is that audiences and acquisition executives working for distributors (more precisely, the assistants and interns working for distributors who are assigned the task to watch the films seeking acquisition) are conditioned to react negatively to films that do not equal the financial expenditures of typically distributed movies. Combine this with the fact that there are literally thousands of new feature-length films created *every* year that are vying for very few distribution spots leads to the conclusion that all filmmakers, especially first-time film-makers, must carefully review their script to determine if it is structured optimally to maximize available funds.

FILMMAKER-WRITTEN SCRIPT

Often independent filmmakers write the script for the film they intend to make, and there was a time, primarily between 1994 and 1999, when it was fashionable for indie filmmakers to brag that they wrote their script in two or three weeks with little or no rewriting. Experience has shown that in making an independent film the best path to a successful outcome is to rewrite a script over a time period of at least a year, to conduct staged readings of the script with actors, to receive feedback from the readings, and then pay a professional writing consultant to review the script and provide notes for more rewrites. Unfortunately, very few filmmakers take these steps. This is especially true for first-time filmmakers. A simple comparison of the initial version of a script with the final version after it has gone through the above steps shows an improvement to the final script which is dramatic; not to mention the positive effect a high quality script has on fund-raising. The fund-raising path is rarely a short one so while the filmmaker is approaching investors he or she is rehearsing the script with actors in a workshop at least once a month, fine-tuning the script and gaining a better understanding of the story and how to best direct the film, which will dramatically improve the final film. The reality is that most filmmakers take a helter-skelter approach. They do a rewrite or two, get feedback, mostly from random people in their lives (regardless of the experience of these random people as a writer or writing teacher), alienate a friend or two (and/or significant other) because of what the writer perceives as "ridiculous" or "stupid" advice for changes in the script and then move directly into preproduction as soon as "enough" money has been raised. One need not be a fortune-teller to predict the outcome of such a process.

CO-WRITING A SCRIPT

Co-writing situations often create legal difficulties because the collaborative process is based more on the goal of writing the best possible script and less on the process of ensuring that the proper contracts are negotiated and signed concerning the ownership and rights of the script that is co-written.

In general, if a script is co-written with no contract signed by the parties, then under US Copyright law the co-writers will be considered "co-authors" as long as they intended that the work would be merged together into a unitary whole and that each has provided more than a de minimis amount to the final product. Each "co-author" in turn is an owner of the final work in equal proportions (i.e., two writers own the script 50 percent each, three writers each own one third of the script percentage, and so on). Of course, these ownership rights can be altered according to an agreement signed by all relevant parties. The customary issues accompanying a contract between co-writers are usually easily identified, negotiated, and agreed upon by the co-authors. These issues include the division of ownership (which does not have to be an equal split), credit for writing the script, any expenses that are allowable and/or reimbursable, the division of the proceeds upon exploitation of the script, and whether the script writing will be subject to the Writers Guild of America Minimum Basic Agreement. These issues are fairly straightforward if the authors wish to sell or option the final script, but it becomes more complicated if one, some, or all of the co-writers want to make their own independent film based upon the script.

Before a co-authored script is made into a film the following questions should be addressed and answered: 1) Do all of the co-writers have to agree to allow any one of the co-writers to make the script into a feature film?; 2) If so, must all of the co-writers be allowed (or compelled) to participate in the making of the film?; 3) What are the consequences if one of the co-writers is opposed to one of the other co-writers making the film? Is that the final word or is there an arbitration process?; 4) What if all of the co-writers want to make their own film version of the script? Is that allowed? If so, is there compensation due and owing?; 5) What if there are rewrites to the script? Are other writers allowed to rewrite the script or must the "assignment" be offered to one or all of the other co-writers first?; and 6) If one or all accepts such an assignment, is compensation due for such services? If so, how much? These are just some of the questions that should be answered if a script written by co-writers is to be produced into a film. Although there are solutions to the above issues which can be reduced to a contract and signed by all of the co-writers, the obstacles are usually so great as to complicate the process to such a degree that the co-writers can't even begin the process of negotiation simply because they do not have the funds required to engage the necessary experienced legal counsel. Even if the writers can engage counsel, the issues are usually so complicated that, in spite of their eagerness to do so, the co-writers will be unable to agree on how to address them. From a practical point of view, the co-writers all need to agree to make one film and all must agree on what the duties/rights regarding that film are to be. Who is responsible for raising money for the budget? Who is the director? How will bona fide disagreements regarding the making of the film be settled? If they decide to allow each co-writer to make his or her own version of a film based on the script it will severely limit the value of the script for the remaining co-writers who have not as yet made a film based on the script (or never will). The latter is true because once a film is made and brought to the market based upon a certain script other production companies and distributors will no longer be interested in purchasing the script, producing a film based on the script, or distributing a film that has already been released in a different version.

REGISTERING THE SCRIPT WITH THE UNITED STATES COPYRIGHT OFFICE

No matter what process a writer/filmmaker goes through to produce a script, from a legal perspective it behooves him or her to register the script with the United States Copyright Office. The process of registering scripts with the United States Copyright Office has recently been changed to encourage registration of works using the "Electronic Copyright Office" ("eCO") online. Works such as screenplays can be registered using the online system for a fee of $35, which is not only cheaper than using other forms but also provides the fastest processing time, online status tracking, online payment by credit card, and the ability to upload copies of the screenplay. If registration online is not applicable or desired by the author there are two other methods available. There is a fill-in Form CO online that uses barcode scanning which makes the processing of these forms faster than traditional Form PA. The Form CO is completed online, printed out and mailed with a copy of the screenplay and a check or money order for the fee, which is currently $50. For those who do not want to use eCo or Form CO, the Form PA remains available to register a screenplay. However, this method is being phased out by the Copyright Office and these forms are only mailed from the Copyright Office upon request. The fee for registration by Form PA is currently $65.

OBTAINING THE SCRIPT

To this point our discussion has been limited to screenplays written or co-written by the filmmaker. There are other avenues to a screenplay which include, but are not limited to: 1) optioning a completed script from another writer for potential purchase; or 2) obtaining the film rights to a book and then writing the script oneself, or hiring another person to write a script based upon the book. It is not common for filmmakers producing a film for less than $1 million to have sufficient funds to obtain the rights to a book and hire a writer to write the screenplay (and rewrites, polishes, etc.), especially since these expenses are incurred at the beginning of the process (i.e., before the funds to make the film have been raised and therefore come from the filmmaker's own pocket). However, if the filmmaker does incur these expenses, they are commonly recouped by the filmmaker from the funds that are subsequently raised to make the film.

OPTION/PURCHASE AGREEMENT FOR A COMPLETED SCRIPT

Another way a filmmaker can obtain the rights to a script is by entering into an option/purchase contract with the writer(s)/owner(s) of a script. A filmmaker may find a script already completed and want to produce it into a film. He or she would want to tie up the rights to the script long enough so as to have the opportunity to try to raise the funds necessary to make the film. An option is a right, within a specified period of time, to purchase the rights to the script. Of course, a filmmaker could skip entering into an option and instead purchase all of the rights to a script outright; however, it is rare for an independent filmmaker (not to mention a first-time film-maker) to have sufficient funds for such an action. Even if he or she does have sufficient funds to purchase the script, most often he or she does not yet have the money to produce the film nor is certain that he or she will ever be able to raise it. In such an event, the filmmaker would be the proud owner of a script sitting on his or her shelf. The goal of the filmmaker is to make a film, not to accumulate scripts which may or may not have value. The option/purchase contract solves this dilemma.

The option/purchase contract is an agreement that gives the holder (in this case the filmmaker or the filmmaker's production company) a certain period of time within which to purchase the script from its owner for an agreed upon sum of money. The option period is usually between six months and two years during which time the holder has the right to develop the film and attempt to raise the funds necessary to make the film. The option holder's right to purchase the script is exclusive during the option period so as to allow him or her to concentrate on raising the funds for making the film with the assurance that if he or she is successful the script can be purchased at a predetermined price. If, on the other hand, he or she is unsuccessful in raising the funds by the end of the option period (i.e., the option "lapses"), then the owner of the script retains all of the rights to the script.

The amount an option holder pays for the option varies from nothing up to $10,000 or more, and is usually not refundable. It is negotiable, and the option price reflects the perceived value. It is not uncommon to find writers who are willing to option a screenplay for a nominal amount, one dollar for example, because they believe in the filmmaker and/or recognize the value of having one of their scripts produced into a feature film. However, when the option price is nominal, it is usually for a shorter period such as six months, and the writer may ask for other concessions such as a higher final purchase price or a producer credit or even profit participation.

The option/purchase agreement may take different forms and include various terms. The two most common agreements are "short-form" option/purchase contracts (usually two or three pages long) and "long-form" option/purchase contracts (between ten and twenty pages long). At the very least, the short-form option/purchase contract should include the following terms: 1) how long the option holder has the exclusive right to purchase the rights to the screenplay (the option period); 2) how much the filmmaker will pay the writer(s) for the exclusive right to purchase the rights to the script (the option price); 3) the mechanisms for the holder to exercise the option (usually by forwarding written notice with full payment of the purchase price); 4) the purchase price to buy the script; 5) what rights are being purchased (the grant of rights); 6) what rights (if any) are reserved by the writer(s); and 7) what credit is due to the writer(s) in any motion picture made based on the script.

The long-form is so-called because it not only incorporates the short-form terms but also includes more complicated terms to be negotiated between parties who may have unique needs. Such additional terms can include: 1) whether the writer(s) of the script has/have a right to write a polish and/or rewrite of the script (and if so, how much compensation shall be paid for such work); 2) whether the writer(s) is/are entitled to any contingent compensation such as Net Profits (with the term Net Profits also then to be defined), this is also known as "profit participation"; 3) writer(s) rights concerning any potential sequels, prequels, and remakes, for example, the right to write sequels or the right to further compensation if the writer(s) are not given such opportunity; 4) who owns the rights to any material created by the option holder during the option period which is based upon the script (for example, any ideas, treatments, loglines, etc.); 5) representations and warranties by the writer(s); namely, that he or she wrote the script, the script is original (i.e., not copied from anyone), that the rights to the script have not been previously transferred to any other party and the writer(s) has/have the right to transfer the rights to the script. In this regard representations and warranties should be in the short form as well, but it is not uncommon to find it omitted since the parties can attach a "Certificate of Authorship" signed by the writer(s); 6) a statement that the writer(s) will indemnify and hold the filmmaker harmless if the writer(s) breach any representations made; 7) whether or not the agreement and the script will be subject to Writers Guild of America Minimum Basic Agreement (if so, the parties will be required to follow the WGA rules); 8) the inclusion of an additional "short-form assignment" which is a one-page agreement that acknowledges the option (this will facilitate filing with the United States Copyright Office for chain of title and notice of the option); and 9) a "Certificate of Authorship" which is a one-page agreement in which the writer(s) certify, among other things, that the writer(s) is/are the only author(s) of the script, the script is wholly original, it does not copy from any other source, it does not infringe on any other work, that the writer(s) own the work, that the writer(s) is/are authorized to transfer the work and have not previously transferred the work.

Whether the agreement is a short-form or long-form, the option period is usually between six months and two years. The filmmaker wants a period long enough to have a legitimate chance to engage in the development and fund-raising activities necessary to be able to produce the film (i.e., pay the purchase price and enter into preproduction in making the film). On the other hand, the owner of the script does not want to tie up the rights to the script with one filmmaker and risk passing up other opportunities to sell or option the script; therefore the owner of the script will want to receive enough money to compensate for that risk. It is not uncommon for both sides to overestimate the value of what they are bringing to the bargaining table. Clearly, the filmmaker likes the script enough to be involved with it for the many years it takes to make an independent film from start to distribution, and believes he or she can raise the money to make the film. However, the fact is that the overwhelming majority of filmmakers who attempt to raise the funds for the film they want to make are unsuccessful—so most likely the script will be tied up for a period of time and the only compensation the owner of the script will walk away with at the end of the option period(s) is the amount paid by the filmmaker for the option period(s). So if this amount is one dollar, then the script owner has precluded other potential deals during the option period for basically nothing.

Looking at the negotiations from the filmmaker's perspective, however, it is reported that over 35,000 scripts are registered with the US Copyright Office every year, so in simple economic terms, the supply of scripts far outnumbers the demand. This is not to say that each and every script is not valuable, it is just to highlight that the perceived "opportunities" that the script owner believes he or she is passing up are probably more "perceived" opportunities than real. The latter is especially true if the owner of the script has had no previous sales or options for any script. If the filmmaker pays 10 percent of the purchase price, for example, then he or she has every right to expect an initial option period of one to two years. From an economic standpoint the time given for the option period will vary based on the amount the filmmaker pays for the option (i.e., the less the filmmaker pays the less time the script owner is willing to allow for the option period). But this is an oversimplification because the fact is that anything less than a year renders the filmmaker's potential for raising the money to pay the purchase price less likely, meaning that the time the script owner will have given would be essentially "wasted" time since the ultimate goal—getting the money, purchasing the script, and making the movie—will have very little chance of occurring.

Quite often the owner of the script will make the decision to grant an option based primarily on his or her confidence in the filmmaker; first, that the filmmaker will successfully raise the money for the film, and second, that he or she will make a "good" film—not to mention that the writer might "like" the filmmaker. These intangibles in the negotiation process are often what influence a script owner's decision to option the script for very little money and for a reasonably long period of time. The fact is that the independent filmmaking process often involves emotions and intangibles as much as it involves decisions based upon hard-core economic analysis. But, the script-owner's readiness to make considerable concessions usually comes with a quid pro quo, which could include provisions for a higher price for any extension of an initial option period, a higher purchase price for the script if and when the filmmaker successfully raises the money to make the film, or a variety of other concessions.

Even if the initial option price is not obtained at a discount, but is set at a "rule of thumb" amount of 10 percent of the purchase price, any successive option periods will generally cost the filmmaker more to obtain. As a note, it is not unusual to find that provisions for subsequent option periods are often omitted from short-form option agreements. As a rule, the option prices are commonly much higher than the first option period price of 10 percent since the filmmaker controls the choice of exercising the option. Also, the initial agreement will escalate the cost of subsequent options because the script owner will want to put pressure on the film-maker to successfully raise the funds during the first option period. The thinking is that it is an incentive for the filmmaker to work as hard as pos-sible if he or she knows that at the end of the first option period there will be a substantial increase in the price for extending the option which would enable the filmmaker to continue working on the project. Further, even if the filmmaker does work hard during the initial option period, it is reason-able to assume that his or her chances of being more successful at raising the money in second or third option periods decrease because it is reason-able to assume that they unsuccessfully approached their "best contacts" in their first efforts. As a result, a script holder will want to escalate the option prices commensurate with the decrease in the probability of success. In other words, the "lost opportunities" risk will be expanding quantitatively with each subsequent option. It should be repeated that the extension terms and costs associated with each successive option term are negotiated and agreed upon before the parties sign the initial agreement. It is customary that the amount paid by the filmmaker for the initial option period is not offset against the purchase price if and when the purchase price is paid. However, it *is* customary for amounts that are paid by the filmmaker for each subsequent option period *will* be offset against the purchase price if and when the purchase price is paid. It should be noted that the parties sometimes alter these latter "customary" provisions regarding the offset of the option price against purchase price.

The final purchase price is also negotiated and agreed upon before the parties sign the agreement. The amount for the purchase price is also open to negotiation, and for a low-budget film it can be as low as $5,000 or as much as required for the WGA minimum amount (the WGA amount is used as a benchmark but the film most often will not be made a WGA signatory film by the filmmaker). For total budgets below $500,000 and between $500,000 and $1.2 million, part of the WGA minimum amount may be deferred based upon the requirements of the WGA low-budget agreement. The purchase price is influenced by such factors as: the experience of the writer (i.e., has the writer ever sold and/or optioned a screenplay before); whether the writer is a member of the Writers Guild of America; and the budget for the film. Writers who are members of the WGA, and who have sold a script before, will not want to agree to a purchase price that is less than the last amount he or she previously received for selling a screenplay, and in any case, he or she will not be open to accepting an amount less than the amount required under the WGA contract. A filmmaker producing a film is not a "signatory" to the WGA unless and until he or she signs up the company and the film with the WGA, thereby agreeing to abide by the WGA rules. A filmmaker is *not required* to take such a step. Therefore, a filmmaker who has not taken that step has the right to pay a writer whatever the market dictates.

However, most filmmakers want to be fair to the people with whom they work when making the film, and in the long run being fair when dealing with the people who work on a film is the best business policy. What many filmmakers decide to do to be fair to both themselves and the writer is to make the purchase price contingent on the amount of the production budget as of the time the film enters production. For example, if the in-going, direct production budget is between $200,000 and $300,000, then the purchase price could be 3 percent of the budget; if the in-going, direct production budget is between $300,000 and $500,000, then the purchase price could be 4 percent of the budget; if the in-going, direct production budget is between $500,000 and $1 million, then the purchase price could be 5 percent of the budget; etc. In the event the amount to be raised exceeds $1 million, then it's not uncommon to set the purchase price as a percentage of the in-going direct production budget, with a ceiling price and a floor price. For example, the purchase price might be a sum equal to 5 percent of the in-going, direct production budget, with a minimum purchase price of $50,000 and a maximum purchase price of $100,000. If a film is subject to completion bond fees, financing fees, or interest, then the in-going, direct production budget is calculated without the inclusion of these types of expenses. Usually, films made for less than $1 million do not involve such fees.

Another issue that is often addressed in the option/purchase agreement is whether or not the writer is to receive "points," which are often referred to as "net profits," "net proceeds," or "profit participation." Points generally encompass the provision that if the filmmaker receives proceeds in amounts that are in excess of the costs incurred in making the film, then certain individuals, such as the writer, would receive a certain percentage of such net proceeds. These amounts are commonly referred to as "monkey points" for obvious reasons (i.e., most independent films never even earn back the costs of the film, let alone earn revenue above the costs). In addition, even if a film does earn revenue above the costs, profit participants end up having to spend money hiring accountants and lawyers in order to obtain money rightfully belonging to them—money the typical participant does not have. The general rule is that profit participants never participate in the profit of a film regardless of how many "points" are promised in a contract. Nevertheless, whether the contract calls them "points," "net proceeds," or "net profits," it is recommended that the definition of any such term be placed in the option/purchase agreement, and such definition should correspond to the definition that the filmmaker has included (or will include) in his or her operating agreement for the limited liability company producing the film (and any other documents regarding the flow of money for the film, e.g., a private placement memorandum). By placing the definition of the contingent compensation in the contract, it avoids disagreement in the future as to how and when the writer's contingent compensation should be calculated. The uniformity of having the "net proceeds" or "net profits" calculated the same across all documents relating to the film avoids a situation where one party, the writer, director, or the investors, for example, unintentionally receives a more favorable position regarding these payments than another party involved with the film.

This discussion of option/purchase agreements is not intended to be comprehensive since there are numerous other issues regarding the negotiation and drafting of such agreements (including the "additional terms" associated with the long-form contract noted above). It would be wise for the filmmaker to engage an attorney in the drafting of an option/purchase agreement to ensure that the agreement clearly reflects the agreements between the parties involved.

OBTAINING THE FILM RIGHTS TO A BOOK

There are many similarities between the process of obtaining the film rights to a book and the process of obtaining the rights to a script that is already completed. However, there are some added complications and costs involved, especially if the book has already been published by a third-party (i.e., not self-published). If a book has been published by a third-party company then there is obviously another party involved who may have a license/ownership right to the book's film rights. Writers often, though not always, hold on to these rights because they view these rights as potentially lucrative. If the book is distributed by an established publisher then more often than not, the writer of the book has an agent and/or a manager who handles any inquiries regarding the writer's business.

The filmmaker should contact the publisher of the book who will ask the filmmaker to submit a written request regarding the availability of the book's film rights. More often than not the publisher will let the filmmaker know if the rights are available, and, if available, refer the filmmaker to the writer's agent who, of course, earns money by receiving a percentage of his or her client's earnings. So when the filmmaker contacts the agent he or she will suggest that a formal offer be submitted. Because low-budget film-makers have little or no money to make an offer, a response from the agent regarding a formal offer is rarely received. As a result, most filmmakers will decide to find the writer and approach him or her directly. There are film-makers who will skip the formal process altogether and go straight to the writer. The goal is obviously to convince the writer to grant the opportunity for developing the book into a script and the opportunity to raise the funds to produce the movie. The strategy for this approach is to demonstrate the passion, integrity, and genuine interest that the filmmaker will bring to the writer's book. Writers, unlike agents, are creative people and often respond positively to other creative people; on the other hand, writers are business people too, and they rely on their agents/managers to help them maximize the potential revenue from their intellectual property. So when meeting directly with the writer the filmmaker should have good answers to several inevitable questions from the writer such as:

1) How much money do you have to option the film rights for the book?
2) How much money is available for the person who will write the script?
3) Who will write the script?
4) Can the writer of the book have the opportunity to write the script, and if so, how and when would the writer be paid?
5) If someone else writes the script how much creative control over the final script will the writer of the book have?
6) What if the writer of the book hates the final script that the film-maker ends up with?
7) What is the amount of the budget for the film the filmmaker is trying to make from the book? Why is the budget so low?
8) What other films has the filmmaker made to this point?
9) For what length of time does the filmmaker want to option the film rights?

For the film rights to a book, the filmmaker should be prepared to spend between nothing and $10,000 for an option period of between six months and two years. Of course, if a book is a bestseller, or the writer is a famous writer, or other parties are interested in optioning the book's film rights, then it will be a whole different story.

Many of the terms found in an option/purchase agreement for a completed screenplay are also applicable to an option/purchase agreement for the film rights to a book (so-called literary option/purchase agreement). An additional document that needs to be obtained with the option/purchase agreement for the film rights to a book is a "Publisher's Release." This document, signed by the publisher of the book, basically states that the publisher has no claim to or interest in the film rights to the book. This document is of particular importance in obtaining the proper errors and omissions insurance for distribution of a film that is made based upon a book. If the filmmaker successfully obtains the option/purchase agreement for the film rights to the book, he or she then needs to obtain a script based on the book. Of course, the filmmaker could always write the script himself or herself which would reduce the cost of obtaining the script, but adapting a book into a film is not an easy, straightforward process. The filmmaker should carefully consider whether he or she can adapt the book into a screenplay; or whether or not a different writer could make a more successful adaptation; or whether the filmmaker has enough time under the option to both successfully complete a screenplay *and* raise the money necessary to produce the film.

If the filmmaker decides that he or she will hire a writer to adapt the book into a screenplay then there is the added process and cost of negotiating, drafting, and signing the writer's contract. Terms for this contract include but are not limited to:

1) What work will be required from the writer? Write a treatment? Write an outline? Write a first draft of the script? Write a rewrite of the script? Write a polish of the script?

2) What are the time periods for delivery of each writing form (i.e., outline, treatment, script, rewrite, polish)?

3) How long does the filmmaker have to read each writing form and make notes?

4) How much shall the writer be paid for each writing form?

5) Is any of the payment deferred?

6) Is the writer entitled to any contingent compensation?

7) Is the writer a WGA member (and if so, does the filmmaker want to be subject to the minimum payments and residual payments required by the WGA)?

8) How will the writer's writing credit be determined?

Clearly, the negotiation and drafting of the writer's contract could take a good deal of time to complete. Usually the filmmaker doesn't want to negotiate and enter the agreement with the writer until the option/purchase agreement with the holder of the film rights to the book is secured, which certainly makes sense. But by doing so, the time spent negotiating and entering a contract with the writer will be time taken away from the option period obtained from the holder of the film rights.

TALENT

One of the most important factors in determining whether or not an independent film achieves distribution through established channels, or even showings at film festivals, is the actors who appear in the film, or are even associated with it. Except for certain rare circumstances it is very difficult to secure the commitment of recognizable name talent during the development phase of the project. However, if a filmmaker wants to secure name talent, then this is the stage at which the process should begin, because it is never predictable, and it may be possible at this stage to secure the services of recognizable name talent without putting forth a pay-or-play offer, which is usually not a realistic option for an independent filmmaker, especially a first-time filmmaker. More importantly, the filmmaker will develop the information necessary to evaluate whether it makes sense to move forward and produce the film without recognizable name talent. Further, the filmmaker will also have laid the groundwork for obtaining the highest level of recognizable name talent if and when the money to make the film and pay the actors is actually secured. *Of course, most independent films are produced without any recognizable name actors.* There are, however, rare circumstances in which a filmmaker can secure recognizable name talent without paying money in a pay-or-play offer. The most common circumstance is when the filmmaker has a previous relationship with the actor. It also happens when an actor decides to produce his or her own independent film and turns to the people he or she has worked with in the past. Even if a recognizable name actor does commit to a film, rarely are contracts signed evidencing such a commitment since it is usually based on friendship.

There are different forms that an actor's commitment to a film can take: a verbal commitment, a "letter of intent" (sometimes called a "letter of interest"), a "deal memo," a "short-form contract" and a "long-form contract" are some examples. From a legal perspective, an oral or verbal contract is enforceable in California. There have been a few Hollywood cases concerning oral contracts, including two more recent high profile lawsuits, one involving Kim Basinger and her agreement to provide acting services to the film *Boxing Helena*, and one involving Francis Coppola and Warner Brothers' claim that he breached an oral agreement to provide directing services to the project *Pinocchio*. The purpose here is not to offer a summary of the legal issues of enforcing oral contracts or implied-in-fact contracts, but to review what a filmmaker needs to follow and needs to avoid in producing his or her film. Verbal agreements should be considered practically worthless, and should be discounted to zero, and the project should move forward as if they didn't exist. It is almost impossible to convert a verbal commitment into hard resources (think along the lines of walking into a bank to obtain a loan for your film and telling them, "don't worry, Tom Cruise is my friend and he told me he was going to be in the film"). And even if you could somehow translate a verbal commitment into hard assets (utilizing the well-known prophesy of P. T. Barnum that "there's a sucker born every minute"), it could turn out to be very difficult to secure such services from the person who gave the verbal commitment. At that juncture the filmmaker would be in the position of explaining to the people who turned over the hard assets why they were told that a certain actor (or other person) was committed to the film, and are now being informed that they are not going to be involved with the project. Even if, in the case of a lawsuit, witnesses can be brought to testify under oath that such person did in fact verbally agree to be in your movie, it won't matter. It's all bad since it will only create obstacles for the project, and will undercut the filmmaker's credibility. Properly drafted "letters of intent" (also called "letters of interest") are not legally enforceable. In general, a legally binding contract contains the parties' manifestation to be bound and contains the essential/material terms of the agreement. A properly drafted letter regarding the interest of an actor to a particular film will contain delimiting language. Here are a few examples.

- *"This letter sets forth certain non-binding terms . . ."*
- *"in no manner or under any interpretation does this letter create a binding commitment for 'actor' to participate in the project . . ."*
- *". . . there is no intention to be bound unless and until a formal, written contract is agreed to and signed by the 'actor' and an authorized representative of your company . . ."*

This does not mean that "letters of intent/interest" are worthless. Without the benefit of having previously produced a feature film there is no way to prove that the filmmaker can actually make one. However, the process that a filmmaker goes through in producing a low-budget feature film creates a track record, and can instill confidence that the filmmaker understands what needs to be done. Most pointedly, that he or she has already laid the groundwork to move ahead when the money is raised. At a minimum it shows that the filmmaker understands that name talent is a favorable asset for a film, and has approached the actor and the actor's representatives, successfully or not, to secure the actor's services. As a note, if a letter is signed by an actor the filmmaker should include a phrase in the letter that allows the filmmaker to use the name and likeness of the actor for development purposes, including, but not limited to, seeking financing for the film. In general, a good letter of intent/interest can help create credibility for the filmmaker and confidence that the filmmaker can accomplish what he or she is claiming he or she can accomplish, and, of course, it must be the "right" actor. Presenting an actor who is not a recognizable name, or for some other reason does not bring value to the film, may, on the other side of the coin, make it appear that the filmmaker will not spend the money raised in an economical, impactful manner. Further, even if the actor is the "right" actor, the filmmaker must be prepared to deftly answer any questions as to why a particular actor was approached to sign a letter, or as to whether the filmmaker would replace the actor if necessary. The best answers are the truthful answers, since the ultimate answer is that such letters bind neither the actor nor the filmmaker, so all roles in the film remain open until the signing of either a "deal memo," a "short-form contract," or "long-form contract."

"Deal memos," "short-form contracts," and "long-form contracts" are generally not entered into during the development phase, but are primarily negotiated and signed when the money to make the film has been raised and available for the filmmaker to spend. A "deal memo" (also referred to as a "term sheet") is a one- or two-page document that contains the basic terms of an agreement. For the actor the deal memo will contain such terms as: the role the actor will play; the compensation; the credit the actor will receive; the start date; the length of time the actor will provide services; the application (or not) of SAG-AFTRA rules; and whether the offer is a "pay-

or-play" offer. A "pay-or-play" offer, if accepted by the actor, means that the filmmaker is required to pay the compensation offered whether or not the film is ever made, or whether or not the producer decides to utilize the actor's services for the offered role. If an actor accepts a pay-or-play offer, the filmmaker is legally responsible for payment of compensation upon the signing of the agreement by the actor. This is the catch-22, that is to say, it is, of course, desirable to attach a recognizable name talent to help attract money, but it takes money to attach recognizable name talent to a project.

For simplicity's sake, it will suffice here to say that a "term sheet" is a one- to two-page document, whereas a "deal memo"—though it can also be a one- to two-page document—is commonly seen as the heading for contracts that are between four and ten pages in length. A "short-form contract" is also generally between four and ten pages in length. In a word, a "deal memo" could also mean a "short-form contract." The number of pages are separate from any "standard terms and conditions," "inducement letters," or "loan-out" terms that are sometimes found incorporated with a "deal memo" or "short-form contract." "Long-form contracts" are rarely used in the independent film world, especially for films with budgets below $1 million. "Long-form contracts" are primarily utilized by studios (and their subsidiaries/affiliates), and for actors can be upwards of fifty or sixty pages in length.

Recognizable name talent most often has an agent, a manager, and an attorney, or at least one or two from this group. The agent is the person responsible for fielding offers, so it is primarily the agent who the filmmaker approaches when making an offer. If a filmmaker is pursuing name talent, then it is very helpful to have an experienced casting director working with the filmmaker during the process of making any offers to talent. An experienced casting director normally will have had a working relationship with the various agencies and other actors, and can be invaluable. Again, the filmmaker will probably be caught in a catch-22 since it takes money to engage the services of a casting director which usually is not available until the money has been raised to produce the film. Sometimes filmmakers will make written offers via actors' agents stating that the offer is "contingent on securing the financing of the film's stated budget" or other such language. The offer can be submitted by the filmmaker or the filmmaker's attorney, but the filmmaker should be prepared for such offers being ignored by the actors' agents, who most likely will not even acknowledge receipt of such an offer. This is not a development that should concern the filmmaker, most players in the industry consider filmmaking a business, and when the filmmaker successfully raises the money to produce the film, he or she will attract the attention of the appropriate agents, at which time only the amount of the guaranteed offer will become the focus. From the agent's point of view, he or she will be reluctant to reject an offer outright because, of the multiple offers an actor receives for potential projects, which one will eventually raise enough money is an unknown. Therefore, it is safest for the agent to simply ignore the offers (neither accepting, rejecting, nor even acknowledging any of them) until an offer materializes with verifiable money available for the project (i.e., available for the agent's client).

CONSIDERING THE TYPES OF FILMS DISTRIBUTORS ARE DISTRIBUTING AND FESTIVALS ARE SCREENING

Considering what distributors and festival organizers are looking for before making a film may appear to run counter to the premise that an independent filmmaker should only be concerned with fulfilling his or her "vision" regardless of what audiences are being fed by the "gatekeepers." I believe the resolution of this conflict is inherent in the matter of sequence, that is, a filmmaker should follow his or her passion in writing the script, or finding the script that he or she wants to make as a low-budget feature film, *and then, once that decision is made* to review what distributors are distributing and film festivals are screening. I believe it is more important to understand what distributors are distributing because I have never met a filmmaker who didn't want an audience for his or her film, and the largest one possible. Further, there doesn't seem to be any particular pattern as to what film festivals will screen from year to year, whereas with distributors there is. Distributors are in the business of making money so they will generally pursue films they are reasonably confident can be sold. So, what is being recommended is that a low-budget feature filmmaker research and find the distribution companies who have distributed films in the past two to three years that are similar to the type of film that he or she plans to make. Then he or she should contact the filmmakers who made those films and ask them about their experiences with the distributor, and specifically what the budget was for their film. It will be relatively easy to get information from the filmmaker regarding his or her experience with the distributor (the key question is: Would you distribute another film through this distributor? Why or why not?). However, it is not going to be easy to get accurate information from the filmmakers regarding the budget because most seem very reluctant to share what their actual budget was. If you already know what things will cost you then you can begin to piece together whatever information you receive (as well as viewing the film) to estimate what their budget was. For example, the following questions should be asked:

1) Did they film on 35 millimeter film or digital video?
2) If it was digital video, was it a consumer camera or a high-end camera such as the Arri Alexa, Red Epic, or Sony F65?
3) Was it a SAG-AFTRA film?
4) Was there any "name" talent in the film?
5) If there was "name" talent, how much per day did they charge?; How many days of production?
6) How was postproduction completed?
7) How many crew members did they have?

A review of a company such as Image Entertainment, Inc. is a good example. This distribution company is a public company so its annual report is subject to certain public disclosures. For the fiscal year ending March 31, 2012, the company reported approximately $88.5 million in accumulated revenue, $73.7 million of which was primarily from DVD and Blu-ray. Image Entertainment, Inc. estimates that more than one hundred and twenty-five thousand DVD titles are available in the domestic market, of which three thousand two hundred titles are Image Entertainment releases, and to which Image adds an average of fifteen to twenty exclusive DVD titles per month. The company further states in its 2011 Form 10-K report:

We are a leading independent supplier of content in the music, comedy, special interest, episodic television, urban, and lifestyle genres . . . The Company has refocused its content acquisition efforts by focusing on . . . cast-driven feature films, which may result in fewer new titles, but have potentially higher consumer recognition and revenue on each release . . . The Company now acquires the greatest variety of distribution rights regarding acquired content in the greatest variety of formats, including DVD, Blu-ray, broadcast, VOD, and digital, for both domestic and international use.

This information tells you what is most important from this distributor's perspective. At the end of calendar year 2012, Image Entertainment, Inc. was purchased and began operating under the RLJ Entertainment umbrella. The chairman of RLJ Acquisitions, Robert Johnson, discussed the new company and provided information that is useful to low-budget independent filmmakers ("Six Questions: Robert Johnson, Chairman of the RLJ Companies," *Home Media* magazine, October 8, 2012, by Erik Gruenwedel). His feedback includes the following:

1) They plan to launch an urban-based subscription video-on-demand (SVOD) through YouTube to get low-budget urban films produced and distributed (he notes that from their perspective SVOD will fill an important niche in distribution because foreign source revenue is usually nonexistent for urban productions without major stars such as Will Smith or Denzel Washington).

2) Approximately 80 percent of their revenue is from physical DVDs.

3) Because there is a "slow migration" to digital distribution they acquire all digital rights from all films that they acquire.

4) They hope to inspire new urban content once producers become aware of Image's desire to distribute it.

5) Mr. Johnson states that since minority producers have great talent but do not get the funds to produce their films, Image is working with their lender to create a "60 million dollar film-financing pool."

6) He states, "the key to all of this is compelling programming with a marketing strategy that gets the consumer aware of the product." These are wise words to consider whether the low-budget film-maker is seeking to utilize an established distributor or plans to self-distribute his or her film.

Image Entertainment's 2007 Form 10-K also provides valuable information by citing the actual budgets for certain feature films it produced. These films should be viewed and evaluated to determine what industry professionals will expect production-wise at those budget levels. Unfortunately, since most distributors are private companies, and are not required to reveal their financial information to the public, it is more difficult to get an entire industry-wide perspective. Nevertheless, much valuable information can be gathered by reviewing the websites of private distribution companies and speaking with the individual filmmakers who have had their films released by such companies.

Thirteen Distribution Companies:
1) Grindstone Entertainment Group: *Nailbiter* (2013); *Black Cobra* (2012); *Knock Knock 2* (2012); *Night Wolf* (2012); *Game Time* (2011); *Removal* (2010); *Living Will…*(2010); *The Righteous and the Wicked* (2010); *Cold Storage* (2009); *The Last Resort* (2009); *Legend of the Bog* (2009); *Nightwatcher* (2008); *Sucker Punch* (2008).
2) CodeBlack Entertainment: *Fatal Consequences* (2011); *Politics of Love* (2011); *Whatever She Wants* (2010); *Something Like a Business* (2010); *Pressure* (2009); *Neo Ned* (2008); *Divine Intervention* (2007); *Nite Tales: The Movie* (2008); *All About Us* (2008).
3) Echo Bridge Home Entertainment: *All Of Her* (2013); *Locked in a Room* (2012); *BreadCrumbs* (2011); *Coming & Going* (2011); *The Last Vampire on Earth* (2010); *Nightfall* (2010); *Zombie Dearest* (2009); *Live Animals* (2009); *Frame of Mind* (2009); *The Woods Have Eyes* (2008); *Saving God* (2008); *American Military Intelligence and You!* (2008).
4) MarVista Entertainment: *Absolute Fear* (2012); *Campus Killer* (2012); *Cruel Will* (2011); *House Under Siege* (2010); *Nowhere to*

Hide (2009); *Cop Dog* (2008); *Resurrection Mary* (2008); *You Did What?* (2007).

5) Anchor Bay: *Love Me* (2012); *The Victim* (2011); *Megan Is Missing* (2010); *Cyrus: Mind of a Serial Killer* (2010); *Growth* (2010); *Frat Party* (2009); *Staunton Hill* (2009); *Soccer Mom* (2008); *The Cook* (2008); *Breathing Room* (2008); *All Roads Lead Home* (2008); *Five Across the Eyes* (2008).

6) First Look: *Bulletface* (2010); *The Locksmith* (2010); *Endgame* (2009); *Into Temptation* (2009); *Anxiety* (2008); *The Breakout* (2008).

7) Image Entertainment: *Prank* (2013); *What Goes Around Comes Around* (2012); *Money Matters* (2011); *Speed Dating* (2010); *Perfect Combination* (2010); *Everybody Dies* (2009); *I Do...I Did* (2009); *Are There Any Questions?* (2008); *Love For Sale* (2008); *Six Reasons Why* (2008); *Comedy Jump Off: The Latino Explosion* (2008).

8) Lionsgate Home Entertainment: *Los Wildcats del Norte* (2012); *Go For It* (2011); *Seconds Apart* (2011); *The Spirit* (2008); *Punisher: War Zone* (2008); *Transporter 3* (2008); *Saw V* (2008); *Meet the Browns* (2008); *A Christmas Too Many* (2007); *Experiment in Torture* (2007); *Knock Knock* (2008); *Bella* (2007).

9) TLA Releasing: *The One* (2011); *Finding Me: Truth* (2011); *Satan Hates You* (2010); *Release* (2010); *Redwoods* (2009); *Shank* (2009); *3 Day Weekend* (2008); *I Dreamt Under the Water* (2008); *Another Gay Sequel: Gays Gone Wild* (2008); *Dog Tags* (2008); *Summer Scars* (2008); *Two Minutes Later* (2008).

10) Magnolia Pictures: *V/H/S* (2012); *Diary of a Tired Black Man* (2009); *A Good Day to Be Black & Sexy* (2008); *Yonkers Joe* (2008); *Julia* (2008); *Donkey Punch* (2008); *Hank & Mike* (2008); *Closing Escrow* (2007); *The Signal* (2007); *Great Wall of Sound* (2007); *The Life Before Her Eyes* (2008).

11) IFC Films/First Take/Festival Direct: *Sleepwalk with Me* (2012); *Autoerotic* (2011); *Lovers of Hate* (2010); *Cold Weather* (2010); *I Hate Valentines Day* (2009); *Looking for Eric* (2009); *Home Movie* (2008); *Che* (2008); *Medicine For Melancholy* (2008); *The Pleasure of Being Robbed* (2008); *Diminished Capacity* (2008); *Ping Pong Playa* (2008);

In Search of a Midnight Kiss (2008); *Hannah Takes the Stairs* (2007); *Nights and Weekends* (2008).

12) Indican Pictures: *The Truth About Angels* (2011); *Bat $#*! Crazy* (2011); *Dark Metropolis* (2010); *Street Poet* (2010); *The Tenant* (2010); *Monster Beach Party* (2009); *The Grind* (2009); *10,000 AD: The Legend of a Black Pearl* (2008); *A Simple Promise* (2008); *Cut'n It Up: Chicago* (2008); *The Legend of God's Gun* (2008); *Fighting Words* (2008); *Rolling* (2008); *Dead in the Water* (2007).

13) Benten Films: *St. Nick* (2010); *Canary* (2010); *The GoodTimesKid* (2009); *Quiet City/Dance Party USA* (2007); *The Guatemalan Handshake* (2007); *The Free Will* (2007); *Team Picture* (2007); *LOL* (2006).

PART II
Producing the Film

4

Equity Financing of Independent Films "Outside the System"

"Remember, George, no man is a failure who has friends."
——It's a Wonderful Life

STUDIO FINANCING

The extreme level of risk involved in the process of making and distributing films, and the disproportionate demand for funding versus the supply available makes obtaining money to make a film the greatest obstacle in the filmmaking process. In general, a producer with a script has two distinct paths to follow in the process of producing his or her project; find financing through a major or mini-major studio, or directly approach funding sources to obtain the necessary funds, these funding sources may be within the "system" or outside the "system."

Studios do invest money in making films. However, the odds of any particular script being chosen for financing through the studio system are very long—staggeringly so. And even if a studio is interested in a script the deal is usually to option or purchase the script without any attachments such as the writer being attached as the director of the film or as an actor in the film. As studios evolved they realized that they maximize their revenue when they act as the distributor and not as financier of the film. As a result, they primarily seek opportunities to distribute films made by other people in exchange for taking a distribution fee "off the top." When studios do decide to finance films in addition to distributing them, they primarily develop and release "tent pole" films that are theatrically released on many screens simultaneously and have strong possibilities of sequel and prequel movies. The basic business model of today's studios, therefore, tends to exclude the overwhelming number of available scripts from obtaining studio financing or, for that matter, distribution either.

Therefore, most producers seek financing for their script outside the studio system (i.e., *independent* of the studios), which is one of the major reasons the films are called "independent films." This chapter will review the process of pursuing equity financing for a low-budget independent film, and the next chapter will explore alternative means of financing a film such as nonequity crowdfunding, loans, nonstudio distributors, tax subsidies, and tax–exempt status and fiscal sponsorship. Chapter 6 will explore the means of financing independent films within the "system."

PRIVATE EQUITY

As noted in the previous chapter, the total budget for any independent film is hard to come by; this is even more so for determining the sources of the funds for the budget. However, an article in *Variety* ("Beggars Banquet," January 14, 2004) sheds some anecdotal light on what is commonly believed to be accurate regarding the sources and amounts of financing for independent feature films. The article evaluated the sixteen films in dramatic competition at the 2004 Sundance Film Festival, and found that ten of the sixteen films were financed by the producers' network of friends, family, and acquaintances. According to a quote of Micah Green, then at Cinetic Media, "financing for most first features is coming from the same source it's always come from: the friends and family network." The reported budgets of these films are within the range that is to be expected of a first or second film (i.e., from $50,000 up to $1,000,000), with the majority of films falling in the $250,000 to $500,000 budget range. I have found Green's observation to be generally true, that low-budget feature film-makers, first, second, or otherwise, utilize what is known as "private equity" (for example, friends, family, and acquaintances) as opposed to loans, non-studio distributors, presales, or tax subsidies. It is not that a low-budget filmmaker never utilizes the finance sources other than private equity; it is just that these other sources are rarely available to a low-budget filmmaker, and when they are, they are rarely cost-effective for a film in the budget range between $50,000 and $1,000,000.

SECURITIES LAWS

The first step in the process of raising private equity money is for the film-maker to determine if he or she is offering a "security" for sale which would require its registration or exemption. Basically, a "security" exists whenever a party invests money which is expended in a common enterprise with the expectation that there will be a return of money primarily through the efforts of others. Under the federal and state securities laws any "offer" to "sell" a "security" must be either registered with the proper authorities or qualify for an exemption from registration. The primary federal exemptions are:

1) Regulation D ("Reg. D");
2) The private offering exemption under Section 4(2) of the Securities Act;
3) The intrastate exemption in Section 3(a)(11) of the Securities Act;
4) Section 4(6) of the Securities Act which exempts from registration offers and sales of securities to accredited investors when the total offering price is less than $5 million.

The question often arises as to whether the investor is an "active" investor or a "passive" investor. If the investor is an *active* investor then the transaction *does not involve a security* and the federal and state securities laws will not govern the transaction. If, on the other hand, the investor is a *passive* investor then the transaction *does involve a security* and the federal and state securities laws will govern the transaction. This is an important distinction because the transaction will be reviewed to see if it involves the expectation of a return of money from the investment "primarily through the efforts of others" (i.e., a "passive" investment). In determining this issue courts have held that in order to trigger the federal and state securities laws, "the most essential management functions or duties must be performed by others" and not by the investor. The determination as to whether an investor is "active" or "passive" is a "facts and circumstance" inquiry, which also includes an inquiry as to an investor's "knowledge and experience" in an industry (in this case, in the film industry). The purpose of such an inquiry is to determine if the investor is relying on the efforts of others even in situations where he or she has had knowledge and experience in a different industry, or in situations where he or she has the right to meaningfully engage in the management of the investment (for example, in a member managed limited liability company). Therefore, filmmakers should be aware that there are multiple requirements in an inquiry to determine whether an investor is the type of investor who needs to be protected by the federal and state securities laws.

The "active"/"passive" issue impacts the filmmaker in a few different situations: a) money that is provided to the filmmaker without any paperwork regarding the receipt and expenditure of the money; b) money provided to a limited partnership that will produce the film; c) money provided to a general partnership that will produce the film; d) money provided to a limited liability company that will produce the film; and e) money provided based on an "investment contract." As discussed in Chapter 7, C corporations and S corporations are rarely if ever used to raise money to produce a low-budget feature film because of the many operational and tax limitations, and are not effective vehicles for these purposes especially when compared to the excellent alternatives of limited partnerships and limited liability companies. However, it should be noted here that, in general, an investment in C corporations and S corporations by a "passive" investor is a "security" transaction subject to federal and state securities laws.

Money Obtained with No Paperwork. Although it does occasionally occur, it is very rare (and not recommended) for an investor to give money to a filmmaker without receiving paperwork relevant to the investment. When it does occur it is primarily in situations where there are one or two relatives of a filmmaker who give him or her money to make the film. In this type of situation the facts can, and often do, lead to the conclusion that these family members had no "expectation of a return of money" so it was not a "security" investment (and therefore not subject to the securities laws), but the money is more properly characterized as a "gift" (although the family members should be made aware of the potential estate and gift tax consequences of the "gift"). Also see the discussion of "gift" in the "Crowd-funding—Nonequity Investment" section of Chapter 5.

Partnership as a "Security." Investors who are limited partners in a limited partnership generally have purchased a security, whereas investors who put money in a general partnership generally have not purchased a security. The reason why a general partnership does not ordinarily trigger securities issues goes back to the "active" versus "passive" evaluation. Limited partnerships are designed to have a general partner who has the sole responsibility of performing the management duties of the enterprise. As such, the investors are relying "primarily on the efforts of others," thereby rendering the investment a security. Conversely, the laws of general partnerships usually consider each investor a partner with the right to participate in the management of the enterprise. Since the investors are *not* relying primarily on the efforts of others, the investment is *not* a security. These are general rules, because if a general partnership agreement is drafted so as to eliminate or severely restrict the partners' rights to participate in the management of the partnership, then the general partnership *will be* deemed a security and will be subject to the federal and state security laws. Similarly, if limited partnership investors are granted "general partner" rights and responsibilities then those investors *could be* "active" investors. In addition, even if a partnership provides the investors with rights and powers, there is a further inquiry to determine if the investors in fact have the ability to exercise those rights and powers. For example, if an investor is so inexperienced and unknowledgeable about the industry in which the investment is made (for these purposes, the film industry), or so dependent on the unique entrepreneurial or managerial ability of the general partner who is effectively "irreplaceable," then the investor could be considered a "passive" investor regardless of the rights and powers the investor might be able to effectively exercise over the investment. In most instances investors will not have experience and knowledge of the film industry so the filmmaker *will* be required to comply with federal and state securities laws.

Limited Liability Company as a "Security." As will be seen in Chapter 8, the most common entity filmmakers use for making a film is the limited liability company, usually a newly created limited liability company formed for the sole purpose of making the film (sometimes referred to as "one-off" companies). The limited liability company is designed to be a flexible entity. The degree of flexibility of the management of the enterprise is drafted in the language of the company's governing document, that is, the limited liability company operating agreement. At one end of the spectrum the limited liability company operating agreement can be drafted similar to a limited partnership, with the investors having no right of participation in the management of the company, and therefore, it *would be* a "security" investment. At the other end of the spectrum the limited liability company operating agreement can be drafted so that it is a "member-managed" company, with each investor ("member") participating in the management of the company. Similar to the general partnership/limited partnership analysis, determining whether the member-managed LLC is a "security" will also need to take into account whether an investor is so inexperienced and unknowledgeable about the industry in which the investment is made, or so dependent on the unique entrepreneurial or managerial ability of the general partner who is effectively "irreplaceable," that the investment is therefore a "passive" investment thus requiring the filmmaker to comply with federal and state securities laws. Most independent films, especially first-time film efforts, are produced using a limited liability company with "passive" investors having little or no participation rights in the management of the company. Accordingly, independent films using limited liability companies with "passive" investors *must* address the federal and state securities laws regarding the money raised to make the film.

Investment Contract as a "Security." The phrase "investment contract" is a "catch-all" for any agreement between filmmakers and investors establishing the rights and obligations of each. The most common investment contracts encountered in film production are "investor financing agreements," "joint ventures," and "strategic alliances." The determination of whether or not an investment contract is a "security" and subject to federal and state securities laws depends on the terms in each investment contract. The standards applied to these types of transactions are the same standards presented above (i.e., a "security" exists when a party invests money that is expended in a common enterprise with the expectation that there will be a return of money primarily through the efforts of others). Also similar to the above analysis the determination often turns on whether the party investing the money will be "active" or "passive." Therefore, the terms of each "investment contract" need to be reviewed in order to determine whether or not it is subject to federal and state securities laws.

"SECURITIES" REGISTRATION AND EXEMPTION FROM REGISTRATION

In the event an enterprise is considered a "security" (whether it is a limited partnership, LLC, investment contract, or other), the Securities Act of 1933 generally requires the registration of the security and the issuance of a prospectus before offers to purchase the securities are solicited or made. Registering a security when raising money to produce an independent film is generally an impractical, time-consuming, and expensive process. It is even more so with films made for budgets between $50,000 and $1,000,000. Therefore, independent filmmakers generally avoid the process of registration and instead take advantage of one of the "exemptions" that are available for certain securities and certain transactions. These exemptions allow the issuer to accept an investment from a "passive" investor without the need to first register the security and provide a prospectus. However, each exemption has specific requirements that must be scrupulously met. The most common exemption relied upon by independent filmmakers is Regulation D. Regulation D provides objective standards that filmmakers can rely upon to avoid the penalties associated with offering or selling a security without proper registration. Other exemptions available include the so-called private offering exemption (Section 4(2) of the Securities Act), the intra-state offering exemption (Section 3(a)(11) of the Securities Act), and the accredited investor exemption (Section 4(6) of the Securities Act).

An Example of the Securities Laws at Work with Independent Film Producing. There are not many reported claims against independent filmmakers brought by disgruntled investors and/or government regulators. However, such claims do occur. It is wisest to take the time to understand the parameters of what can and cannot be done when raising money for an independent film. Further, once such understanding is obtained, one should not be fooled into believing that potential negative consequences will not occur simply because of a lack of high-profile reported claims against filmmakers. The following reported incident is an example of some of the securities laws that can cause a filmmaker to run afoul and some of the potential consequences of violating such laws. The independent films *From Mexico With Love* (2009) and *Eye of the Dolphin* (2006) were produced by Cinamour Entertainment, LLC, and Q Media Assets, LLC, respectively. In June 2011 the Federal Bureau of Investigation (FBI) and the Internal Revenue Service (IRS) arrested and charged eighteen individuals on the grounds that in the process of raising funds for producing films the defendants allegedly lied, provided half-truths, and concealed material facts from investors. The authorities claimed that the defendants obtained "lead lists" of potential investors and obtained film financing by making false claims and failing to disclose material facts. It was charged that the defendants claimed that a certain percent of the funds would be used solely to produce the films, that investors would receive up to 1,000 percent return on investment (ROI) and that a film would be completed which was eventually never produced (the authorities identified the film as one entitled *Red Water: 2012*). Two films that were produced with the funds raised: *Eye of the Dolphin* reportedly earned $70,000 at the domestic box office with a budget of approximately $4 million and *From Mexico With Love* reportedly earned $550,000 at the domestic box office with a budget of approximately $5 million.

Among the charges brought by the authorities were: 1) "sale of unregistered securities"; 2) "mail fraud"; and 3) "wire fraud." It was reported that the sale of unregistered securities carries a maximum possible sentence of five years in prison and the mail fraud and wire fraud carry maximum sentences up to twenty years in prison. It is not surprising that the situation caught the attention of federal regulators when it was reported that the situation included unfulfilled promises to complete certain films, the claim that the funds were raised in a "boiler room" manner and less than one-third of the money raised was actually spent on producing the films. This situation serves as a sobering reminder of the legal standards and penalties that can be applied to an independent filmmaker who may find himself or herself on the wrong side of the laws. A filmmaker would be wise to carefully weigh the potential risks inherent in the language provided to potential investors when asking for financing for his or her independent film. See Chapters 9, 10, and 11. [1]

Regulation D Exemption. Regulation D ("Reg. D") provides three exemptions from the registration requirements which are found in Rules 501 through 506 of the Securities Act. Rules 501, 502, and 503 provide general rules applicable to the Regulation D exemptions, and Rules 504, 505, and 506 provide the three exemptions that filmmakers rely upon.

Rule 504 of Regulation D. Rule 504 provides an exemption from the registration requirements for certain issuers when they offer and sell up to $1,000,000 of their securities over any twelve-month period. To qualify, an issuer must have a stated business plan or purpose (i.e., not be a so-called blank check company), the issuer cannot be a reporting company and the company is not allowed to solicit or advertise the securities to the public.

---

1. Epilogue: It was reported in June 2012 that eight of the defendants facing trial plead guilty, three were found guilty at trial and one was acquitted.

A reporting company is one that is required to file a registration statement under the Securities Act, which is basically a company that offers securities to the public, or is listed on a national stock exchange or has over 500 investors and assets greater than $10 million. A non-reporting company is one that is not required to file a registration statement. A "blank check company" is one that solicits offers for securities when the company/issuer has no specific business plan or purpose, or a business plan to engage in a merger or acquisition with an unidentified company or companies. A "one-off" entity formed to make a film generally will be neither a reporting company nor a "blank check company." Rule 504 does not require the issuer to provide investors any specific information; however, an issuer must comply with antifraud provisions of the securities laws, which can be achieved by providing sufficient information regarding the offering that neither contains false information nor omits any material fact or information. Therefore, a disclosure document (a private placement memorandum or "PPM") is an important step to ensure compliance with the antifraud provisions. This is discussed further in Chapter 10. The securities sold under this exemption are considered "restricted" securities (see below).

Rule 505 of Regulation D. Rule 505 allows companies to offer and sell up to $5 million of its securities during any twelve-month period. The company may sell to an unlimited number of *accredited* investors and up to thirty-five other investors who do not need to satisfy the sophistication or wealth standards associated with other exemptions. Similar to Rule 504, the securities are also "restricted" securities and the company cannot use general solicitation or advertising to sell the securities.

An "accredited investor" includes the following: a) a bank, insurance company, registered investment company, business development company, or small business investment company; b) an employee benefit plan, within the meaning of the Employee Retirement Income Security Act, if a bank, insurance company, or registered investment adviser makes the investment decisions, or if the plan has total assets in excess of $5 million; c) a charitable organization, corporation, or partnership with assets exceeding $5 million;

d) a director, executive officer, or general partner of the company selling the securities; e) a business in which all the equity owners are accredited investors; f) *a natural person who has individual net worth, or joint net worth with the person's spouse, excluding the value of his or her primary residence, that exceeds $1 million at the time of the purchase;* g) *a natural person with income exceeding $200,000 in each of the two most recent years or joint income with a spouse exceeding $300,000 for those years and a reasonable expectation of the same income level in the current year;* or h) a trust with assets of at least $5 million, not formed to acquire the securities offered, and whose purchases are directed by a sophisticated person. The two italicized groups, f) and g), are the ones most often associated with independent filmmakers. Issuers can decide what information to give accredited investors as long as they do not violate the antifraud provisions of the federal and state securities laws. However, non-accredited investors under Rule 505 must receive specific information, that is, generally the same kind of information that is provided in registered offerings. This will be discussed in Chapter 10.

Rule 506 of Regulation D. Rule 506 is considered a "safe harbor" for the private offering exemption of Section 4(2) of the Securities Act. Issuers using the Rule 506 exemption can raise an unlimited amount of money. To utilize this exemption the issuer: a) must not use general solicitation or advertising to sell the securities (there is an exception to this general rule within the "Jumpstart Our Business Startups" (JOBS) Act that was signed into law on April 5, 2012; see "General Solicitation or Advertising Prohibited" below); b) can sell to an unlimited number of "accredited investors" and up to thirty-five other purchasers (*unlike Rule 505, all non-accredited investors also must be sophisticated investors, that is, they must have sufficient knowledge and experience in financial and business matters to make them capable of evaluating the merits and risks of the investment*); c) must provide non-accredited investors specific information, that is, generally the same type of information provided in registered offerings; and d) must provide information that does not violate the antifraud provisions of the federal and state securities laws. The securities offered and sold are also *restricted* securities.

Securities Purchased Are "Restricted Securities." The parties who purchase securities under the Regulation D exemption are purchasing "restricted" securities meaning that they may not be resold unless subsequently registered with the SEC or unless the new purchaser(s) meet the requirements for another exemption from registration. The Securities Act doesn't provide a direct exemption for resales of privately placed securities (such as when a filmmaker relies on a Regulation D or other exemption). However, the so-called four, one and one-half, 4 (1 ½), exemption is a court created exemption allowing certain parties to resell securities acquired in a private placement. There are numerous requirements to claim the exemption which forces the issuing company, the initial investor, and the prospective purchaser to incur further legal fees and shoulder the burden of proving the fulfillment of these requirements, which is not without risk. Overall, the filmmaker should be aware, and communicate to potential investors, that the paperwork his or her attorney will prepare (the PPM, Operating Agreement, Subscription Agreement, etc.) will explicitly state that the securities are "restricted," so the initial investor must invest without the intention of reselling the investment, and that any such proposed transfer will require the approval of the company which it may withhold with absolute discretion.

General Solicitation or Advertising Prohibited. Rules 504, 505, and 506 prohibit general solicitation or advertising in the offering of securities under these exemptions, but there are two minor exceptions, one under Rule 504 and one under Securities and Exchange Commission Rule 1001, and one pending exception under the JOBS Act which revised Rule 506 (see below). Examples of general solicitation include advertisements, for example, on a website and mass mailings. Obviously, what facts constitute a "general" solicitation is a gray area. A guideline as to whether general solicitation or advertising has been used is whether or not the issuer has a "pre-existing" relationship with the party that is receiving the offer to purchase the security, that is, if the issuer has a "pre-existing" relationship, then it would not be engaging the general public.

There are two scenarios in which an independent filmmaker can utilize a "general announcement" of a proposed offering: first is Securities and

Exchange Commission Rule 1001, which provides an exemption from the registration requirements for offers and sales of securities in amounts of up to $5 million that satisfy the conditions of Section 25102(n) of the California Corporations Code; and second is Regulation D Rule 504 coupled with the Model Accredited Investor Exemption (MAIE). A third possible scenario is the JOBS Act which eliminates the prohibition of general solicitation or general advertising regarding offers and sales of securities made pursuant to Rule 506, provided that all purchasers are "accredited investors" and the issuer takes reasonable steps to verify that purchasers of the securities are "accredited investors." As of the writing of this book the Securities and Exchange Commission (SEC) issued proposed rules (outlined below) but has not adopted final rules. The new JOBS Act eliminating the prohibition of general solicitation or general advertising under Rule 506 does not become effective until final rules are adopted by the SEC.

The California law exempts offerings from California state registration when made by California companies to "qualified purchasers" whose characteristics are similar to, but not the same as, accredited investors under Regulation D. This exemption allows some methods of general solicitation prior to sales. Certain issuers (such as California corporations and other entities organized in California) are permitted to make a "general announcement" of a proposed offering to be published by written document with the following information: 1) the price of the security; 2) a brief description of the issuer's business; and 3) a statement "For more complete information about the Issuer and the Security, send for additional information from (name and address) by sending this coupon or call (telephone number)." After the issuer provides disclosure documents and subscription information to the prospective purchaser it must then wait at least five days before either a sale or commitment to purchase can be accepted. This exemption and general announcement is rarely utilized by independent filmmakers because it is applicable for California residents and most independent filmmakers plan to approach investors outside of California, which disqualifies this exemption.

Of more use to independent filmmakers, especially low-budget independent filmmakers, is the Model Accredited Investor Exemption (MAIE), coupled with Regulation D Rule 504, compliance for offers and sales of up to $1 million. The MAIE was adopted by the North American Securities Administrators Association (NASAA) and a majority of the states have passed laws that adopt the MAIE or a similar version with variations, including the following states: Arkansas, California, Colorado, Connecticut, Delaware, Hawaii, Indiana, Kansas, Kentucky, Maine, Maryland, Nevada, New Jersey, New Mexico, North Dakota, Oklahoma, Puerto Rico, Rhode Island, South Dakota, Utah, Virginia, Washington, West Virginia, and Wyoming. The good news is that under the exemption an issuer can make a general announcement of the offering "by any means," including the Internet if the issuer meets other requirements of the exemption. This potentially increases the number of prospective investors that can be reached. The bad news is that there are many requirements that must be fulfilled to qualify for the exemption, and many states have certain requirements specific to offers and sales in its state which increases compliance costs. In addition to complying with the requirements of Rule 504, an issuer can only sell its securities to parties it reasonably believes are "accredited investors," as defined above. Other requirements include certain information that must be provided in a "general announcement," the proper investment intent of any prospective purchaser and other state filing requirements.

The Securities and Exchange Commission (SEC) issued proposed rules regarding the JOBS Act repeal of the prohibition against "general solicitation" and "general advertising" when utilizing a Regulation D, Rule 506 exemption. In general under the proposed rules, an issuer must: 1) take reasonable steps to verify that the purchasers are accredited investors; 2) all purchasers must be accredited investors either because they meet one of the definitions or the issuer reasonably believes that they do at the time of the sale; and 3) all terms and conditions of the definition of accredited investor, the integration rules, and the rules limiting resale must be satisfied. The SEC stated that they decided against providing bright line or specific methods that are required to verify accredited investor status of purchasers. To increase flexibility the SEC decided to base the determination of whether steps taken are "reasonable" on the facts and circumstances of each transaction, but it has provided a number of factors to be considered when determining if an issuer used reasonable steps to verify accredited investor status, including: 1) the nature of the purchaser and the type of accredited investor that the purchaser claims to be; 2) the amount and type of information that the issuer has about the purchaser; and 3) the nature of the offering, including the manner in which the purchaser was solicited and the size of the investment among other terms.

The SEC believes that the amount and type of information that an issuer has about a purchaser will inform the issuer of what additional steps are required to verify the purchaser's accredited investor status. For example, if investors are solicited through a website accessible by the general public, or through email or social media, then an issuer is required to take greater measures to verify accredited investor status. As opposed to a situation where a reliable third party, such as a registered broker-dealer, creates a database of prescreened accredited investor parties that an issuer accesses to solicit investors. The SEC specifically advises that asking investors to complete a signed questionnaire confirming its accredited investor status would not be sufficient where investors are solicited through a website accessible by the general public, or through email or social media. An issuer would have to consider the additional time and expense with the prospect of obtaining the information necessary to secure the investment. This is especially critical for low-budget filmmakers who often do not have additional time or funds to meet these additional expenses. The SEC gives the following examples of the types of information an issuer should obtain from purchasers to verify the purchasers' accredited investor status: a) Form W-2 (income reports); b) tax returns; c) recent pay stubs; d) tax assessments; e) valuations and appraisals; f) a list of liabilities, including a sworn statement that all material liabilities have been disclosed; g) organizational documents; h) balance sheets and quarterly statements; i) personal and company bank statements and brokerage statements; and j) verification of accredited investor status by a broker/dealer, attorney, or accountant.

The Rule 1001 and the MAIE/504 rules for "general announcements" have generally provided the opportunity for website providers to create a form of "online dating service" where the website provider invites companies to create a company "profile" (in compliance with the exemption requirements) on the website and then invites prescreened "accredited investors" to peruse various listed companies, hoping for an investment "date" that matures into an investment "marriage." The JOBS Act revisions to the "general solicitation" and "general advertising" under Regulation D, Rule 506 have not yet become operative law as of the writing of this book, so the extent of its usefulness to the low-budget independent filmmaker remains to be evaluated, especially in light of the fact that even one sale to a purchaser that is not an "accredited investor" precludes reliance on the changed law. It should be noted here that low-budget filmmakers often find their financing among friends, family, and acquaintances, within which there is usually at least one purchaser who is not an "accredited investor."

For those who do decide to sell only to "accredited investors," when the changes do become operative law, they will alleviate past concerns about what was generally regarded as a "gag" law on a company engaged in selling securities reliant upon Rule 506. For example, the new law would alleviate concerns if a filmmaker who is relying on a Rule 506 exemption informs visitors to its website that the company is raising funds for a film, and it also would alleviate concerns attached to "pitch seminars" or "pitch meetings" in which the filmmaker provides information about investing in his or her film to attendees who have become aware of the gathering through "general advertising." However, reliance will require more administrative time and expense to verify the accredited investor status of each purchaser. In any case, independent filmmakers generally should not consider the ability to provide a "general announcement," "general solicitation," or "general advertisement" regarding investment in their film under these exemptions as a tool that will necessarily increase the prospects of obtaining investor financing for their film. The terms "general announcement," "general solicitation," and "general advertisement" are misnomers since the exemptions only apply if the prospective investors are "qualified purchasers" or "accredited investors," which by definition are a very small percentage of the general United States population. Further, independent filmmakers, and particularly low-budget filmmakers, primarily obtain the funding for their films from people they know and who know them. Having the ability to reach certain members of the general public does not change the basic fact that investing in independent films is a high risk endeavor so even if an investor is interested in a high risk investment, it is most often based on the relationship between the investor and the people involved in the endeavor and not on the economic prospects of the investment.

Providing General and Financial Information. A company offering securities under Rule 504 is not required to furnish specified information to purchasers. Under Rule 505 and Rule 506 a company *must provide* non-accredited investors disclosure information that is basically the same as those provided in registered offerings. Under all of the Regulation D exemptions, the company making an offering must also provide information sufficient to avoid violating the antifraud provisions of the federal and state securities laws. To comply with the foregoing, a company must meet certain requirements depending on whether it is a reporting or non-reporting company. A reporting company will generally provide either: a) the annual report to investors for the most recent year (and any updates), information contained in the most recent proxy statement, and a Form 10-K if requested in writing; or, b) the Form 10-K, a registration statement on Form S-1, or a registration statement under the Exchange Act on Form 10, whichever is the most recent. A reporting company must also provide a brief description of the securities being offered, the use of the proceeds from the offering, and any material changes not reflected in the documents it has provided. A non-reporting company must have a private placement memorandum (PPM) prepared, and provide it to prospective investors within a reasonable timeframe before the sale of the securities. The private placement memorandum must include information "to the extent material to an understanding of the issuer, its business, and the securities being offered." First-time filmmakers almost always utilize a "non-reporting company," and therefore must have a private placement memorandum prepared by a qualified person (i.e., a qualified attorney).

Filing Form D. To be eligible to utilize Regulation D, a company must file a Form D with the Securities and Exchange Commission no later than fifteen days after the first sale of securities pursuant to one of the exemptions. If the issuer fails to timely file a Form D, the Commission can obtain an order from a court, and, once such order is issued, the exemption under Regulation D will no longer be available to the issuer for future transactions. The disqualification can be waived, however, upon a showing of good cause by the issuer that the exemption should not be denied. For purposes of Form D the first sale is deemed to have taken place upon receipt of the first subscription agreement and the first deposit of funds into escrow even if the funds placed in escrow are subject to the realization of a specified minimum amount. As of March 2009 the SEC no longer accepts paper filings of Form D but requires them to be electronically filed using the SEC's Electronic Data Gathering, Analysis, and Retrieval system (EDGAR).

Private Offering Exemption. Section 4(2) of the Securities Act (the so-called private offering exemption) exempts from registration "transactions by an issuer not involving any public offering." To qualify for this exemption, the purchasers of the securities must: a) have enough knowledge and experience in finance and business matters to evaluate the risks and merits of the investment (i.e., be a "sophisticated investor"), or be able to bear the investment's economic risk; b) have access to the type of information normally provided in a prospectus; and c) agree not to resell or distribute the securities to the public. There also can be no public solicitation or general advertising in connection with the offering. There are factors that make qualifying for the private offering exemption a challenge, not the least of which is determining when an offering in fact becomes "public" so as to make this "private" offering exemption unavailable. Regulation D has created a "safe harbor" for situations that comply with the requirements of Regulation D, which makes the private offering largely redundant for the low-budget filmmaker.

Intrastate Exemption Of Section 3(a)(11). This exemption in the Securities Act is available where all offers and sales are made to bona fide residents of a single state, that is, the state laws where the company offering the security is organized and doing business. The doing business requirement has been difficult to implement and requires the company to have its principal place of business in the appropriate jurisdiction, and must plan to use most of the proceeds within that jurisdiction. This exemption is also more problematic than other available exemptions because a single offer or sale to a nonresident of the applicable state will destroy the availability of the exemption of *all* sales reliant on the exemption.

Section 4(6) Exemption. Section 4(6) of the Securities Act is an exemption available for offers and sales by any issuer made exclusively to accredited investors if the aggregate offering price of the sale does not exceed $5 million. Similar to the rules under Regulation D, there can be no public solicitation or advertising in connection with the offering. Accredited investors are identical to those as defined in Rule 501 in Regulation D. There are relatively few factual circumstances in which transactions exempt under Section 4(6) would not also be exempt under Rule 505, and as such the exemption is largely redundant. However, there are certain factual circumstances under which an issuer may not qualify under Rule 505 (such as "investment companies"), and issuers are not prohibited from using this exemption even if the persons associated with the company were the subject of certain previous administrative, civil, or criminal actions (so-called bad boy provisions). A first-time low-budget filmmaker will most likely not be in these latter factual circumstances.

Accepting Equity Investments Through Crowdfunding—The JOBS Act Exemption. The JOBS Act created a new provision that exempts from registration the offer and sale of up to $1 million of securities within any twelve month period to an unlimited number of investors using the Internet. Under this new law the amount sold by any issuer of securities cannot exceed: 1) the greater of $2,000 or 5 percent of the investor's annual income (or net worth for investors with an annual income or net worth less than $100,000); or 2) 10 percent of the investor's annual income or net worth if the latter is equal to or greater than $100,000, but not to exceed a maximum aggregate amount of $100,000 invested by any investor.

Any offering and sale must be conducted through a registered broker or a "funding portal" and the issuer must comply with filing and disclosure requirements. The issuer must file a disclosure document with the Securities and Exchange Commission (SEC), the broker or "funding portal" and all potential investors. The disclosure document must provide at least the following information:

1) the names of directors and officers and each person holding more than 20 percent of the issuer
2) a description of the business and anticipated business plan of the issuer
3) a description of the financial condition of the issuer, including either
   a) the issuer's latest income tax returns and financial statements certified by the principal executive officer if seeking less than $100,000
   b) financial statements reviewed by an independent public accountant if seeking more than $100,000 but less than or equal to $500,000
   c) audited financial statements if seeking more than $500,000.

The issuer also cannot advertise the terms of the offering except through notices that direct investors to the broker or "funding portal." Further, no person may be compensated to promote the offering other than in accordance with rules to be prescribed by the SEC. In addition, an issuer must provide "investors reports" at least annually that summarize results of operations and financial statements—these documents must also be filed with the SEC.

Under this new exemption, crowdfunding intermediaries (brokers and "funding portals") must register with the SEC and a self-regulatory agency (currently, Financial Industry Regulatory Authority, "FINRA"). Intermediaries must provide information to ensure that each investor: 1) reviews investor education material; 2) affirms that the investment carries the risk of loss of the entire investment and that each investor can bear such a loss; and 3) is able to answer questions demonstrating an understanding of the level of risk generally applicable to investments in start-ups and emerging businesses, as well as being able to answer questions regarding small issuers, the risk of illiquidity and any other matters the Commission determines by rule.

Intermediaries must also take measures to reduce the risk of fraud, including, but not limited to; 1) obtaining a background and securities enforcement regulatory history check on each officer, director, and person holding more than 20 percent of the outstanding equity of each and every issuer using the intermediaries' services; 2) disseminating the information provided by the issuer to investors and the SEC at least twenty-one days prior to the first sale; 3) complying with administrative procedures to ensure that the issuer complies with the crowdfunding exemption rules; 4) not compensating promoters, finders, or lead generators for providing the intermediary with personal identification information of any potential investor; and 5) any other such requirements as provided by the SEC. The following are additional restrictions that funding portals have to adhere to: they cannot provide any investment advice or recommendations; they cannot solicit purchases, sales, or offers to buy securities offered or displayed on its website or portal; they cannot compensate employees, agents, or other persons for such solicitation or compensate based on the sale of securities displayed or referenced on its website or portal; they cannot hold, manage, possess, or otherwise handle investor funds or securities; and other rules by the SEC that are forthcoming.

The bottom line is that an issuer shall be liable for any untrue statement of a material fact or omission of a material fact which might render statement(s) misleading. Liability may not exist if the purchaser does not know of an untruth or omission and the issuer did not know, and in the exercise of reasonable care, could not have known of such untruth or omission. Issuer is defined as any person who is a director or partner, principal executive officer, controller or principal accounting officer. The parties who purchase securities under the crowdfunding exemption are purchasing "restricted" securities just as those who use the Regulation D exemption; that is, the securities may not be resold unless subsequently registered with the SEC or unless the new purchaser(s) meet the requirements for another exemption from registration. States must receive the information to be provided by the issuer and state laws that restrict such an offering are not overruled. So, for example, if a state exempts purchases by no more than thirty purchasers, then an issuer who is subject to the laws of such state and is relying on a crowdfunding exemption from federal securities laws must further comply with such state's maximum number of purchasers, and any other state requirements.

The JOBS Act exemption allowing equity investments through crowdfunding via the Internet *is not effective law until the Securities and Exchange Commission (SEC) adopts and issues final rules,* which has not occurred as of the writing of this book. The rules were required to be issued by January 1, 2013, but the SEC missed this deadline. Because the chair of the SEC stepped down at the end of 2012, and the inherent complication of creating new equity crowdfunding rules, and the fact that the Financial Industry Regulatory Authority (FINRA) will also have to issue regulations regarding the crowdfunding equity rules, it has been stated by industry pundits that the new law will probably not become effective until 2014. *It is important to note that issuers, including independent filmmakers, cannot rely on the new law until the SEC and FINRA issue and adopt final rules.*

ANTIFRAUD PROVISIONS APPLICABLE TO ALL OFFERS AND SALES OF SECURITIES

Even if an offer and sale of a security is exempt from registration, the transaction remains subject to the antifraud sections of the applicable securities laws. Although there are different antifraud laws under the Securities Act, the Exchange Act and state laws that have different requirements, the primary standard is generally that the issuer of securities is prohibited from making any untrue statement of material fact or omission of material fact. Any determination of what is an untrue statement or omission of material fact will depend on the facts and circumstances of any given situation. However, a statement or omission is generally "material" if there is a substantial likelihood that a reasonable person would consider it important. As mentioned, there are numerous requirements under each specific antifraud section that must be fulfilled, such as whether the issuer had an intent to defraud, negligently or recklessly made any untrue statement or omission, or even had knowledge of an untrue or omitted fact. In addition, there are defenses available to an issuer accused of making an untrue statement or omission that apply to each specific antifraud law. For example, the inability of the issuer to discover the untrue or omitted fact through the exercise of reasonable care, or the untrue statement or omission was not "material," or a determination that the issuer's actions did not cause the investor to purchase the securities. This is another area in which a filmmaker would be wise to rely on the counsel and advice of his or her qualified attorney who is able to discuss the filmmaker's specific circumstances and review the filmmaker's securities paperwork. This issue often arises in connection with the film-maker's desire to include financial projections or similar information in his or her paperwork. For a discussion of the issues in this context, see Chapter 11, "Inclusion of Return on Investment (ROI) Analysis and Financial Pro-jections."

FINDERS

The use of finders to seek funding for a project is a strategy with its own set of problems. In the simplest terms a finder is a party who brings the party with money to the party who wants the money. The securities laws provide that no party is permitted to effect or solicit securities transactions unless the party is registered as a "broker-dealer" or is a person "associated with a registered broker-dealer." Similar to other securities laws, this law exists to regulate these intermediaries in order to protect investors. Whether a party will be considered a "broker" or a "dealer" is a determination of "facts and circumstance." It depends on whether the party: a) is "engaged in the busi-ness" of securities transactions (i.e., whether the finder acts with certain reg-ularity of participation in securities transactions or is involved in an isolated occurrence); b) receives a transaction-based compensation, for example, a percentage of the money raised; c) advertises for clients; d) solicits investors and gives advice regarding the transaction; e) negotiates the terms of the transaction; and/or f) takes custody of the securities at any time.

The law looks to the presence of payments and the manner of pay-ments for the services as being transaction-based as a primary indicator. A commission on the money raised is often the determining factor regarding the "broker-dealer" analysis. However, a "no-action" letter the SEC issued regarding the entertainer Paul Anka is an example of the circumstances in which the SEC determined that a finder was not required to register as a "broker-dealer." Paul Anka proposed to provide the names and contact information of potential investors regarding an offer and sale of limited partnership interests in exchange for a finder's fee of 10 percent of the sales price of the securities sold. The SEC decided that Paul Anka was not acting as a "broker-dealer" since he made no recommendation regarding the investment, did not contact the potential investors about the offering, provided no advice to the potential investors, had not previously acted as a finder nor had any plans to be a finder in the future, and did not make any independent analysis or engage in any "due diligence" activities. It is important to note that "no action" letters provide the view of the SEC staff in response to a specific inquiry. These decisions can be reconsidered and are not binding law. However, the letters give a basic framework to guide an issuer's decision process regarding the use of a finder. In practical terms, for a filmmaker to safely utilize a "finder," the finder must do no more than provide the names and contact information of the parties being introduced to the filmmaker. One of the most problematic variables in the equation is whether the finder seeks to receive compensation that is transaction-based (i.e., a percentage of the money the finder secures), which would support that the finder is acting as a "broker/dealer," and he or she would have to register with the proper authorities as such. The producer, on the other hand, wants and expects a finder to do more than simply provide contact information of parties being introduced to the producer; that is to say, the filmmaker also wants a finder, in some way or another, to explain the benefits of the investment to such contacts and to encourage them to invest, etc. Therefore, finders are rarely engaged since the legal guidelines for utilizing a finder are rarely fulfilled based on what a filmmaker or a finder would want from this type of transaction.

Rule 3a4-1, Safe Harbor Rule. A "broker" is basically anyone engaged in the business of effectuating securities transactions for others while a "dealer" is basically anyone engaged in the business of buying and selling securities for his or her own account. "Brokers" and "dealers" are required to comply with licensing requirements before they are allowed to act either as a broker or dealer in any securities transaction. However, partners, officers, directors, and employees of a company issuing its own securities usually do not fall under "broker-dealer" licensing requirements, although their actions could easily deem them to be "brokers." This is based on a safe harbor from broker-dealer registration found in Rule 3a4-1 under the Exchange Act (17 Code of Federal Regulations Section 240.3a4-1). The safe harbor provides that an associated person of a company offering securities shall not be deemed a broker solely through his or her participation in the sale of the company's securities if such person: a) is not subject to certain "bad boy" provisions (e.g., a conviction of a securities laws felony or misdemeanor within the ten years before the issuance); b) is not compensated in connection with his or her participation in the offering by the payment of a commission or other transaction-based compensation; and c) is not an associated person of a broker or dealer. In addition, such a person will not be considered a broker if he or she meets certain conditions. The group of conditions most often applicable to producing a film requires that the associated person: a) primarily performs, or intends to perform at the end of the offering, substantial duties on behalf of the issuer other than duties connected to transactions in securities; b) was not a broker or dealer, or a person associated with a broker or dealer, within the preceding twelve months; and c) did not participate in selling an offering of securities for any issuer more than once every twelve months.

The SEC has noted in its "no action" letters regarding this safe harbor that their conclusions are based on all of the facts and circumstances of a situation, using the above factors for guidance. In determining whether a person is a bona fide employee, the SEC has sometimes looked to whether or not the company is paying social security, unemployment and state disability tax for the individual and whether the company is withholding and paying federal and state taxes for the individual. Withholding and paying these taxes supports a conclusion that the person is a bona fide employee and helps support a conclusion that Rule 3a4-1 safe harbor is available. Perhaps the most important factor is whether the person is paid a percentage of the securities sold. Fixed compensation helps support a conclusion that the person does not need to register as a "broker/dealer." The SEC has stated that providing substantial duties on behalf of the issuer other than duties connected to transactions in securities "can be measured in terms of the percentage of time devoted to activities other than selling securities and the volume of work performed not related to selling securities." Further, each state has its own broker-dealer laws that vary as to if and how they follow the federal rules and are generally more restrictive than the federal rules.

The broker/dealer issue is generally not problematic regarding the company, the filmmaker, and the other few principal partners/officers of the company. The issue often arises when a filmmaker meets a person whom he or she wants to bring on board to help raise money and the person wants to provide more than the names and contact information of the parties being introduced to the filmmaker (i.e., more than a "finder," see above). If such an individual would fall under the Rule 3a4-1 safe harbor laws, then it naturally expands the pool of potential investors for the filmmaker because an "associated person" includes a partner, officer, director, or employee of the company. The benefit stems from the fact that such partner, officer, director, or employee brings with him or her an extended number of "pre-existing relationships" that the filmmaker would not have been able to approach since they were not within the filmmaker's *own* "pre-existing relationships."

The bottom line is that failure in any way to comply with the requirements of Rule 3a4-1 will expose the filmmaker to potential federal and state securities ramifications, so a filmmaker would be wise to consult a qualified attorney regarding these issues and carefully follow his or her advice.

5

Nonequity Financing of Independent Films "Outside the System"

"Stop wasting my time. You know what I want. You know what I need. Or maybe you don't. Do I have to come right flat out and tell you everything? Gimme some money, gimme some money."
—This Is Spinal Tap

NONEQUITY CROWDFUNDING

Crowdfunding has become a valuable addition to the independent film-maker's financing tools and involves using third parties to provide money to produce a film project. For example, Kickstarter and IndieGoGo are two high profile crowdfunding sites each with specific rules regarding the utilization of their sites. Independent filmmakers producing a low-budget independent film most often raise only enough money through crowdfunding sites to assist small, specific segments of their fund-raising requirements. Facts gleaned from the Kickstarter website support this conclusion. From April 2009 through October 2011 approximately 27,000 film and nonfilm projects were launched on Kickstarter, and approximately 10,000 projects successfully raised money. Of the 10,000 successful projects, approximately 97 percent raised $25,000 or less and approximately 84 percent raised $10,000 or less. It should also be noted that about 3,000 of the projects were for film and video endeavors (documentaries, narratives, shorts, webseries, and animation projects). Kickstarter also reported that from April 2009 through January 2013 there were 2,331 narrative film projects that collected $31.74 million, which is an average amount of $13,616 collected per project.

As will be seen in Chapter 9, there are hard costs associated with producing an independent film, and some of those hard costs must be incurred before the filmmaker raises any money from investors. Therefore, it is advisable for low-budget filmmakers to attempt to raise between $5,000 and $10,000 at the beginning of the fund-raising process to cover these hard costs. If successful, these funds can be utilized to pay for start-up costs necessary in order to approach investors. Start-up costs include such things as: hiring a unit production manager/line producer to break down, schedule, and budget the script; legal fees; entity set-up and maintenance fees; travel costs; copy costs; and other similar expenses. It is wise to segregate the few potential investors who the filmmaker believes may provide large investments (more than $5,000) from the crowdfunding campaign. The reason for this is so that the filmmaker will not have to ask such individuals to provide funds twice. It should be all too obvious that asking an individual for money a second time is much more difficult simply because the individual will feel he or she has already fulfilled his or her obligation during the crowdfunding campaign. This leads to a broader question. Should the filmmaker attempt to raise the entire budget through a crowdfunding campaign? There is no bright-line answer to this question, but it would be wise for the filmmaker to note that between April 2009 and October 2011 only 259 projects raised between $25,000 and $100,000 and only twenty-three projects raised more than $100,000, which accounts for approximately 3 percent of *all successful projects* on Kickstarter. Even more sobering is the fact that film and video projects represent only a fraction of that 3 percent. The best answer to the broader question is to "do the math."

Each website permitting a filmmaker to raise money through crowd-funding will have its own specific rules, so it is recommended that the rules be carefully read before planning and launching a crowdfunding campaign. *Warning*: if a filmmaker fails to follow all the rules, a fund-raiser usually retains the right to demand the return of all the money raised by them (most, if not all of which, may have already been spent by the filmmaker). In addition, the filmmaker may be held responsible for additional damages. There are several questions that need to be asked before contracting with a crowdfunding site. For example, what "types" of crowdfunding campaigns are allowed? IndieGoGo allows campaigns to raise money for a wide variety of endeavors, whereas Kickstarter only allows campaigns for projects in the creative fields while specifically prohibiting other types of campaigns. Are the funds raised refundable to contributors? For example, IndieGoGo does not allow refunds; funds are disbursed as soon as they are received. On the other hand, campaigns through Kickstarter must be fully funded at the end of a certain time period before any of the funds are released to the campaign organizer. Another example is whether or not giving "perks" or "rewards" to contributors is required. IndieGoGo does not require "perks" or "rewards" but highly recommends them, whereas offering "rewards" is a requirement with a Kickstarter campaign.

Crowdfunding is a relatively new method of obtaining funding for a project, so the legal guidelines are still evolving; however, there are a number of legal issues of which a filmmaker utilizing crowdfunding should be aware, including but not limited to: 1) securities laws; 2) breaches of contract; 3) income tax consequences; and 4) state sales tax consequences. First, *securities laws*, which were discussed in Chapter 4, apply to crowdfunding as well. However, crowdfunding sites such as IndieGoGo and Kickstarter have established their own rules designed to render the securities laws nonappli-cable to their operation. Specifically, crowdfunding sites such as IndieGoGo and Kickstarter limit a campaign from soliciting or offering equity invest-ments by prohibiting the offering of ownership in the project, financial incentives, returns of money/investments, net profit payments, or any other similar type of return that would support a conclusion that a "security" is being solicited, offered, and/or sold. As discussed in Chapter 4, the JOBS

Act added an exemption for selling securities through crowdfunding. If a filmmaker is not taking the required steps to comply with the laws and rules for the crowdfunding exemption under the JOBS Act (when this law becomes effective) then it is wise to avoid providing any potential "reward" or "perk" that may create unintended security law issues, and it is highly recommended to have a qualified attorney review any proposed offering in exchange for a contribution.

A second legal issue regarding crowdfunding is *breach of contract*. Simply defined, breach of contract is promising to provide something (in this case a "reward" or "perk") that the filmmaker does not deliver to those who contribute money. For example, a common reward might be a promise to deliver a copy of the film on DVD, which may become an issue if the film is not completed. This arises in situations where the fund-raiser releases funds to the campaign organizer even if the full amount is not obtained. As mentioned above, IndieGoGo is an example of a site which allows this. This seems to be less of a concern with a Kickstarter campaign since the funds will not be obtained from contributors unless the full amount is raised. However, it can still become a concern if the "full amount" received by the filmmaker is less than the "full amount" needed to complete a film and transfer it to DVD. Since it is common for many different "rewards" or "perks" to be offered based on the amount contributed, a filmmaker should carefully review each one to avoid the possibility of a breach of contract, since it may become impossible to deliver every such "reward" or "perk." Some examples of these types of "rewards" or "perks" for a film include but are not limited to flying the contributor and guest to a New York City premiere to walk the red carpet and have photos taken, a guaranteed role in the film, or the producer promising to fly anywhere in the world to personally screen the film.

Third, the precise *income tax consequences* with regard to a crowdfunding contribution will depend on the facts and circumstances of each situation. But to put it as simply as possible, the first thing to recognize is that every transaction that involves the exchange of value in the United States falls under the rules of the Internal Revenue Code (IRC), and it is the IRC that provides the basic guidelines for determining tax consequences, supplemented by interpretations by the Internal Revenue Service. What follows is a brief overview of some of the tax issues a successful crowdfunding campaign must consider. For tax purposes, the receipt of "value" (that is, money, goods, services, etc.) via crowdfunding can generally fall within one of four categories: a) an investment; b) income; c) funds provided to a tax-exempt organization; or d) a gift, and deserve further discussion.

a) *An Investment.* In general terms, an investment occurs when one party provides money that is expended in a common enterprise with the expectation that there will be a return of money primarily through the efforts of others. From a tax perspective investments are great for the parties involved since there is generally no immediate tax gain or loss to report. Unfortunately, primarily because of the extensive federal and state securities laws applicable to offers and sales of investments (that is, "securities"), crowdfunding sites such as Kickstarter and IndieGoGo clearly state that participants are precluded from offering an investment. This means participants cannot offer or receive an ownership interest, return on investment, profits, or anything else that could be perceived as an investment. Therefore, the rules of the crowdfunding sites will usually *preclude* the crowdfunding money, initially received from third parties, from obtaining the favorable tax consequences the IRC provides for investments. It should be noted that offers and sales of securities (i.e., investments) require compliance with federal and state securities laws whether or not a crowdfunding mechanism is utilized. If an offer and sale of a security investment is made in compliance with the JOBS Act crowdfunding exemption (when such law becomes effective: see Chapter 4), then such investments will be eligible to claim no gain or loss, but they will still be subject to all other applicable tax rules. An example of an applicable "other" tax rule affecting the transaction is when donated property is subject to debt, in which case the applicable tax rules will affect the amount to be "counted" toward the "investment."

b) *Income.* There are several points of importance regarding income tax. To begin with, the IRC broadly defines "gross income" as "all income from whatever source derived." For example: compensation paid for services; income derived from business; gains derived from dealings in property; etc. Accordingly, unless categorized as funds provided to a "tax-exempt" organization or a "gift," money initially received from a successful crowdfunding campaign is required to be included in the recipient's "income," and can be subject to federal and state taxes. For example, with regard to a crowdfunding campaign, the funds could be "income" to an organizer of a campaign upon receipt (reported for tax purposes as such); however, when or if, as an individual, the organizer provides those funds (in his or her name) to the film project as an investment then the transfer would be eligible for the favorable tax treatment. Even if the money is included in income, the amounts subsequently expended on producing the film may be deductible as an "ordinary and necessary" business or trade expense (or capitalized and deducted over future years), if, of course, the recipient is operating a business. If an individual is operating a business as a sole proprietor, or an LLC with only one owner, then the income and deductions from producing the film would be reported on the individual's Schedule C with his or her Federal Tax Form 1040, as well as with any corresponding state tax forms. If the funds are provided by the initial recipient to an S Corporation or a limited liability company with more than one owner, then the funds and expenses would be accounted for within the respective entity, and a Federal Schedule K-1 form would be issued at the end of the year reflecting the percentage of ownership of such entity and the corresponding income or loss to each owner. *This is another area where it is imperative to consult with your tax professional since there are other issues that affect the final tax outcome.* The limitation of deductions for expenses incurred in activities that are not deemed engaged in "for-profit" (the so-called hobby loss rules) and the passive activity rules are just a couple of such issues.

c) *Funds provided to a tax-exempt organization.* There are unique considerations regarding funds provided to a tax-exempt organization. If a filmmaker has a "tax-exempt" organization then the amounts received through crowdfunding will generally not be subject to federal, state, or local taxes. There are, however, extensive reporting requirements regarding funds received and expended by "tax-exempt" organizations. For example, "tax-exempt" organizations are required to file a Form 990 with the Internal Revenue Service and corresponding forms for state and local taxing authorities. However, it is not very common for an independent filmmaker to have his or her organization recognized as "tax-exempt" by federal and state taxing authorities because the filing of the applicable forms is a relatively expensive and time-consuming process. It is more common to apply for fiscal sponsorship and then receive the crowdfunding receipts through that fiscal sponsor. (Tax-exempt status will be addressed in a subsequent section.) Briefly, fiscal sponsorship is when a party (in this case, the filmmaker) wants to receive "grants" and/or "tax-deductible" donations but lacks the required "tax-exempt" status. To comply with the "tax-exempt" requirements, the party (filmmaker) enters a contract with an existing "tax-exempt" entity (the fiscal sponsor) which receives such "grants" and "tax-deductible donations" on behalf of the filmmaker. Examples of such organizations providing fiscal sponsorship are the International Documentary Association and Fractured Atlas. It should be noted that the "tax-deductible donations" are deductible by the party that provides the funds to the fiscal sponsor, which is an added attraction to this type of crowdfunding campaign. There are several different structures utilized by "tax-exempt" organizations in establishing sponsorship agreements. Each structure will have unique rules. As a general rule the tax-accounting consequences of various fiscal sponsorship arrangements include but are not limited to: 1) each fiscal sponsor accounts for all funds received and expended on its own Form 990 and corresponding state and local tax forms (in such case there are generally no tax consequences to the filmmaker unless he or she receives a salary from the payments which would be subject to personal income taxes); 2) the project (filmmaker's company) is a separate "tax-exempt" organization and it accounts for all funds received and expended on its own Form 990 and corresponding state and local tax forms (in which case there generally are no tax consequences to the filmmaker unless he or she receives a salary from the payments which would be subject to personal income taxes); 3) the funds are transferred to the filmmaker (to the individual or his or her entity that is not a "tax-exempt" organization), and are accounted for on the filmmaker's personal tax forms or the entity's tax forms. Almost all of the arrangements with fiscal sponsors for films are as described in 3). Therefore, it is important for the filmmaker to recognize that, when utilizing a fiscal sponsor, the funds received from that fiscal sponsor will most likely be considered "income." Such income will have to be reported on the filmmaker's appropriate federal and state tax forms (depending on whether it is received by the filmmaker as an individual or his or her entity) and is potentially subject to taxes.

d) *A Gift.* The receipt of a "gift" creates no tax obligation for the recipient (filmmaker). Therefore, if the money received in a successful crowdfunding campaign is a "gift," the filmmaker has no tax consequences when it is received. However, there may be tax consequences to the party providing the gift, because current rules allow an individual to gift only up to $13,000 per year per individual to an unlimited number of individuals without tax consequences. The determination of whether money or other value received is "income" or a "gift" is not as simple as it may seem. The decision as to whether the money is a gift or income must be made for each party that provides "value," and on the facts and circumstances of each transaction. For example, if contributions are received from twenty parties then the facts and circumstances of each one of the twenty contributions must be examined. Some may be ruled a gift and others not. Further, although the IRC clearly excludes "gifts" from "income," the process of determining when a "gift" occurs has been primarily left to the courts to decide. These cases provide certain guidelines; however, most situations will fall within a vast grey area leaving the filmmaker to decide (if challenged by the Internal Revenue Service) whether he or she is willing to have a court ultimately decide if the filmmaker's "gift" determinations are correct. The courts have concluded that the highest controlling factor regarding a "gift" is the *transferor's intent* in making the transfer. In other words, why is the money given to the filmmaker? In examining the question of intent the courts have identified some important factors which include the following:

1) A "gift" most likely has not occurred if the transferor had a legal or moral obligation to make the transfer. This can become an issue if a crowdfunding campaign provides items of value in return for donations. Are the transferors providing money because they have the legal or moral obligation to do so because they are receiving "free" DVDs of the film signed by the star and director? Or might they be receiving "free" tickets to the premiere of the film and "free" transportation to and from the premiere screening of the film? These are some of the issues which may arise. The fair market value of such items must be determined. In general, the transaction will be considered a "gift" for tax purposes only if the market value of goods, services, or other "perks" received by the transferor from the film-maker is *substantially* less than the value of the monies provided by the transferor to the filmmaker.

2) A "gift" most likely does not occur if the transferor is making the transfer because he/she/it expects economic value in return. In addition to the examples of the items in 1) above, the courts have stated that even "intangible" economic returns are considered "value." Intangible returns have been judged to include such things as the protection of a business' "goodwill" or an enhanced "public image." On the other hand, a "gift" most likely does occur when a transfer is made from "detached

and disinterested generosity," "out of affection, respect, admiration, charity and the like…"

3) Finally, a "gift" most likely *does not* occur if it is made by an employer to an employee, but *does* most likely occur if it is made by a family member.

In light of all the above, an organizer should provide all relevant information to his or her tax professional and apply the foregoing factors to his or her circumstances when attempting to claim that all, some or none of the funds initially provided are a "gift." As can be seen by the extensive discussion in the last several pages regarding the legal issues of "income tax consequences" in crowdfunding, it cannot be emphasized enough that providing complete and accurate information to your tax professional is a key factor, because the tax consequences related to a crowdfunding campaign are based on *all* of the facts and circumstances of *each* transaction. At the very least, your tax professional will need to know the following: the relationships between the filmmaker and each party providing funds; the amount each party provides; what the party receives in return from the filmmaker (and its fair market value); whether the filmmaker receives the funds directly or an entity initially receives the funds; the owners of an entity that initially receives funds; whether the filmmaker has a "tax-exempt" organization that receives the funds; and whether the filmmaker is producing the film "for profit."

Another legal issue in crowdfunding, together with the other three (i.e., securities laws, breach of contract, and income tax consequences), is *state sales tax*. The potential sales tax liability is obscured because "rewards" or "perks" are not offered as items "for sale," in other words, the transfer of funds in exchange for "rewards" or "perks" does not immediately present itself as a sales tax transaction. However, the following scenario will shed more light on the issue. If the book *Independent Film Producing: How to Produce a Low-Budget Feature Film* is offered for sale on Amazon.com, and someone provides $25 in exchange for receiving the book, it is clear (assuming that certain other sales tax requirements are met) that this transaction is a sale of a good that is subject to state sales tax that must be collected from the sale and remitted to the appropriate state sales taxing authority. On the other hand, if the book is offered as a "reward" or "perk" to an individual who provides $50 to a crowdfunding campaign, is the transaction a sale of the book that is subject to sales tax? The precise answer depends on a multitude of factors, including: a) what state the seller is in; b) what state the buyer is in; c) if they are in different states, whether either the buyer or the seller has sufficient connection to the state the other is in; d) whether a good or service provided is "exempt" from state and local sales tax; e) the value of the good or service provided relative to the amount of funds provided; and f) whether the state identifies a "sale" when the money is received by the "seller" or when the customer takes possession of the item.

This is another area where it is best to consult a tax professional, and have him or her review the "rewards" and "perks" to handle potential sales tax issues.

LOANS

Generally, loans from established lenders are not available to first-time film-makers. These types of loans generally include presale loans and loans with negative pick-up agreements. Presale loans are when a bank lends the film a percentage of the total production budget. Usually, the amount is equal to approximately the amount of presales estimates acquired by foreign sales agents. These types of loans are primarily only available to the largest, most established film companies, and certainly not to a first-time filmmaker unless partnered with a more established company. A negative pick-up deal is when a distributor (usually a major studio) agrees to purchase ("pick-up") a film after it is completed in exchange for a certain amount (usually the full amount of the budget). Since the studio will not provide the money for the pick-up unless and until the producer makes and delivers a completed film, banks will be looked to for a loan of the money to produce the film, using the distributor contract as security. Only parties with established studio rela-tionships obtain negative pick-up deals, and even among those producers, such arrangements have become a less common model for film financing.

Although not commonly used, the primary loan instruments that can be utilized by independent filmmakers are promissory notes, and loans that are convertible to an equity investment, ("convertible loans"), the latter falling within the definition of a "security." Whether or not a promissory note is a security depends on the specifics of the promissory note. In general, short-term loans not exceeding nine months are not considered securities, although courts have found short-term notes to be securities in certain circumstances. For other loan agreements, a security generally is not present when a loan is purely commercial (as opposed to an investment), or is for a relatively short term, has a commercially applicable rate, and does not have a variably adjusted repayment based on the profitability of the borrower. Filmmakers should rely on experienced finance and legal counsel in the drafting and reviewing of any and all promissory notes to evaluate if there are any securities law issues. Other issues with regard to promissory notes are when and how the loan will be repaid in relation to the investors (i.e., Are the loans repaid before or after the investors are repaid?), and whether the loans are recourse or nonrecourse loans (i.e., whether or not the film-maker will be personally liable for the repayment of the loans).

CREDIT CARDS

The primary means of lending that independent filmmakers have historically utilized are credit cards. Until the recent bank implosion, banks had made credit cards widely available to a broad spectrum of borrowers, regardless of a borrower's credit worthiness. There have been numerous stories reported about filmmakers who made their films by obtaining and using numerous credit cards, some reporting the use of over ten different credit cards. I have never worked with an independent filmmaker who has not utilized at least some credit card debt in the making of his or her film. However, credit card debt comes with personal liability and risk, so a film-maker would be wise to limit his or her use to times when it is absolutely necessary and only in amounts that the filmmaker reasonably believes he or she can pay in future monthly minimum required payments. For every story of a filmmaker who gambled and won at credit card roulette, there are thousands of filmmakers whose personal credit is damaged for many years, precluding him or her from obtaining credit for items such as a car, a lease, a home purchase, or other personal expenditures, even if the film-maker can prove at a future time that he or she has steady work income. As I mentioned, if you are making an independent film, you will at some point utilize unsecured credit card debt, so there are some important aspects of the terms that a filmmaker should review, notably whether the annual percentage interest rate (APR) is fixed or variable and any finance charges and fees associated with the use of the card.

NONSTUDIO DISTRIBUTORS

On occasion a nonstudio distributor will provide money to a filmmaker before the film is made in exchange for certain distribution rights to the film. From the filmmaker's perspective, these types of preproduction offers are usually not as favorable as they would be if the filmmaker approaches a distributor after the film is completed. The obvious reason for this is that a distributor has tremendous leverage in preproduction deals because of the increased risk for a distributor at this point in the process. First, the film may never get produced, and second, if it is produced it may not be considered a "quality" film by the distributor. The filmmaker should carefully scrutinize the amount of money that is being offered, the rights (theatrical, home video, video-on-demand, and others) that the distributor wants to obtain, and any other terms of "control" that the distributor may be demanding. For example, it's not unusual for the distributor to require someone from the distributor's company to be involved in each aspect of the production of the film, and it is not uncommon for the distributor to expect this person's salary to be paid out of the production budget of the film. As a practical matter, since the supply of independent films is far greater than the demand, distributors generally will not enter these types of agreements. From a dis-tributor's point of view it is more cost effective to review the films that have already been completed, when it is easier to evaluate the potential value of a completed film as opposed to a film in the script stage that will be produced by relatively inexperienced filmmakers and without the benefit of a completion bond. A completion bond is basically a guarantee given by a completion guarantee company that such company will assure a third party (usually a financier, or in this case a distributor) that a film will be completed in accordance with an agreed upon budget and time frame. If the producer fails to complete the film within the agreed upon budget and time frame then the completion guarantee company will provide the funds to complete the film as well as deliver the film if the producer fails to do so. Low-budget independent films do not engage the services of completion guarantors. These companies usually require a minimum budget of $1,000,000 since their fee is calculated on a percentage of the budget. However, even if these companies would provide their services, low-budget filmmakers would most likely choose not to spend their limited funds on a completion bond but on production expenditures that will tangibly contribute to the ultimate goal, which is a completed film that looks like it cost three to five times the actual cost.

TAX SUBSIDIES

Tax subsidies are offered by some states as incentives for filmmakers to make films in their states. Some countries offer similar incentives for films made in their countries. These tax subsidies are usually offered in the form of money rebates, tax credits, or exemptions from sales tax, use tax, or other taxes. A *rebate* is money paid to the production company based on the amount of money the company spends in a jurisdiction, or on other economic criteria (e.g., jobs created). In general, a *tax credit* is money that a company can receive from a jurisdiction's tax agency, usually with the requirement that the company must file a tax return in that jurisdiction in order to utilize the tax credit. If the company owes tax, then the tax credit offsets any such amounts and the remainder is paid to the company. If a company wants to receive money for the tax credits before filing a tax return in the relevant jurisdiction, then the company must find a third party who will exchange cash for the credits, naturally at a discount, which would, of course, reduce the amount the company would receive. Some jurisdictions do not allow the company to transfer these credits to other taxpayers in the jurisdiction and some do not refund the tax credit amounts in excess of tax owed, but instead allow the company to carry the credit amounts forward each year to offset any tax the company might otherwise have to pay in subsequent years. *Exemptions* from sales, use, or other taxes are also widely available to film projects in many states. These exemptions are subject to state and local rules including minimum expenditure amounts, applications to be registered vendors, limitations on the types of items for which the exemption is available and other requirements. In theory tax subsidies are great sources of "revenue" for independent filmmakers, but in practice many obstacles and associated costs have to be overcome in order to acquire state or foreign tax subsidies. The costs and minimum budget thresholds associated with utilizing tax subsidies for films in the lower budget ranges (approximately $50,000 to $500,000) generally make most tax subsidies either unavailable or cost prohibitive. As a budget rises above $500,000 and certain minimum budget requirements are attained, the benefits begin to outweigh the costs, at which point tax subsidies can become a real source of potential "revenue" for an independent film. If a filmmaker meets requirements and has the resources, it is worth investigating the applicability of tax subsidies, because the films that do meet all of the requirements for a jurisdiction can access tax subsidies of up to 40 percent of qualified expenditures in certain states and even larger percentage savings in foreign locations. Exemptions, on the other hand, are widely available and accessible to films in almost all budget ranges. "Revenue" as used above is in quotes because filmmakers should not view these tax subsidies in the same way that they view private equity or loans because there is a "timing" issue associated with tax subsidies. Although jurisdictions have different requirements, in general films that qualify for tax subsidies will not receive the subsidy until after the film is completed and the company files the proper paperwork supporting the claimed tax subsidy, (e.g., proof of the expenditures and filing a tax return in the jurisdiction). Tax incentives add nothing to the pool of money needed to produce the film since they come in after the film is completed, unless a third party can be found who will provide the funds at the beginning of the production in exchange for the projected subsidies. A problem with the latter arrangement is that, of course, these third parties charge a fee, which in turn reduces the amount of the tax subsidy that can be utilized in making the film. This option is unavailable is some jurisdictions, since not every jurisdiction allows the tax subsidy to be "transferable" to a third party. It should be pointed out that tax credits and rebates allow a producer to reduce the amount of revenue a film needs to generate in order to recover the costs of production, which may be of interest to potential investors. For example, if a $5 million film receives 25 percent tax subsidies that effectively nets the producer $1 million after costs to obtain the subsidy, then this means that the film needs $4 million in revenue to cover production costs although it has the production value of $5 million.

Many issues need to be addressed before a filmmaker is able to access state or foreign tax subsidies. These issues require the engagement of professionals experienced with the process and the expenditure of a certain amount of money to cover up-front costs. However, even if a filmmaker can cover these up-front costs it is not wise to allow the prospect of subsidies to override sound production decision making. The primary consideration should be whether the proposed jurisdiction will provide all of the elements needed to properly complete principal photography (and postproduction, if applicable). The filmmaker should work closely with his or her unit production manager/line producer, location manager, and other crew members to determine whether or not the jurisdiction has enough skilled, trained crew members available to provide professional services for the film and whether or not the jurisdiction can provide the types of locations called for in the script. It is important to remain focused foremost on making sure that the film can be properly produced in the jurisdiction and not on incentives offered to filmmakers by a state or foreign nation.

Securing subsidies from local, state, or national sources is made more difficult since each jurisdiction will have peculiar restrictions (sometimes literally "peculiar"). In general these categories of restrictions include but are not limited to: a) certain eligible types of projects (for example, motion pictures and television series but not commercials or music videos); b) a certain percentage of the crew who must be local residents of the jurisdiction; c) a specific minimum number of days the company must be present in the jurisdiction; d) a specific minimum amount of money the company has to spend in the jurisdiction (for example: in Arkansas it is more than $50,000; in Colorado it is more than $250,000 for out-of-state companies; in Illinois it is more than $100,000 for projects over thirty minutes; in Massachusetts it is more than $50,000; and in West Virginia it is more than $25,000); e) certain "types" of expenditures that qualify for the tax subsidies (for example, wages paid to certain crew members and equipment rentals but not costs to develop a screenplay, etc.); f) a maximum amount of tax subsidy that a company can receive for a project; and, often the most cumbersome restriction, g) strict requirements as to evidence of the expenditures, including production expense reports and an audit with an auditor's opinion stating that the expense report is true and accurate and completed in accordance with the jurisdiction's requirements.

Some jurisdictions also have a limit on the total amount that can be allocated to tax credits for all projects in a given tax year, so the filmmaker should take care to find out if there is enough left in the jurisdiction's budget to cover his or her project. A filmmaker must seek certain guarantees that if sufficient funds are available when the project is "approved," the funds will actually be disbursed upon completion. Some jurisdictions retain the sole discretion as to who will receive the subsidies among the pool of "approved" applicants. Issues such as determining the tax consequences for actors and crew who will work in the jurisdiction should also be clarified. Do they have a loan-out company? If they do, what are local laws with which the loan-out company needs to comply, including state and local taxes? Finally, because of international laws and the increased costs associated with filming in foreign countries, these types of subsidies are even more difficult to access when the total budget for a film is between $50,000 and $500,000. Canada stands out as a notable exception, having offered lucrative incentives to films with budgets under $1 million. Canada's close proximity to the United States and the ability for productions to comply with the Canadian Federal Program and Canadian Provincial programs (for provinces such as British Columbia, Nova Scotia, and others) are chief reasons for this. However, other issues that make it more difficult to access international tax subsidies in general include: the exchange rate for the currency of a foreign territory; increased travel and lodging costs to the foreign jurisdiction; and the increased legal costs, since local counsel in the foreign territory must be engaged.

This discussion is not intended to discourage a filmmaker's attempt to secure such subsidies, but merely to ensure a realistic approach to the process, and a recognition that months or even years may elapse until a final guarantee of receiving any tax subsidies can be secured.

Internal Revenue Code (IRC) Section 181. Section 181 basically allows a taxpayer to deduct up to $15 million in qualifying production costs in the years the costs are incurred. This is a change from how film and television costs have traditionally been required to be deducted under the IRC. Previously these costs were required to be capitalized and amortized— small, equal amounts were required to be deducted over many years into the future. As of December 31, 2013, IRC Section 181 is set to expire if not extended by the legislature. If it is allowed to expire, then as of January 1, 2014, it will not be available for any taxpayer that did not meet the terms of the code section and the regulations issued by the Internal Revenue Service as of December 31, 2013. In any case, it is generally recommended that the paperwork regarding the production of an independent film not provide tax information regarding the potential tax outcomes for investors in the film. There are numerous IRC requirements for a taxpayer to utilize losses from investments, including "passive activity losses" for individuals, and "recapture provisions" in certain circumstances, when there is a license or sale of the film after a taxpayer has taken IRC deductions. Any paperwork that a filmmaker provides to a prospective investor should provide a statement that includes language such as: "prospective investors are not to construe the contents of this document as tax advice, but each investor should consult his, her, or its personal legal counsel, accountant, and other professional advisors as to the legal and tax aspects of investment and its suitability for such investor."

TAX-EXEMPT STATUS & FISCAL SPONSORSHIP

As stated earlier in the chapter, it is not common for independent feature narrative films, low-budget or otherwise, to be produced as not-for-profit endeavors, primarily because most independent filmmakers want to produce their independent film as a commercial enterprise. Commercial endeavors are disqualified from obtaining "tax-exempt" status. Put simply, they want their film to return funds in amounts equal to or greater than the budget, thereby generating a profit for investors and the filmmakers, which would render the endeavor incompatible with the "charitable" or other requirements for a project to receive "tax-exempt" status. Another reason is that it is a relatively time-consuming process with additional costs. Nevertheless, it is important for a filmmaker to appreciate the potential benefits of obtaining "tax-exempt" status (also referred to as "nonprofit" or "not-for-profit") for a specific project.

Often the decision to seek "tax-exempt" status is made when producing a documentary rather than a narrative film. However, whether producing a narrative or documentary, a filmmaker should be aware that once a decision is made to produce a project as a "nonprofit" endeavor, converting the project to a "for-profit" project at a later date will have consequences; specifically, the tax benefits that were obtained when funds were accepted under the "nonprofit" tax rules would have to be addressed. This commonly entails returning the funds obtained if a "fiscal sponsor" was utilized (the terms "fiscal sponsor" and "fiscal sponsor agreement" will be addressed below); furthermore, whether or not a fiscal sponsor is utilized, revoking the tax deduction each donor received may entitle the donor to recall its funding and demand repayment of any amounts previously paid to the filmmaker, which will, most likely, already have been spent. Therefore, a filmmaker should be aware of the latter consequences if a film's fiscal sponsor has a policy that allows a film project to begin as a "nonprofit," "noncommercial" project with the understanding that if the producer decides to convert the project to a "for-profit" project, then all the producer needs to do is terminate the fiscal sponsorship at that point. Such a policy will assist the fiscal sponsor if questioned by the Internal Revenue Service (IRS), but it will create substantial financial and legal issues for the producer.

In light of the fact that exemption from taxes has the potential to be abused, the granting of "tax-exempt" status by the IRS is meticulously scrutinized, and there are strict regulations governing the operations of not-for-profit organizations. As a result, tax exemption is associated with higher costs. Unfortunately, most independent filmmakers do not have the time or resources to complete the necessary paperwork to obtain and utilize "tax-exempt" status. For example, the federal application, Form 1023, is thirty pages in length and the information required can span from five pages to hundreds of pages. In addition, approximately ten to fifteen documents must be provided, including, but not limited to, the organizing documents, special corporate by-laws, power of attorney, tax information authorization, project explanations, financial data and projections of expenditures, and printed materials and publications. As discussed above in the "Non-equity Crowdfunding" section of this chapter, it is not very common for an independent filmmaker to have his or her organization recognized as "tax-exempt" by federal and state taxing authorities; rather, if it is decided to obtain "tax-exempt" donations when producing a noncommercial, not-for-profit film, then it is more common to apply for fiscal sponsorship and receive the donations through that fiscal sponsor.

An organization seeking to qualify for "tax-exempt" status must be organized and operate for one of the purposes specifically designated in the IRC. The most common exemption sought by endeavors in the arts is under IRC section 501(c)(3) which requires that an organization:

1) be organized and operated exclusively for religious, charitable, scientific, testing for public safety, literary, or educational purposes, to foster national or international amateur sports competition, or for the prevention of cruelty to children or animals;

2) have no part of the net earnings of the organization benefit any private shareholder or individual;

3) have no substantial part of the activities of which is carrying on propaganda or otherwise attempting to influence legislation;

4) does not participate in, or intervene in (including the publishing or distributing of statements) any political campaign on behalf of (or in opposition to) any candidate for public office.

Therefore, if any film project seeks to qualify for "tax-exempt" status on its own (by completing and filing the proper documents with the IRS), then such film project must satisfy a tax-exempt purpose (usually under 501(c)(3)). Further, if a fiscal sponsor is utilized by a film project seeking "tax-exempt" status, then the project must further the fiscal sponsor's stated "tax-exempt" purpose, which in the arts is most often a "charitable" or "educational" purpose. This is a primary reason why it is extremely difficult, some may argue impossible, to produce a film project under fiscal sponsorship that utilizes "tax-exempt" status for some of the funds received, and "for-profit" status for other funds received for the project. The IRS is wary of abuse so it will most often take the position of denying the "tax-exempt" status of such arrangements (that is, a film project accepting tax deductible donations in addition to accepting for-profit investments) by stating that these organizations are neither organized nor operated exclusively for "charitable" or "educational" purposes, nor do they further the "nonexempt" recipients' purposes rather than the fiscal sponsor's "tax-exempt" purposes, nor meet the requirement that "tax-exempt" organizations serve a public rather than a private interest. It is correct to state that the fiscal sponsor can challenge such a determination arguing that, a) even if such expenditures are not in furtherance of the fiscal sponsor's exempt purpose, it comprises only an insubstantial part of its activities; b) the fiscal sponsor's "primary" activities are in the performance of exempt activities; c) the fiscal sponsor has maintained control and discretion as to the use of the tax-exempt funds; and d) it has also maintained records establishing that the "tax-exempt" funds have not served a private interest.

However, since a violation of the "tax-exempt" rules jeopardizes the fiscal sponsor's "tax-exempt" status for *all* of its endeavors, most "fiscal sponsor contracts" commonly contain provisions that protect the fiscal sponsor, including, but not limited to: a) all funds must be expended for educational and/or charitable purposes; b) the project must be a "noncommercial" project at all times; c) there must not be any investments accepted for the project; d) the fiscal sponsor can unilaterally withhold, withdraw, or demand immediate return of any funds if the fiscal sponsor determines, in its sole and absolute discretion, that the filmmaker or the project breaches the fiscal sponsorship agreement or jeopardizes the fiscal sponsor's "tax-exempt" status; e) the fiscal sponsor can unilaterally redirect any funds away from the filmmaker and to any other party who can fulfill the stated goals of the film project; f) the right of the fiscal sponsor to approve any and all funding sources for the film project; and g) the filmmaker is required to periodically file reports documenting all expenditures made with the funds and any changes to its legal or tax status.

If there are any future tax liabilities for a fiscal sponsor that arise from a filmmaker's acceptance of both "tax-exempt" funds and "for-profit" funds regarding a project, the filmmaker should be prepared for the fiscal sponsor to exercise some or all of its foregoing rights as found in the fiscal sponsorship agreement signed by the filmmaker. The long and short of it is that an independent filmmaker should be aware of the potential consequences of signing a "fiscal sponsorship agreement," should be certain that choosing the "tax-exempt" path fulfills the filmmaker's expectations and goals, and should have any agreement reviewed by an attorney experienced in such matters before signing.

6

Financing Independent Films "Inside the System"

By Michael Blaha, Esq.

" Independent" film financing is just that—independent of the studios and devoid of the loss of creative and business control that inevitably comes from essentially turning a project completely over to another party. However, there are some transactions that a filmmaker might conceivably make to raise some or all of the financing for his or her film which, while requiring the surrender of varying levels of independence and authority, are nevertheless deemed worth the trade-off. This section will briefly look at two of the least independent approaches, "PFDs" and "negative pick-ups" and then discuss in more detail a more traditional independent model, bank financing from foreign "presales" (selling distribution rights in a film before completion and, usually, before production has even begun).

PRODUCTION-FINANCING-DISTRIBUTION AGREEMENT

With a PFD or "production-financing-distribution" agreement, a studio basically "buys out" the producer of the film, acquiring all rights in the film in all media throughout the world by purchasing the screenplay and any other necessary literary or intellectual property rights. In that event, the first-time independent filmmaker might at best be engaged as a producer on the film but would be a "hired gun" of the studio with little, if any, final approval or control of how the film is made or distributed. In addition, although the filmmaker will receive the rights purchase payment and possibly a producing fee, he or she will not retain any ownership of the film or proceeds from its distribution, beyond possibly a small percentage of net profits, which in most cases does not generate any additional payments.

While the majority of studio films are made using some species of a PFD, by definition few if any independent films are financed this way, unless one invokes a broader meaning of "independent" to include studio films of certain sensibilities or genres, and not just those that are financed "outside the system." Ironically, some of the "independent" divisions of the major studios, such as Fox Searchlight or Universal's Focus Features, undoubtedly use some of the traditional independent methods, such as equity investments or presales, to purchase the rights from the filmmaker. For example, Fox Searchlight may have a sufficient volume of "output" deals with foreign territories, whereby film projects that fit certain criteria (e.g., genre, cast, director) are automatically sold to those territories for preordained minimum amounts, so that Fox already knows it is guaranteed to recover some or all of the rights purchase price.

NEGATIVE PICK-UP

Another method of financing, which falls somewhere between PFDs and presales with respect to the amount of control and ownership the independent producer must cede, is the "negative pick-up" arrangement. In a negative pick-up transaction, a studio or other production and distribution company agrees to pay a set price for certain distribution rights upon delivery of the finished film to the distributor. The rights acquired could range from worldwide rights in all media, which would make it closer to a PFD agreement, to the more common all domestic rights, which would be more similar to a presale agreement.

Because the studio is not advancing the cost of production in a negative pick-up deal, but only paying upon delivery, it will not have the same level of creative control over the production of the film as in the case of a PFD or presales arrangement. However, the studio will still insist on a certain level of input and may retain approval over certain elements of the film, such as cast director, and script.

Like with presales, under a negative pick-up agreement the distributor does not pay anything until after the film is completed and delivered. The producer will have to obtain a loan against the studio's promise to pay upon delivery, and the bank will require a "completion bond" (a.k.a. "completion guarantee"—more on that later) to ensure that the film will be delivered so the bank will be repaid their loan. Accordingly, the discussion below regarding the process of obtaining bank loans against presales also applies in most relevant respects to negative pick-up arrangements.

PRESALES AND THE BASIC ELEMENTS OF A FILM PACKAGE

Historically, one of the main methods of financing independent films has been through bank loans secured by "presales" of the foreign distribution rights of the film being financed. Although the value of preselling rights has arguably waned in recent years due to a number of factors, including a reduction in the amount of money foreign territories have to spend, and an uptick in native productions. Presales have been and continue to be a significant source of independent film financing.

Since presales are usually made before the film has even begun preproduction, let alone actual photography, there is no finished or even partially finished film to show to potential foreign distributors. Instead, the buyers will base their purchasing decisions on such factors as the filmmaker's prior experience, if any, as well as the genre, the script, the cast of the film, and even the proposed "one-sheet" (poster) artwork for the film. One only has to walk through the halls of the American Film Market ("AFM"), held every November in Santa Monica, California, to see how prominently one-sheets figure into the presales equation.

As a result, one of the first steps that must be taken by any filmmaker who is interested in raising money through presales is to put together a "package" for the film. The package includes the screenplay, the director and stars, if any have been attached, and the one-sheet (poster) artwork. Ideally, the package would be assembled in consultation with the sales agent who will actually be the one trying to sell the film to the foreign buyers. At whatever stage a sales agent is retained, the selection of that sales representative is an important decision, because the ability to raise presale financing and/or gap financing (see below) is largely dependent on the ability of that agent to make sales and the reliability of their sales estimates in the eyes of the lender.

The sales agent would then take the film package to major film markets throughout the world, which include the European Film Market during the Berlin Film Festival (in February), the Hong Kong Filmart (March), Le Marché du Film during the Cannes Film Festival (May), and, perhaps the most important one, the American Film Market (November) and try and make presales of the film on a country-by-country (or territory-by-territory) basis.

BANK LOANS BASED ON PRESALE COMMITMENTS

Once the sales agent has made a sufficient number of presales of the film, the producer then goes to a bank that specializes in film financing (e.g., Comerica Bank, Imperial Bank, or City National Bank) and tries to obtain a production loan secured by those presale commitments and other collateral. The collateral, or security, which the producer grants to the bank to secure the loan, is central to a film production loan transaction. Typically, a bank will want a security interest in all of the film assets including the script, the copyright, all of the physical elements of the film, the contracts for the sale of the film, and the accounts receivables (even those unrelated to the presold territories).

The security interest "attaches" to the property by virtue of the loan documents. "Perfection" of the security interest involves filing it with the correct governmental entity (e.g., clerk of the county in which the borrower resides). In the event the borrower defaults on the loan, the bank theoretically can foreclose on the security interest, take possession of the collateral, and sell it to try and recoup its losses (much like a bank forecloses on a house when the lender does not pay the mortgage). Even if the producer files for bankruptcy, a properly "perfected" security interest (recorded to give notice to other possible claimants) in the pledged property will prevent the assets from being sold without the sales proceeds being paid to the holder of the security interest.

There are of course many factors which go into the bank's decision whether to loan against the presale commitments and other collateral and if so, in what amount and at what interest rate. For example, depending on the reputation of the "prebuyer" and the experience the bank has had, if any, with loaning against that buyer's presales commitments in the past, the bank may require the buyer to post a letter of credit to guarantee payment upon delivery of the film, or increase the amount of the presale contract that the bank will "discount" (e.g., if the presale is for $1 million, the bank might discount that amount 20 percent or more, resulting in a loan of no more than $800,000 [$1,000,000 x 80% = $800,000]).

The interest rate for the loan is almost always expressed as some number of percentage points linked to a benchmark rate like prime rate or LIBOR, the London InterBank Offered Rate. In addition, the bank will normally require an up-front "commitment" fee that may be 1 to 2 percent of the total loan amount.

The bank will expect the producer to sign a "commitment letter" which commits the bank to virtually nothing but usually commits the producer to paying all of the legal fees which the bank incurs in connection with negotiating and documenting the loan (in addition to the borrower's own legal fees). Usually the producer will be on the hook for these fees, even if the loan transaction is never completed, regardless of the reason. As a result the producer should try to avoid execution of such a commitment letter for as long as possible, and in any event try to cap the amount of legal fees that he or she may be obligated to pay.

Another standard requirement which may catch the inexperienced producer/borrower unawares is that banks will often ask the *borrower's* attorney for a legal opinion that the loan documents are valid and enforceable and that the lender's security interest in the collateral is properly perfected. Since the documents are usually prepared by counsel for the bank, and it is the bank's lawyer, not yours, who is responsible for perfection of the security interest, such request should be opposed. If the borrower's attorney must render such an opinion, he or she should make sure to include references to the applicable ABA (American Bar Association) and equivalent state bar provisions which minimize the risk in issuing such an opinion.

The loan is of course paid back out of the proceeds from the distribution payments received by the producer, upon delivery of the film, including the money generated from guarantees from the various presold territories. However, the bank does not receive 100 percent of those receipts. There may be deductions due to foreign withholding taxes, or sales agent expenses and some or all of the sales agent's commission (depending on the sales agent's standing and agreement with the bank). Some portion of the distribution proceeds may also need to be set aside for residuals and third party participations.

The documents which make up the bank loan package include the Loan Agreement between the borrower/producer and the lender bank (including the security agreement), the Completion Guarantee (and the related documents specified below), the Distributors' Notices of Acceptance (whereby the distributors agree to pay the agreed purchase price for the distribution rights in the presold territories to the bank upon delivery of the picture), and an Interparty Agreement (an agreement between the producer, lender, sales agent, completion guarantor, and, to the extent applicable, investors and gap or bridge lenders to set forth the order of payment and the priority of the applicable security interests).

GAP LOANS AND BRIDGE LOANS

As noted above, it has become harder to obtain production financing loans in the last couple of years, and when this negative trend is coupled with the increased aversion to risk most banks are experiencing, it becomes less and less likely that an independent filmmaker will be able to raise the entire amount needed to make his or her film. That is where "gap" financing comes in.

Gap financing, which also has become more difficult to obtain in the recent past, is designed to fit the "gap" or shortfall between the amount the bank will loan and the actual budget for the film. The amount of gap financing a bank (and it will not necessarily be from the same bank who makes the main presales loan) may be willing to make will be based on the sales agent's estimates of sales in territories that were not presold.

For example, if $5 million is needed to produce a film and there are presale guarantees of $5 million, a bank may be only willing to lend $4 million. In that case, there is a $1 million gap between the presales loan amount and the production budget for the film. If the sales agent has estimated that distribution rights in the film could be sold in some or all of the territories which were not presold for another $2 million, then a gap loan for the remaining $1 million of the budget may be secured against those estimates for the as-of-yet unsold territories.

Since they are just that—estimates as opposed to contractual commitments like the presales—a gap loan is riskier than a presales loan and is therefore more costly in terms of both the up-front fees and the interest rate. The lender might also seek contingent compensation, in addition to the interest payment, based on some percentage of film revenue. Like the presales loan, the borrower will need to acquire a completion guarantee as a condition of the loan.

Last but not least are "bridge" loans, which are used to fund preproduction expenses before the completion bond is in place. They are repaid from presales or proceeds of the gap loan when it is funded once the completion bond is in place. Since these loans do not require a completion bond guaranteeing that the film will actually get made, they are the riskiest loans, and lenders, which may also be gap lenders, charge very high points (up-front fees as high as 10 percent of the loan amount) and a very high rate of interest.

COMPLETION GUARANTEES

Since a presale loan is repaid from the payments due from the presold distributor upon delivery of the film, the bank must have some assurance that the producer will be able to complete and deliver the movie on time and on budget. That is where completion guarantees, or completion bonds, come into play. The bank will require a completion bond from a third party insurance company (the "completion guarantor") such as Film Finances, Inc. or International Film Guarantors, who will guarantee, in return for a premium (typically 2 to 3 percent of the budget), that the producer will be able to finish the film and deliver it to the prebuyers, triggering their payments under the presales contracts to the bank to pay off the loan.

If the producer encounters difficulties in completing the film, a completion guarantor will either loan additional monies to the producer to address the problems, "take over" the production and complete the film itself, or, in the most extreme cases, "abandon" the production and repay the loan amount including interest, to the bank. If monies are advanced, then the completion guarantor recoups those advances against film revenues (such advances would normally be deemed a "nonrecourse loan," so that the sole source of repayment is those revenues (that is, the producer itself would not be liable for repayment), subordinated to the bank's loans.

Because the completion guarantor's main priority is making sure the film is completed on time and within budget, it will require that the film budget include a line item for contingencies of at least 10 percent (or higher if the director or producer of the film are inexperienced filmmakers or unknown to the completion bond company). The completion guarantor also will require the producer, director, production manager, and key department heads to approve the budget and script and agree they can perform their services within the time and money constraints of the proposed budget.

The definition of what constitutes "delivery" of the film (which is essentially what the completion bond company is guaranteeing) is usually consistent with the distribution agreements upon which the lender has based the production-financing loan. If those agreements contain excessive or subjective approvals, those approvals will usually have to be deleted before the completion guarantor will bond the film. Similarly, if there are any "elements" that a distributor or distributors have required as a condition of payment upon delivery (e.g., a particular actor or director), then the completion guarantor will try to work with the distributors to arrange for a method to replace those elements if necessary, usually by way of the Distributors' Notice of Acceptance form that makes up part of the overall loan documentation.

A completion guarantee should not be confused with other types of production insurance, such as cast and crew insurance, negative insurance, general liability insurance, or errors and omissions insurance. Indeed, a completion guarantor will require the producer to maintain these standard types of coverage as a prerequisite to issuance of the completion guarantee. In addition, the completion guarantor will always exclude certain types of risks or claims from its coverage, including but not limited to chain of title (e.g., confirming the producer owns the necessary intellectual property rights, such as copyright, to make the film), a particular MPAA rating, the artistic quality of the film, and the insolvency or creditworthiness of a distributor who is obliged to pay on delivery.

There are several agreements that make up the typical completion guarantee package. These agreements include 1) the Producer Agreement— the agreement between the producer and the completion guarantor setting forth their respective rights and obligations; 2) the Completion Guarantee (or Bond) itself—the agreement between the completion guarantor and the lender/bank whereby delivery of the picture is guaranteed on certain terms; 3) the Production Account Takeover Letter and Takeover Agreement— giving the completion guarantor the right to control the production bank account and under some circumstances, take over the entire production; and 4) the Lab Access letter—giving the completion guarantor access to and control over the physical film elements.

Few movies are fully taken over contractually, because it is bad publicity for the film and harms the reputations of the producer and the director of the film. Usually, a completion guarantor will first try a so-called soft takeover, where it doesn't take over the production entirely but rather exercises increasingly stringent controls over the production, including the production bank accounts and budgetary expenditures. Under a soft takeover, the producer will have to follow cost-cutting suggestions made by the completion bond company. However, the producer might be permitted the opportunity to raise additional production financing (which cannot dilute the bank's position) before having to implement those cost savings.

These are some of the ways an independent film producer might raise production financing "inside the system." As can be seen by this analysis, the main trade-off is the loss of creative and business control as well as loss of possible upside potential; however, if you are able to raise the funds "outside the system" (for example, by selling equity in your project), you will remain in control of the creative and business aspects of the production and have a much better chance of receiving a substantial share of the film's profits if it becomes a commercial success.

7

Entities

*"You must choose. But choose wisely. For as the true grail will
bring you life—The false grail will take it from you."*
—Indiana Jones and the Temple of Doom

REASONS FOR CREATING AN ENTITY

One of the questions a filmmaker needs to ask is: "Do I need to set up
an entity right now?" The answer is: "It depends." Eventually, however, when the filmmaker is ready to solicit investments to make the film,
the entity receiving money will need to legally exist. A primary advantage
in setting up an entity is that it creates limited liability for the owners,
relieving them of personal liability for the debts of the entity (absent certain
special circumstances). When making a film there are many contracts that
need to be entered into, and there are many activities that have to occur in
order for a film to get made. Each one of these endeavors opens the filmmaker to the risk of liability. Creating an entity provides a buffer of protection between the individual filmmaker and the hundreds of people and
thousands of interactions that occur in making a film. Although, as stated
in the introduction, the primary motive of the independent filmmaker for
making his or her film should be the compulsion for artistic expression, it

should never be forgotten that making a film is also a business endeavor. In pursuing any business it is helpful for tax and accounting reasons to have a separate entity in which activities that are not associated with the filmmaker's personal affairs are separated and accounted for. In addition, the filmmaker will most likely be raising money from other people, and to do that he or she will need to create a separate entity in which the individuals will invest their money, usually in exchange for a percentage ownership interest in the entity. Individuals who invest in feature films most likely are not interested in being involved in the daily operation of making the movie, nor does the filmmaker want the investors to have the power to control the daily operation of making the film. Certain entities, such as a limited liability company, grant the filmmaker a structure that can have management of the entity separated from the investors in the making of the film. In return, the investors are able to limit their personal liability to the amount they provide in exchange for the ownership interest. So, for example, if an individual invested $5,000 in exchange for an ownership interest in an entity that is producing the film, then that individual's maximum risk of liability is the $5,000 he or she invested. This principle operates under the assumption that the individual remains uninvolved in producing the movie or running the operations of the entity.

Potential investors in a film will be interested in knowing the plan for the return of their investment and the process of dividing any potential profits when and if the film is sold, as well as the "rules" by which the filmmaker will be playing in making the film and running the business. Having an entity and creating the necessary paperwork for the entity provides the mechanism for return of any revenue and the rules of operation. It is easiest to think of creating the entity as creating a "club" that has certain rules that must be followed (by law) and other rules that are created and agreed upon by the members of the "club" (by agreement). Each type of entity has advantages and disadvantages in allowing the filmmaker the most flexibility and protection in making the film. Partnerships, corporations, and limited liability companies have different rules regarding the management and control of the operation of the company, the personal liability of the participants, the raising of money to make the film, the allocation of profits and losses, the costs involved, and many other issues that will affect the successful completion of the film.

COSTS OF CREATING AN ENTITY

Filing Costs. It costs somewhere between seventy dollars and four hundred dollars to file the paperwork to form an entity in a state (depending on the state).

Attorney vs. Legal Document Service Company. Further costs would accrue if an attorney drafts any of the proper documents and files them. Some independent filmmakers will use a document service company, such as LegalZoom.com, to create their entity, which will send them standard forms. For example, if the creation of a corporation is intended, then the filer will receive standard by-laws, or if a limited liability company is intended, then he or she will receive a standard operating agreement from the vendor. This is definitely less expensive than hiring a lawyer to create the documents. However, a filmmaker should recognize that these documents are designed to be used in conjunction with an attorney who will tailor the documents in accordance with the facts and circumstances of the filer's particular business endeavor, in this case, the film and filmmaker(s). Boiler-plate documents can be dangerous unless modified to specific circumstances, since there are as many different needs in creating and running a business as there are different businesses. It probably is a wise choice, from a cost/benefit perspective, to use standard documents in the case of a company formed with one owner and that one owner (i.e., the filmmaker) will be the only individual providing money to the entity. However, most filmmakers have one, two, or three other partners, a slate of films (i.e., scripts) that they plan to develop or create, and they probably plan to raise money from other individuals. They also usually plan to invest some of their own money in the project with other investors. Situations involving people working and investing with the filmmaker are best addressed by engaging an experienced attorney to draft the paperwork, even if a corporate service company formed the entity with the proper state authority. Experienced attorneys charge between two hundred dollars and seven hundred and fifty dollars per hour. The amount of time an attorney will need to devote to a particular situation depends upon how complicated it is. For example, if only two people are involved, one providing the script, direction, and producing and one person contributing the money, then it will be less complicated to handle than a situation with four different individuals bringing four different types of skills and resources to the project. If they plan to raise the financing from other private individuals, that adds another layer of complexity. Basically, anything that adds more time for an attorney to handle will cost more money.

C Corporations and Double Taxation. An often overlooked aspect of choosing the type of entity is the taxation questions. Herein lie some perilous traps for the unwary. Just as an example, one of the main drawbacks of a C corporation is that it has two levels of taxation. That is, the C corporation is taxed twice: once on the entity level and a second time when the individual shareholders (investors) receive distributions from the corporation. If the corporation is taxed on the first dollar of profit, assuming the highest current federal corporate tax rate (i.e., 38 percent), then sixty-two cents are left to be distributed to shareholders. When the shareholder receives the sixty-two cents in the form of an ordinary dividend, the shareholder is taxed again—let's assume at the current highest federal personal income tax rate (i.e., 35 percent)—leaving forty cents of the original one dollar profit for the individual. On the other hand, if the same dollar was received in a limited liability company, which has no first level of taxation at the entity level, then the amount the individual receives would be sixty-five cents (one dollar multiplied by the highest personal tax rate of 35 percent).

THE STATE WHERE ENTITY SHOULD BE FORMED AND STATE AND LOCAL TAXES

Most states have a minimum tax payable for each year of an entity's existence. Many cities (Los Angeles, for example) also require businesses to pay local taxes based upon the county or city in which the business is based.

For example, entities in California are generally required to pay a minimum tax of $800 per year. There is some debate as to whether or not it is better to form the entity in a state that has a more favorable tax structure so as to avoid taxes like that of California's $800 minimum. Because of its favorable state tax structure regarding entities, Nevada is often cited as a preferred state in which to form an entity. Generally, the requirements regarding paying entity tax in a state are dictated by where the company will transact its business. Where it will conduct its business is determined by a "facts and circumstance" evaluation to determine whether or not any company has engaged in sufficient business in any one particular state to require the company to have to register and pay taxes in such state. This is not as simple as it may appear. The record of a company's activities will determine which state's (or states') laws it will be subject to, but in general an entity must have a sufficient amount of transactions within any particular state for it to become subject to that state's requirements to register (and pay tax) in that state.

Let's look at one example: a Nevada entity performs all preproduction, production, and postproduction in Nevada, but also contracts with a company in California, which rents all of the camera lenses used in the making of the film to the company in Nevada, and mails the lenses from California to the company in Nevada. Assuming this is the only transaction that the Nevada company has in California then the Nevada company is not required to file with the California Secretary of State as a "foreign company" doing business in California and thereby pay the minimum tax, because the Nevada company does not have a sufficient connection or "nexus" with California (to use the technical term). However, if the facts are modified so that the Nevada company is engaging in preproduction in Nevada and shooting principal photography in California, and then does most of the postproduction in California, then the Nevada company has become subject to California jurisdiction and must register as a "foreign entity" transacting "intrastate business in California." A filmmaker is advised to consult with a local attorney in each state in which the filmmaker is conducting numerous transactions in order to determine whether or not such registration and tax requirements are triggered. Each state has its own specific language defining what determines whether or not there is enough of a connection with the state to require an entity to register and pay tax in that state. For example, in California "transacting intrastate business" is basically defined as entering into "repeated and successive business transactions" in the state, and would require the entity to register in California. For tax purposes a company is subject to California entity taxes (such as the minimum $800 tax) when the company is "doing business" in California, which is basically defined as when a company "actively engages in any transaction for the purpose of financial or pecuniary gain or profit." The point is that if the filmmaker forms a Nevada company to avoid taxes and then makes the film in another state, all that has been accomplished is the incurring of extra and unnecessary expense of creating a Nevada company since the filmmaker will need to register and become subject to the tax structure of the state in which the film is created anyway. From a practical standpoint this is usually not a major cost issue because the film is usually made in one state. However, films pursuing state tax subsidies and films that require location shooting in more than one state need to be aware of the potential issues regarding registering and paying tax in any relevant state.

CHOOSING AN ENTITY WHEN PRODUCING AN INDEPENDENT FILM

The rest of this chapter provides a brief survey of the different types of entities available, and the major aspects of each one. As stated above, it is recommended that at least one vehicle should be created by the filmmaker. The one actually chosen will depend on the facts and circumstances of each particular project, and the filmmaker should rely on the advice of his or her personal attorney. It should be noted here that in general the limited liability company has become the prominent entity used in making films and the one most recommended in making feature films (whether it is a first feature film or not). However, depending on the circumstances, a limited partnership can be utilized and be just as effective as the limited liability company.

A number of filmmakers have also created a subchapter S corporation, either as the only entity in making their film, or in addition to creating a limited liability company. The circumstances in which filmmakers have created an S corporation as the only entity has been when the filmmaker or the filmmaker and one other person are the only ones contributing all of the money to finance the film. The other situation when the S corporation may be created in addition to the limited liability company is when a few individuals (as few as two and as many as six or seven) plan to make more than one feature film, and/or hold themselves out as a production company available to produce/create music videos, commercials, industrials, and corporate videos. In this type of situation, they are creating the S corporation to provide limited liability, and the benefits of one level of taxation, and they plan to have this S corporation exist for many years in the future. When and if the time comes to make their feature film, they can then create a limited liability company with the S corporation as the managing member, and the interests in the limited liability company may be made available for purchase by investors. In the future when the feature film has been fully exploited the limited liability company can be dissolved, but the S corporation will remain active for involvement in other projects. Having the S corporation creates another layer of insulation from personal exposure for the owners, but it also creates more paperwork and more cost, which will be discussed in more detail later in this chapter. I will discuss various available entities here, but more space is devoted to the S corporation and the limited liability company because they are the most widely used entities by filmmakers in making a first feature film.

THE SOLE PROPRIETORSHIP

When a person operates a business by himself or herself, he or she is operating a sole proprietorship. The main disadvantage of a sole proprietorship is that the individual has no protection from the liabilities created in the daily operation of the business. As a general rule this means that any asset owned by the individual can potentially be claimed to satisfy any liabilities claimed against the business. In addition, because the sole proprietorship is not considered an entity separate from its individual owner, the individual can not sell interests to other parties who may wish to invest. For these reasons, the sole proprietorship is of little value to the filmmaker producing his or her feature film, and is generally not recommended for producing a film.

THE PARTNERSHIP

A partnership is an association of two or more people who come together to operate a business for profit. In California, partnerships are covered under the Uniform Partnership Act, but this form of entity is very flexible in allowing the partners to contract among themselves regarding the management, control, and division of profits and assumption of losses. When a partnership is created, every partner is personally responsible for the obligations created by every other partner (as long as the partner's action is within the scope of the partnership's activities). Not only are partners personally liable for their actions while making the film, in a partnership they may be liable for the actions of the other partners under certain circumstances as well. On the other hand, partnerships provide only one level of taxation, and the tax consequences of running the business (whether profits or losses) pass through to each partner. A delimiting factor is that individuals who invest money in the project have joint control over the partnership, and therefore have control over the production of the film. If an individual wants only to invest money in the project and not have any other exposure to liability, then the partnership model is not the proper entity. Overall, because of the personal liability of the partners and the divided control over the production of the film, this is not an entity filmmakers generally choose for making their film.

LIMITED PARTNERSHIP

In California, limited partnerships are governed by the California Revised Limited Partnership Act, and the other states in the country have adopted the Revised Uniform Limited Partnership Act in some form. The operation of a limited partnership is similar to a general partnership with the added feature of allowing interests for limited partners to invest and be shielded from liability for the obligations of the partnership. The individual investor is only at risk to the extent of his or her investment. A limited partnership must have at least one general partner and at least one limited partner. The general partner acts in a similar capacity as a partner in a regular partnership, while limited partners are merely investors. The limited partners contribute money to the limited partnership, that is, the money to make the film, but they do not exercise control over the actual making of the film or the operation of the partnership. As mentioned above, their exposure in the endeavor is limited to the amount of money invested in the limited partnership and does not extend to other liabilities incurred in making the film. The limited partnership blends the advantages of the corporation and the advantages of the partnership in that it provides limited liability for the investors who exercise no control over the making of the film or the operation of the venture. Of course, the general partner(s) of a limited partnership is (are) still liable for the activities pertaining to the making the film. In most instances, but by no means all instances, the filmmaker is the general partner who is then exposed to personal liability for the actions in making the film and operating the partnership—obviously not a desired position for the filmmaker. This problem has historically been solved by the formation of an S corporation which then becomes the general partner of the limited partnership. In this way, the filmmaker still retains control over the production of the film, while at the same time adding another buffer of protection from personal liability. Naturally the latter arrangement carries a greater expense with it since it requires the formation and operation of another entity (i.e., the S corporation). Before the limited liability company became widely available and popular, the limited partnership was the entity of choice for filmmakers and it remains a viable option today.

CORPORATIONS

Overview of C Corporations and S Corporations. There are two types of corporations, a C corporation and an S corporation. Both C corporations and S corporations consist of shareholders, a board of directors, and corporate officers (president, vice-president, etc.). Both corporations are entities separate from their owners, allowing investment by individuals with exposure generally limited to the amount of the investment. C and S corporations can utilize voting and nonvoting classes of stock so that investors have no direct control over the daily operations of the company thereby generally giving the filmmaker both control over the operations and limited personal liability. In terms of making an independent film, the C corporation is generally avoided because of the two levels of taxation. When a corporate entity is desired, the S corporation is generally the entity of choice because it eliminates double taxation. There are, however, numerous restrictions in qualifying for the creation of an S corporation, which reduce the flexibility of the entity and most often render the use of the S corporation inappropriate for producing an independent film.

Both a C corporation and an S corporation are created under state law and operationally they function in the same manner. To become an S corporation, a C corporation must first be created and then the corporation files with the IRS, electing to be treated as an S corporation by the IRS. Both entities have articles of incorporation, by-laws, shareholders, a board of directors and officers. The powers of each of the latter, as well as the structure and management of each type of corporation, and the relationships of the participants are all governed by the laws of the state in which the corporation is created. Because these differences are complex, and vary from state to state, the filmmaker should consult with his or her attorney before making the decision to incorporate and in which state. However, there are basic general elements of the corporate form that are important for the filmmaker to understand before deciding whether to choose this form of entity.

General Rules of How Corporations Operate. Other aspects of a corporation can be viewed as advantageous or disadvantageous to a filmmaker depending on the circumstances. These aspects generally play out in the management and operation of the corporation which is governed by 1) the articles of incorporation and 2) the by-laws of the corporation. The articles and by-laws are the technical terms for the "rules" of the corporation by which the filmmaker must play. The members decide who is in charge, who can join, and the rules by which they will operate. The incorporators have wide latitude and can make up just about any rules they like for the operation of the company as long as these rules comply with the general rules mandated by the governing state where the corporation is created and operates. In California, for example, some permissible variations include granting more or less than one vote per share for any class, providing for election of the director(s) only by certain classes of stock, and supermajority or unanimous voting for certain corporate actions.

The following is a brief overview of how corporations generally operate. Shareholders buy an interest in the corporation with the hope of someday receiving back their investment plus a profit. They are also generally given "voting" stock with the power to elect and remove members of the board of directors and to amend the articles of incorporation and its by-laws. The board of directors has the right and responsibility to oversee the daily operation of the corporation, and is initially chosen by the individual(s) who incorporate the entity. But in most cases, the board of directors does not actually run the day to day operations of the corporation, instead they delegate the authority to people they choose to do the work, that is, the "officers" of the company, which at a minimum include the President/Chief Executive Officer (CEO), the Treasurer/Chief Financial Officer (CFO), the Vice-President and the Secretary. The board of directors and the officers are the two groups of people who run the company, that is, have control over the making of the film. The investors (i.e., the shareholders) are given the right to choose the board of directors, so, in theory, the investors can vote out the board of directors, appoint officers other than the filmmaker, and essentially gain control over the making of the film. As mentioned above, there are changes to the articles of incorporation, by-laws, and stock that, if agreed to, can alter this basic operation.

Articles of Incorporation. Minimally, articles of incorporation should state the following: the name of the corporation, the statement of the corporate purpose, the name and address of the corporation's initial agent for service of process, and the number of shares the corporation is authorized to issue. In California, the law states that the articles may also stipulate "any other provision not in conflict with the law, for the management of the business, and the conduct of the affairs of the corporation." It is through the language of the articles of incorporation (and the by-laws) that the filmmaker may minimize the control the shareholders will have over the corporation. It should be needless to say that the filmmaker should use an experienced attorney to draft the appropriate language. It is a general principle of corporate law that the shareholders should have the power to choose the board of directors of the corporation who in turn choose the executives who manage the corporation. It must always be kept in mind that any attempt to limit the shareholders' power in the articles and by-laws is moving away from the natural operation of corporations. Making planning more difficult is the fact that S corporations are allowed to have only one type of stock, which limits flexibility. This is another reason why the S corporation is reserved for those situations where the filmmaker is the only shareholder, or where there are only one or two other shareholders who do not hold a majority of the shares, that is to say, less than 50 percent of the outstanding shares.

Corporation By-Laws. Although there is no requirement in California for a corporation to have by-laws, almost all corporations do have them. In conjunction with the articles of incorporation, the by-laws operate as the rules for the governing of the corporation. The articles of incorporation are filed with the Secretary of State in California whereas the by-laws are not filed with the state. In the event of any conflict between the articles and the by-laws, the articles govern. The names of the board of directors may be stipulated in the articles of incorporation or in the by-laws, and in general the minimum number of board members allowed in California is three. However, California allows that if there is only one shareholder, the number of board members can be only one or if there are only two shareholders, then only two board members are allowed.

Management and Control of the Corporation. Management and control of the corporation will be based on the number of people on the board of directors, the number of shares the corporation can issue, the "par value" of those shares, who can issue more shares and for how much, and who can decide when in the future more shares can be issued by the corporation. The number of shares to be issued is determined by the incorporators and that number is recorded in the articles of incorporation. In California, either the board of directors or the shareholders can decide when more shares can be issued and at what price. In most situations, it is perfectly appropriate for the filmmaker to name himself or herself to the board of directors as well as to the positions of President, Vice-President, or any other positions. The filmmaker is still responsible to the shareholders who have rights under the law which they can exercise if they are dissatisfied with the manner in which the board and officers are running the company (i.e., making the film). Traditionally, examples of shareholders exercising their legal rights against the filmmaker have not been especially successful, mainly because of the time and expense that is involved in so doing, especially in comparison to the amount invested by the shareholders, and the modest expectations of those who invest in such projects. Nevertheless, if not properly planned for, a small number of motivated shareholders could at the very least exercise their rights to vote for a new board of directors, which, in turn, could lead to a whole new group of officers, which in turn could completely alter the direction of the project. As mentioned above, a simple drafting technique, which is perhaps the absolute best protection for the filmmaker in these circumstances, is to always be the majority shareholder in the corporation. However, this technique often creates a tax liability for the filmmaker since the filmmaker is most often receiving the shares in exchange for services (not money like the other investors) thereby creating "income" for the film-maker which the IRS would expect to be reported as such on the film-maker's tax return. A filmmaker who finds himself or herself facing the prospect of losing control over the original vision for the film or with an unexpected tax liability might well wonder why he or she didn't anticipate these possibilities before choosing to use a corporation.

RULES FOR CREATING AN S CORPORATION

To this point the discussion regarding the corporation has been of a general nature covering both C and S types. The C corporation is usually avoided as the entity of choice for making a feature film primarily because of the two levels of taxation and the issues of control over the entity. This fact does not render a discussion of the general nature of corporate structure moot because there are filmmakers who create an S corporation when making their low-budget film. An S corporation is created by filing a request with the IRS asking to be recognized as such. However, before the election is filed with the IRS, a C corporation must have already been created. An S corporation still operates under the same laws as a C corporation, so the workings of the C corporation discussed above are by and large applicable to an S corporation. A primary difference is the issue of taxation; the S corporation allows the profits and losses to be passed through to the shareholders who then declare the profits or losses on their personal income tax returns.

To convert a C corporation into an S corporation certain requirements must be met which include the following: 1) the corporation must be a domestic corporation; 2) the corporation can have no more than seventy-five shareholders; 3) shareholders can only be individuals, estates, exempt organizations, and certain trusts; 4) none of the shareholders can be nonresident aliens; 5) the corporation can have only one class of stock; and 6) every shareholder must consent in writing to the S corporation election. After a C corporation is created in the state of choice, the filmmaker must obtain Internal Revenue Service Form 2553, fill it out and send it to the IRS.

Not all states recognize S corporations created on the federal level so a filmmaker should consult with his or her qualified attorney regarding his or her circumstances. The federal law requires that the election be made before the sixteenth day of the second month of the tax year in which the corporation first has owners, has assets, or does business. A failure to timely file the election means S corporation status will not go into effect until the next tax year. This fact is not without importance. If, for example, the filmmaker creates the corporation and does not file to be an S corporation in time, then for tax purposes, the corporation is treated as a C corporation for that year and is treated as an S corporation beginning January of the next year. Failure to recognize this small quirk has cost some filmmakers thousands of dollars. Imagine a filmmaker who creates a C corporation in April but fails to timely file his or her S corporation election. The filmmaker begins making the film in August of that year, spending $60,000 by the end of the year. The next year the filmmaker continues making the film and spends another $100,000 to finish it. The first $60,000 spent (cost) is owned by the C corporation and the following $100,000 is owned by the individual shareholders of the S corporation. The tax rules basically treat the C corporation and the S corporation as noncompatible tax entities with the result that the C corporation's earnings (if any) and losses (in this example the first $60,000 spent on the film) are now "trapped" in the C corporation and are subject to the two-level taxation system of C corporation rules, while on the other hand, the subsequent $100,000 spent (loss) can be passed directly to the shareholders. These facts may seem esoteric to the reader; however, one of the curiosities of investing in film projects is that losses and other tax activity passed through to investors is often considered a "benefit" associated with the investment.

Tax laws and IRS rulings can seem bizarre to the uninitiated, but they can usually be traced to some past abuse or another. In the past, some very enterprising people realized if they could find and buy a C corporation that had built up losses over the years (bought of course at a sharp discount), and turn it into an S corporation, they could then sell it to some other S corporation that had built up profits over the years, and the profits and all the taxes owed could be wiped out. Everyone would be happy except the IRS. The fact that these rules serve a purpose does not alter the fact that they can easily represent a trap for the unwary filmmaker. Fortunately, the IRS has provided a way to avoid the trap by providing that a taxpayer may file a request for relief for a late S corporation election pursuant to an applicable revenue procedure, that is, Revenue Procedure 97-48, Revenue Procedure 2003-43, Revenue Procedure 2004-48, or Revenue Procedure 2007-62. It still remains at the discretion of the IRS as to whether or not to grant the S corporation status in the first year the corporation is created. However, the IRS has stated that if a corporation is eligible for relief under an applicable revenue procedure, it will grant S corporation status notwithstanding the late election for the first year. The benefit of obtaining the election is that the corporation will be considered an S corporation for tax purposes from the first day it is created, and no profits or losses will be "trapped" in the C corporation. There are specific requirements which must be met in order to obtain the relief under the cited revenue procedures so it behooves the filmmaker to consult with his or her tax attorney in order to make sure they can be utilized. It is an issue that is often missed among the paperwork surrounding the making of a film using an S corporation, and missing the issue has cost filmmakers substantial amounts of money.

8

Limited Liability Company

"You have chosen wisely."
—Indiana Jones and the Temple of Doom

The limited liability company (LLC) is a relatively new entity. Wyoming is widely credited as being the first state to allow a "limited liability company" in the late 1970s. However, because of the uncertainties as to whether the Internal Revenue Service would treat an LLC as a "pass-through" entity like partnerships (as opposed to having two levels of tax like a C corporation), states were slow to pass laws allowing LLCs. By the early 1990s the Internal Revenue Service had clarified the issue by deciding to allow "pass-through" tax treatment for LLCs and by the late 1990s every state had passed laws allowing LLCs to be formed. The LLC has become so much the favored entity for filmmakers today that it warrants a more extensive treatment than any of the other entities described in the previous chapter.

ADVANTAGES OF A LIMITED LIABILITY COMPANY

LLCs fuse the best of the different entities by providing maximum flexibility to a filmmaker in regard to formation and operation, while retaining the advantage of one level of taxation. Similar to limited partners in limited partnerships, members of an LLC, who are not also managers, are treated only as investors. The "nonmanager" members contribute money to the LLC for the production of the film, but they do not exercise control over the actual making of the film or the operation of the LLC. Their exposure is limited to the loss of any money invested in the LLC and not other liabilities of the company which may be incurred in the making of the film. As stated above, the general partner(s) of a limited partnership remain liable for the activities generated in making the film. This is where an LLC is different than a limited partnership. The manager(s) of an LLC are not liable for the LLC's obligations simply on the basis of being a manager. This eliminates the time and expense of needing to create another entity to act as the manager when using an LLC. A manager also is not required to own any amount of the LLC as a prerequisite to being named a manager. These are some of the aspects that make the LLC a more flexible entity than the limited partnership.

CREATING A LIMITED LIABILITY COMPANY

Each state has its own requirements for filing paperwork necessary for the formation of an LLC. In California the articles of organization must be filed with the Secretary of State in order to initiate the existence of the LLC. The articles must be filed using Form LLC-1, which is obtainable from the Secretary of State's website. There is a filing fee of $70 (as of 2013). The organizer must provide the following: the name of the LLC; the initial agent for service of process; and information as to whether the LLC is member-managed, managed by one manager, or more than one manager. Form LLC-1 provides a standard statement of the purpose of the LLC, which is required by statute and should not be altered. Filmmakers should carefully review the requirements for the state in which the LLC is being created since the requirements of other states will be different than California's. For example, New York requires that a notice containing certain information (such as the name of the LLC, the date of filing, the LLC address, etc.) must be published in two newspapers within 120 days of formation and once a week thereafter for a period of six consecutive weeks. After the LLC publishing is complete, affidavits of publication must be obtained from the newspapers which then

must be filed with the state. Failure to comply with the publishing requirement within the 120 days of formation will cause the LLC to lose certain
privileges. Some of the issues which need to be addressed in setting up an
LLC include: 1) whether there is one or more classes of ownership; 2) how
much money each member is to invest; 3) the distribution of gross receipts; 4)
the authority of the manager(s) and member(s); 5) the responsibilities of the
manager(s); 6) the transferability of a member's interest in the LLC; and 7) the
rights and responsibilities of the manager(s) and member(s) upon dissolution
of the LLC. The rules of formation and operation of an LLC (including 1
through 7 above) are contained in a written "operating agreement."

MAJOR ISSUES IN ESTABLISHING A LIMITED LIABILITY COMPANY

The Operating Agreement. The operating agreement functions in
a manner similar to the by-laws of a corporation or like the partnership
agreement for a limited liability partnership. In California an LLC is not
required to have a written operating agreement, but if it does not then it is
governed by the default provisions found under the *Beverly-Killea Limited
Liability Company Act*, which provides guidelines for matters such as the
formation, operation, and dissolving of an LLC. The operating agreement
is a document most filmmakers need and to which they should give careful
consideration. An attorney should draft such an agreement specifically tailored for producing an independent feature film, and based on the specific
facts attendant to each individual filmmaker's situation. What follows is a
slightly more detailed discussion of some items mentioned above.

Management. The management of an LLC can take many forms. It may
be member managed or managed by one or more managers who may or
may not be members of the LLC. Generally, in a member managed LLC the
members each vote on the actions of the LLC based upon the percentage of
ownership of each member. However, the members can alter this arrangement by giving certain members more voting control than others, or by
eliminating the participation of any individual member from the management of the LLC. These decisions are made before the potential investors

commit to membership in the company. The flexibility of the LLC, especially in defining the rights, obligations, and powers of the manager(s) and member(s), is its primary advantage.

Classes of Ownership. If the filmmaker intends to produce one film then only one class of ownership may be needed. However, there are times when a filmmaker may wish to have the ability to approach investors for the purpose of obtaining development money; or he or she may wish to create a class of ownership to be owned solely by him or herself; or the filmmaker may want to create two or three films with the intention of producing them over several years into the future. In these situations the formation of different classes of ownership might be a better alternative (for example, Class A, Class B, Class C, etc., with each providing different obligations and rewards). To illustrate, an LLC could provide for Class A ownership which would be offered to investors who wish to invest "development money" for the project, while Class B ownership would be offered to investors who wish to invest in the full production and completion of the feature film. The Class A funds would be used for such expenditures as engaging a casting director, hiring a writer to polish the script, paying certain expenses such as office space, or to make pay-or-play offers to actors. Since the money invested in Class A will be spent with no guarantee that the filmmaker will ever be able to raise Class B money, which goes for producing the actual film, it entails greater risks for investors. This is because all of the Class A investment could be spent to "develop" the project, and yet at the end of the process no feature film may exist to generate revenue. Class A investors in this example can only expect some return if Class B investors are found. If there is no feature film then it is virtually impossible to generate any revenue from the project so in essence the Class A investment would be a total loss. However, Class A investors are generally given a greater return on their investment, so if the money *is* raised and the film *is* made, then the Class A investors will get a greater return on their investment than Class B investors (assuming the film generates revenue). How much more of a return varies depending on the circumstances, but it can be as low as an extra 25 percent to as high as an extra 300 or 400 percent. The goal is to offer a return commensurate with the extra risk to which the investor is exposed.

Allocation of Gross Receipts. The distribution of the gross receipts generated from a film is another issue to be decided. There is no "standard" formula for the independent film industry. However, it is an item that should be determined in the earliest stage of the creation of an LLC. Very often a basic framework for the distribution of gross receipts is as follows: 1) The first revenues are distributed to the investors until they have received a return of all of their original investment; 2) Subsequent revenues are then distributed to the investors until they have received a 10 percent cumulative preferred annual return for three years; 3) After items 1 and 2 are satisfied, subsequent revenues are distributed to any cast and crew members who have entered into deferred compensation agreements; and 4) All subsequent revenues will be distributed 50 percent to the investors and 50 percent to the filmmaker(s) after the satisfaction of items 1, 2, and 3 above. The integration of these decisions into a private placement memorandum will be discussed in Chapter 10.

Relationship of Loans to Investments. A fact not always appreciated by investors is that there is a marked distinction between an investor and a lender. A major issue that is often overlooked is the right of the manager of the LLC to enter into loan agreements in making the film. Often the operating agreement allows the manager to enter into such loans, and more than likely, the repayment of these loans is required before the repayment of the investors' money. A filmmaker must consider whether he or she wants to have the ability to secure loans in the making of the film (the answer is generally yes), whether the loans are to be repaid before or after the investors receive return on their investment (generally before), and whether the filmmaker wants to place a cap on the amount he or she can borrow while making the film. Often the placement of a cap on the amount the filmmaker can borrow will be a note upon which an investor's lawyer will insist. A critical issue is the amount of the cap. The filmmaker's concern is that he or she might reach the cap and still need to borrow more money to complete the film (or to go to film festivals or to pay for the delivery items in a distribution contact, etc.). On the other hand, the investor will be concerned that the amount of indebtedness will render it more difficult (if not impossible) to receive any return on the investment or even the investment itself. It is not uncommon for borrowing to be capped at 10 percent of the film's total budget, so that a filmmaker would be able to borrow $5,000 for a $50,000 budget and $100,000 for a $1 million budget, and so forth.

Cumulative Preferred Return. A filmmaker usually does not provide a cumulative preferred return for investors. A cumulative return is designed to account for the "time value of money" for the period the investor's money is tied up in the film and is not in the market generating returns. If a cumulative preferred return is provided for, it is usually for three years, which is a reasonable estimate. It will generally take three years for the full return to materialize, from the time an investor gives money to a filmmaker until the time a film is released to the market and can generate revenue. However, a cumulative preferred return is usually eliminated because of the recognition of the extreme risk inherent in independent filmmaking. The paperwork associated with the investment will clearly note this extreme risk, and generally the investors who do invest in this type of endeavor are well aware that they most likely will lose all of their investment, which makes them less likely to be concerned about the loss of their "time value of money." On the other hand, it might be a good faith gesture by the filmmaker to provide for a cumulative preferred return to any investor who provides money in such a risky endeavor.

Net Profits. In regard to the division of the net profits of the film (i.e., number 4 listed in "Allocation of Gross Receipts"), 100 percent of the net profits can be divided in any percentage the filmmaker decides. The broad categories include the filmmaker, other producers, actors and crew members, and investors.

Authority of the Manager(s) and Member(s). As mentioned in Chapter 2, it is the LLC operating agreement that primarily establishes the authority of the manager or managers; however, if a producer is also a manager then a number of the issues covered in the LLC operating agreement will be identical to many of the issues covered in a separate producer agreement. Member-managed LLCs are not common when making a feature film but could be useful in a situation where it is only the filmmaker or the film-maker and one other person who contribute all of the money to finance the film and they are actively making the film together. However, most filmmakers need to solicit investors and it will be recalled from an earlier discussion that, when dealing with investors, the filmmaker wants to retain control over the making of the film. In this regard, the best entity is usually an LLC in which the members (i.e., the investors) have no control over the LLC (and therefore no control over making the film). Because this is the best course of action, LLCs formed to make feature films almost always have the management and control of the LLC exclusively held by the manager or managers. If there is one filmmaker then this is an easy issue to address because the filmmaker becomes the manager and has control over the LLC, that is, the producing of the film. Difficulties arise in situations where two or more individuals (or entities) are going to be appointed as managers of the LLC.

If more than one person or entity is to be named as a manager then it is imperative to determine what percentage of voting would be necessary in order to put any management decisions into effect; that is, would a simple majority or a super-majority (66 2/3 percent) be necessary, or would some decisions require unanimity? The filmmaker must carefully consider how a final decision will be made when a disagreement between the managers arises. If there are three managers and decisions are made by majority vote, then two of three managers must vote together. If the filmmaker is the sole dissenting vote then he or she has *effectively lost control* of producing the film. The filmmaker can allocate himself or herself fifty-one percent of the vote which would alleviate this issue. However, the other two managers may be reluctant to agree to give the "filmmaker" so much control. This would be the first opportunity for the parties to address the issue and, in fact, how each one of them approaches the issue will provide a good clue to the filmmaker as to how future disputes will be handled. This is a particularly difficult decision-making process, because very often the managers are the writer(s), director and producer(s) who are merging their talents in a manner that they all believe is equally important to the film. Each one, therefore, will be reluctant to give one of the other managers greater control over the project. Instead of one vision there may be three, even if subliminally. From a practical perspective it is easy for a filmmaker to overlook this issue or not give it sufficient consideration because, in fact, the participants will not have a formal meeting every time a decision needs to be made. Rather, the participants will primarily do the job that is expected from each one. Perhaps more importantly, at this stage in the process the participants usually have not had any disagreements and are very positive, if not euphoric, about the process of collaborating together, which can foster an underestimation of the importance of the allocation of the voting power between them. When, in the process of making the film, events don't go as planned (which includes just about every film ever made), the provisions regarding the voting rights of the managers will become paramount.

Another issue to be considered is the removal of a manager if it becomes necessary. Like any of the other terms in an LLC operating agreement, the provisions regarding removal are flexible and can be drafted to meet the needs and desires of the participants. In general, the LLC operating agreement for making a movie grants the manager(s) wide latitude limited only by removal upon the unanimous vote of all of the members, and solely on the grounds of fraud, gross negligence, or willful malfeasance, which must be determined pursuant to entry of a final order of a court of competent jurisdiction from which no appeal is taken. The bottom line is that the members are relying on the manager(s) to use their best efforts and judgment to produce the film just as each manager has "promised" to do. Potential investors evaluate the filmmaker's "promises" from what is presented in the paperwork given to them (as well as what the filmmaker says in conversations with such potential investors). This is another reason why the information presented in the business plan and the private placement memorandum (to be covered in Chapters 9 and 10) must be accurate, and why, if there is any doubt or uncertainty about certain information to be presented to an investor, it is better to err on the side of caution.

Responsibilities of Manager(s). On the most fundamental level, the manager(s) of an LLC are obligated to run the LLC in good faith and in a manner that is in the best interests of the company. This doesn't mean that the manager(s) need to be infallible; it basically means the manager(s) must take actions that are reasonably prudent in the process of making the film. Other important responsibility issues include the time the manager is expected to devote to the LLC, any competing businesses in which the manager(s) may have an interest, and whether the manager(s) are to be paid for the management services provided. Usually a manager is not required to spend any more time than is deemed appropriate to further the business of the LLC (i.e., make the film). Also, usually a manager is allowed to engage in competing businesses (i.e., allowed to also make other films), and is not paid for management services (however, if a writer, director, producer, etc. is also a manager, then each one normally receives compensation for providing such services to the film).

Transferability of a Member's Interest. It is important to note that the LLC interests owned by members are subject to restriction of transfer. In general, no member may transfer all or any portion of their LLC ownership without the prior written consent of the manager(s). Consent may be given or withheld at the sole discretion of the manager(s). In addition, the consent of the manager(s) is usually dependent upon receiving a legal opinion that the proposed transfer is subject to an effective registration under, or exempt from, the registration requirements of the applicable state and federal securities laws (see Chapter 4, "Securities Purchased Are 'Restricted Securities'"). It is also usual for the manager(s) to receive from the potential transferee such information and agreements that the manager(s) may reasonably require, including, but not limited to, an agreement of the transferee to be bound by all the terms and conditions of the LLC operating agreement. Confirmation that the member will pay all expenses incurred by the LLC in connection with such potential transfer is also usually required. The bottom line is that interests are generally not transferable and if they are transferred it will cost the transferor significant additional expense.

TAX TRAP WHEN OBTAINING LLC OWNERSHIP IN EXCHANGE FOR "SWEAT EQUITY"

"Sweat equity" is when a party receives ownership in an endeavor or company in exchange for providing services to that endeavor or company. Filmmakers are always caught off guard to discover that the Internal Revenue Code (IRC) will treat sweat equity as income to the filmmaker when he or she receives ownership in a limited liability company (or other entity) in exchange for providing services. This issue arises when a filmmaker teams with a partner who will provide funds to the company in exchange for ownership in the company, while the filmmaker will receive ownership in the company in exchange for such services as writing, producing, and directing the film. For example, if one partner provides $50,000 in exchange for 50 percent ownership, while the filmmaker receives his or her 50 percent ownership in exchange for services provided or to be provided instead of money, then the IRC requires the filmmaker to report income in the amount of the ownership interest. It is important to note that such amount will be subject to income tax, social security tax, disability tax, and any other applicable tax. Placing a monetary value on the ownership interest received by the "sweat equity" partner is a real challenge. The value is supposed to be equal to the fair market value of the interest; however, since a market for such ownership interest usually doesn't exist, the Internal Revenue Service has taken the positions that the value is equal either to the liquidation value upon receipt of the ownership interest or that it is equal to the amount that the owner, who paid cash, put up for such ownership interest. In the above example the "sweat equity" owner would be required to report $50,000 as income in the tax year he or she received the "sweat equity" ownership interest, or one-half the liquidation value at the time of receiving the equity position.

There are two common solutions often used to avoid the "sweat equity" tax trap. The simplest solution is to eliminate the "sweat equity" partner's ownership interest so that the cash partner would be a 100 percent owner. This may appear to be unfair, but an operating agreement can be drafted so that all relevant parties (the two owners in the example above) are joint managers of the company, thereby providing both with control over the company's affairs. The agreement can contain provision for a split of revenue generated by the film which first pays back all cash investors (the full $50,000 in the above example) and thereafter splits "net profit" fifty/fifty (50/50) between each party. At the present time, the latter could side-step the tax issue if other requirements are met, but a filmmaker should consult his or tax advisor. The tax consequences of receiving a "profits interest" in exchange for sweat equity was subject to uncertainty until the IRS issued guidance, but that guidance was amended and is subject to proposed regulations that are not effective until finalized, which have not yet occurred. If a filmmaker insists on receiving an ownership interest in exchange for services then a second solution can be to issue the 50 percent ownership to each party in exchange for a small amount of cash, for example $100 each, and then have the one party provide a loan/promissory note to the company in the amount of necessary capital, a $50,000 loan in the above example. When selecting this loan/promissory note alternative, the filmmaker should be guided by legal counsel experienced in such matters. An IRS rejection of the transaction as a loan and its recharacterization as equity will only give rise to the "sweat equity" trap, and should be avoided. At the least the loan should be memorialized in a formal promissory note that states an interest amount, the maturity date, and other similar terms; the company should show the transaction as a loan for accounting purposes and the company should pay interest on a quarterly or semi-annual basis. It should be repeated that such arrangements should be handled by an attorney with specific experience in such matters.

A SCENARIO ILLUSTRATING THE IMPORTANCE OF PROPER FORMATION OF AN ENTITY

The following is a situation of a filmmaker who produces a feature film with a budget of approximately three hundred and fifty thousand dollars. There are six principal individuals involved and they all contribute money and work on the production of the film. One individual contributes the majority of the money; one person contributes the script; one person directs the film; and one person primarily produces the film, while the other two individuals work in different capacities in the physical production of the film.

They have no written agreements defining control over the production of the film or the rights and responsibilities of the participants; in other words there were no rules to their "club." The film is shot and edited and the individual who contributed the most money obtains a producer's representative who lines up two offers for distribution of the film in two different media formats, pay television and DVD. The total amount being offered is less than 25 percent of the amount spent on making the film, and, having invested the bulk of the money, and bringing it to the market, the person who obtained the producer's representative believes he should retain the bulk of the money from its distribution.

Although the group who made the film had a smattering of contracts signed with various people who worked on the film, they fell far short of having the complete package necessary to address producing and distributing a film. Believing the script was the value of the film, the person who wrote the script believes she is entitled to some of the proceeds even though she didn't invest any money in the film. The person who worked in various capacities on the production of the film without being paid any money believes he deserves some of the money. The main producer did all of the work producers need to do, and therefore believes he should receive the majority of the proceeds, while one of the individuals who worked in various capacities in production and also invested a relatively small amount of money in the film believes she should at least get her investment back first. Finally, the director believes he should receive *all* of the proceeds because, after all, he is the director.

Who is legally entitled to the proceeds from the distribution company? Who *should* get the proceeds from the distribution company? What will happen to the film if the parties don't agree upon the resolution of these issues? The information presented in this chapter and the preceding chapter provides a framework for understanding why an entity is created when making a film and why it is critical that the issues be properly addressed by the participants at the beginning of the process. In the long run, the time and money spent at the beginning of the process to address these issues is clearly worth it.

9

The Business Plan

"See, I'm an idea man, Chuck." —Nightshift

INTRODUCTION AND DEFINITIONS

In simplest terms, a business plan is a description of an existing or proposed business that provides general information regarding the goals that the business wishes to achieve and the strategies it will employ to achieve them. It is needless to say that many independent films have been produced without the preparation of a business plan, and its necessity for producing a film is not cast in stone. A private placement memorandum or a "PPM" (to be discussed in Chapter 10) is a document that discloses all relevant, material information required under federal and state securities laws and is written to enable a potential investor to make an informed investment decision. A PPM is drafted to be a "stand-alone" document used in the process of raising money from passive investors for the production of a film (or for other types of business endeavors), and does not need to be accompanied by a business plan. However, to enhance the filmmaker's prospects for raising funds to produce his or her film, it is advisable to create a PPM *and* a business plan. Taken together, these documents will convey a clearer picture to potential financial backers as to the project's potential.

A basic function of a business plan is to provide information about the proposed film, the people involved in making the film, any special circumstances regarding the film or the people involved, and how the filmmaker believes the film can best be brought to the market after it is completed.

A PPM, on the other hand, is designed to provide a potential investor all relevant information, including "negative" information such as the risks associated with investing in the project. For example, a PPM commonly uses language such as: "The business of the company will be to finance, produce and exploit the screenplay and the film. In such a venture, the risk of loss is especially high in comparison to the prospects for any profit. The motion picture industry is a highly competitive industry and the market appeal and profitability of a particular motion picture cannot be predicted with any degree of certainty." A PPM (with the proper paperwork for a corporation, limited liability company, or other appropriate entity) is sufficient in order to present passive investors with an "offer" to sell the securities (i.e., sell an investment in the film) thereby generating the funds necessary to produce the film. The business plan, on the other hand, is not a document designed to be relied upon by a passive investor for investing money in a film production. The latter holds true even if the business plan is accompanied with the proper paperwork for a corporation, limited liability company, or other appropriate entity.

In this chapter a general review of the key elements which should be present in a business plan for producing a film will be set forth. A general review of the key elements of a PPM will be considered in Chapter 10, and a review of the practical interaction between the business plan and the PPM for a film project will be covered in Chapter 11.

EXECUTIVE SUMMARY

Although there are no iron clad rules, a business plan of between twenty-five and forty pages (excluding exhibits) probably represents the best balance between providing sufficient information and maintaining reader interest. Business plans usually have an "executive summary" section of about five to ten pages at the beginning, which should digest each of the major sections found in the body of the plan. Although not the only model, the one proposed here will consist of six sections: "The Filmmakers"; "The Film Project"; "The Motion Picture Industry"; "The Market and Marketing"; "Distribution"; and "Conclusion." The executive summary is designed to allow a quick read by business people, like venture capitalists, who are reading numerous business plans at once. Having an executive summary at the beginning of the business plan is not absolutely essential for a filmmaker who will be approaching a limited number of individuals who are presumably sufficiently motivated to read the entire document. However, including a well-written executive summary is recommended because it is a good opportunity to get the reader excited about the project and the people involved and should induce an individual to read the entire document.

THE FILMMAKERS

This section of the business plan should provide an introduction to the individuals who will be involved in the production of the film. The names of writer(s) and director, casting director, if hired, and such other individuals as the director of photography, foreign sales agent, or actors who have been secured should be included along with their bios. The aim here is to get the reader excited about the project by presenting as much relevant, truthful information as possible about the film and the people involved. For example, if the writer of the script of the film has previously been, or still is, a writer of a recognizable network/cable television show, or the director has directed award-winning commercials, or the casting director has secured recognizable name talent in other recognizable television programs or films, or the actors that are attached are recognizable actors, then this section should show them off and that will lend more credibility to the project and the filmmakers.

Attaching name talent most often requires expenditures of money the filmmaker does not have and is trying to raise. Sometimes a business plan will attempt to deal with this catch-22 dilemma by stating that the filmmaker "plans to approach" a certain name actor or director (and then proceed to add that actor's or director's headshot and bio). The filmmaker should be aware however that stating that the company "plans to approach" these individuals, although not necessarily untrue, may tend to undercut the filmmaker's credibility and entails certain risks. There is nothing legally associating these people with the film, and from a legal perspective, there is a question as to whether copying these individual's photographs (name and likeness) and including them in the business plan is even permissible. For these reasons it is better to present only what the company has accomplished when including other participants in the business plan.

The case of Jesse Eisenberg, a well-known actor, whose credits include *Zombieland* and *The Social Network,* is a good example. Mr. Eisenberg filed a lawsuit alleging a cause of action for appropriation of name and likeness, among other claims, when his picture and name appeared on the cover of the film's DVD in which he had a cameo role. Mr. Eisenberg asserted in his lawsuit that although he did appear in the film as a favor to his friends who produced it and reportedly received $3,000 compensation for one day of acting, he was suing to stop the use of his picture and name. Mr. Eisenberg's attorney stated in the lawsuit that Mr. Eisenberg "had valuable rights of publicity and property rights with substantial commercial value, which he did not agree to license or transfer, in whole or in part…" The fact that the film in question gained more notice once it was acquired and distributed by Lionsgate Entertainment (through a subsidiary company) often leads independent producers to conclude that there is little or no risk in including an actor's or director's headshot and name in his or her business plan documents in the early stages of the project because at that point they are still "flying under the radar." However, it would be wise to keep in mind that Hollywood players zealously guard their name and likeness rights even if it means having to sue a "friend," so it is always better to properly address this issue at the first instant that it is contemplated.

There is also a question as to whether or not it is wise to include the names of writers/directors/casting directors/actors who do not have recognizable accomplishments in their respective fields. Including the name(s) of unrecognizable actor(s) or director(s) in a business plan, regardless of their talent, may lead a reader to question the financial viability of the project as well as the judgment of the filmmakers. Measuring the potential success of a film on the basis of "recognizable" names involved may not be a fair assessment (there are numerous stories of nonrecognizable actors and other talent who break through in a hit film); but even if it turns out that for artistic and business reasons an actor is "right" for the part, it is more prudent not to associate any element that could create doubt and prevent the project from moving to the next level.

The business plan may also identify (when advisable) such associates as attorney(s), accountant(s) and other consultants, such as film marketing gurus, who will help guide the film. It might also be useful to identify a prominent distribution executive, or a prominent director who might act in the capacity of "executive producer." The idea here is to present a well-rounded group of advisors indicating that the filmmaker understands the need to reach out to advisors with expertise in a variety of areas. Hopefully it will show that there are individuals who are committed to the project and who have the requisite experience in filmmaking, all of which will be assets in the process of producing the film.

FILM PROJECT

Of course, the project the filmmaker is proposing should be described in a business plan. The log line or one paragraph synopsis should be presented with reference to a full synopsis or treatment available as an exhibit or addendum to the business plan. Also, the projected cost to produce the film should be presented in a brief budget form with reference to a "top sheet" of the budget. A top sheet is a summary of the major categories in the full budget and should be made available as an exhibit at the end of the business plan. See Appendix B for a sample budget top sheet. It should also be noted in the body of the business plan that the full budget (usually between twenty and forty pages in length) will be made available for review upon request. The full budget, however, should not be included in either the body of the business plan or as an exhibit. A "top sheet" (summary) budget is prepared after the full budget has been created.

In order to create a full budget the script needs to be "broken down" into its elements (i.e., the number of actors, the number of locations, the number of day shoots, the number of night shoots, the types of props and locations needed, and so on). It is then necessary to schedule the number of days required to complete the film, as well as what will be accomplished on each day. This is a time-consuming process, and must be completed by an experienced professional. An experienced line producer/unit production manager will charge between $3,500 and $7,000 to create the scheduling, the full budget, and the top sheet for a film. It is possible to find an individual who will "guesstimate" what the "top-sheet" numbers will be for a film for approximately $1,000 to $2,000 without performing the necessary steps of breaking down the script, scheduling, and creating a full budget. A top-sheet budget created by guesstimation is most often no more than an inaccurate budget. To include a top-sheet budget that has not been prepared after both the scheduling and full budget have been created is to present information that is probably not accurate. Including a top sheet prepared as a "guesstimate" is not recommended since in the eyes of a sophisticated reader it undercuts the credibility of the filmmakers and the project. In addition, since the budget informs the filmmakers as to how much money they will ultimately seek to properly produce the project, they would, in effect, be misleading themselves—never a good idea.

Ownership rights should also be made clear in the business plan. Has the script been written by the filmmakers? If yes, then the registration of the screenplay with the copyright office should be presented as an exhibit. Has a writer been commissioned as a "work-for-hire"? If yes, then the contract with the writer should be included as an exhibit. Has the screenplay been optioned/purchased? Again, if yes, that contract should be attached to the business plan as an exhibit. Any other project or projects the filmmaker may be planning should also be mentioned in the business plan, including the budget for each additional project.

INFORMATION ON BUDGETS OF INDEPENDENT FILMS

The following information is not for inclusion in the business plan for the project, but it is information that a filmmaker would be wise to take into account when drafting the plan. It is not easy to obtain accurate numbers regarding the budgets of independent films. By searching film articles in the press and reviewing online sources (such as the Internet Movie Database and Baseline Studio Systems) one may find cost estimates or budgets of independent films, but these resources lack concrete, verifiable information. Below is a chart of *reported* production budgets of a few high-profile and lesser-known independent films:

FILMS	REPORTED BUDGET
El Mariachi (1992)	$7,000
The Blair Witch Project (1999)	$130,000 up to $350,000
Swingers (1996)	Up to $400,000
Pi (1998)	$60,000 to $100,000
Open Water (2004)	$130,000
Napoleon Dynamite (2004)	$400,000
The Signal (2007)	$50,000
Swedish Auto (2006)	$700,000
Splinter (2006)	$437,000
The Hunt (2006)	$426,000
The Battle of Shaker Heights (2003)	$1,000,000
Brick (2005)	$475,000
In Search of a Midnight Kiss (2007)	$25,000
Forgiving the Franklins (2006)	$100,000
August Evening (2007)	$40,000

The only two budgets that are remotely reliable above are the reported budgets for *Splinter* and *The Hunt* which were reported by Image Entertainment in the company's 2007 Form 10-K filed with the Securities and Exchange Commission. Federal securities laws require publicly traded companies to disclose certain information annually on a Form 10-K or other required forms. Since there are potential criminal and monetary sanctions for misrepresentations on such forms, there is a greater degree of certainty regarding the information they contain. Unfortunately, there are very few publicly traded distribution or production companies involved with films at the budget level of $1 million or less.

Even assuming these budgets to be accurate, they are not really useful as a model for an independent filmmaker attempting to make a feature film. A film's budget expresses the money necessary to convert a script into a film. From the perspective of what it will cost to make each film, no two scripts are remotely comparable. Looking to the budgets of other films is not a particularly useful gauge for determining what it would cost to make another film with a unique script; this is especially true for low-budget films. Even if a reported budget for a film could be found which is very similar to the one being proposed, the comparison would only be useful if each and every line item in the budget, for the previously produced film, was available for review and comparison (i.e., a breakdown of each item spent on the film, grouped into above-the-line and below-the-line categories). Making such a comparison is made more difficult by virtue of the fact that the accounting for each independent film is a reflection of the talents and shortcomings of the people involved, the thousands of choices made by the people involved, the resources that the people involved bring to the film, the general economic climate at the time a film is made, and other factors and circumstances not reflected in the final accounting for the film.

If at all possible, what the filmmaker needs to acquire for his or her own film is a budget that accurately reflects the amount necessary for the least qualified people to be able to make a film based upon the filmmaker's script and under the reasonably predictable variables that the filmmaker will face (always keeping in mind that it is best to provide for the worst case scenario). Most often the talents, resources, and circumstances of the people who eventually make the film will be greater than this low-bar approach, so a budget will be generated that will be more than adequate to successfully complete the film. However, the nature of making a low-budget independent film is such that there are many unexpected events which will more than offset any savings. I have never heard of or been involved with an independent film that was not legitimately concerned about running out of money before the film was completed—never, not once.

The most appropriate time for the creation of an accurate budget is before the filmmaker approaches people with a business plan, and in fact anytime that he or she approaches potential investors with any legal documents necessary to obtain money (e.g., a PPM; see Chapter 10). These documents should contain the estimated budget needed in order to complete the film. The accuracy of the budget is obviously a key consideration in convincing people that the film can be made, and made for the amount of money claimed to be sufficient for it to be made. More importantly, it is essential in enhancing the filmmaker's credibility in terms of being qualified to make the film and being diligent in running the project. It is not that budgets don't change, of course they do, but approaching people with different budgets at different times, regardless of the reasons, is not wise because it conveys, whether true or not, that the filmmaker is unsure of what he or she is doing. By the time the money is raised and the preproduction phase begins, an accurate budget covering all reasonably foreseeable contingencies will be the foundation for successfully making the film.

The most common cause of failure for successfully completing a film project occurs when a filmmaker bases the budget on the amount of money he or she thinks can be raised. This is putting the cart before the horse. Almost invariably in this scenario, the money that is raised will be gone while he or she is still far from completing the film. This is obviously a very frustrating position in which to end up and can sabotage any future for a filmmaking career. These results can be avoided if the filmmaker performs due diligence in obtaining an accurate budget at the beginning of the process. A residual benefit of putting the *horse* before the *cart* is that if the filmmaker discovers that the budget for making the film is greater than the amount he or she can raise, having an accurate line-item budget will enable the filmmaker to ascertain whether certain imaginative producing strategies may be found to make the film with the funds available, and precisely how such strategies can accurately alter the numbers. It is always wisest to consider Lord Bardolph's observation:

> When we mean to build,
> We first survey the plot, then draw the model;
> And when we see the figure of the house,
> Then must we rate the cost of the erection;
> Which if we find outweighs ability,

What do we then but draw anew the model
In fewer offices, or at last desist
To build at all? Much more, in this great work,
Which is almost to pluck a kingdom down
And set another up, should we survey
The plot of situation and the model,
Consent upon a sure foundation,
Question surveyors, know our own estate,
How able such a work to undergo,
To weigh against his opposite; or else
We fortify in paper and in figures,
Using the names of men instead of men:
Like one that draws the model of a house
Beyond his power to build it; who, half through,
Gives o'er and leaves his part-created cost
A naked subject to the weeping clouds
And waste for churlish winter's tyranny.

—*Henry IV* Part II, Act I, Scene III

Unfortunately, the independent filmmaking landscape is strewn with aborted film projects which stand as naked subjects to the weeping clouds.

Part of the due diligence in creating an accurate budget entails three things: 1) the script must have been completed; 2) an experienced line producer/unit production manager must have been hired; and 3) the line producer/unit production manager must have "broken down" and scheduled the script. Breakdown of the script is the process of categorizing all of the major elements within a script. For example: the number and type of locations; whether the locations are inside or outside; whether a scene occurs during the day or night; the cast involved in each scene; etc. The schedule of the script represents what will be filmed each day of principal photography. If a script is not put through these steps, the final budget that is created cannot be considered an accurate budget. The budget that will be created for a script that does go through these steps will be the "line-item" budget which covers all elements and their costs in the production of the film. From this line-item budget a "top-sheet" budget is created. The top sheet is a one-page summary of the major categories found within the full line-item budget. (See Appendix B for a sample budget top sheet). Categories in the top sheet should include costs for: story rights; producer unit; cast; travel; production staff; extra talent; set design; and so on.

One of the items which should be included is the cost involved in preparing the budget itself. The essential expense of engaging the services of an experienced, qualified line producer/unit production manager will most often require the filmmaker to pay money out of pocket (i.e., before any money is raised from investors). Raising money to produce an independent film is a highly speculative endeavor, and there are hard costs that need to be incurred before any investor money can be raised. Hiring a line producer/unit production manager to create a budget is one of these hard costs. It is not uncommon for filmmakers, especially first-time filmmakers, to fall to the temptation of saving money by finding a one-page top sheet (or line-item budget) from a film with a budget under $1 million, and then simply change the names and dates and represent that as the budget for his or her film. It is also not uncommon for filmmakers to succumb to the temptation of hiring someone to guesstimate the numbers on the one-page top sheet for the film, rationalizing that the person they hired is an experienced line producer/unit production manager and should be in the ballpark with the budget numbers based on his or her experience. After the money is raised from investors, the logic goes, a full line-item budget will be prepared anyway. The probable outcome of such "shortcut" budgeting is highly predictable.

From a standpoint of credibility and ethics, when the filmmaker ultimately approaches investors, he or she wants a budget that can be reasonably relied upon as being sufficient to complete the film, and the assurance that any assertions being made are based on diligent preparation. From a legal standpoint, if money is raised based upon the "shortcut" budget and it turns out that the film can't be completed for that amount, the filmmaker is open to legal claims from unhappy investors claiming that certain laws have been violated because a budget was provided by the filmmaker which proper due diligence would have exposed as inaccurate. For this reason alone, an experienced, qualified line producer/unit production manager should be hired to create a line-item budget for the film at the beginning of the process. An added benefit derived from hiring an experienced person is that their name and their biography is usually added to your business plan and any legal documents that reference the budget. This demonstrates that the filmmaker understands the need to build a qualified team for the making of the film, and lends greater credibility to the project. If the line producer/unit production manager has high profile credits in his or her biography, all the better since "names" are not only a plus in casting, but in all areas of talent attached to the film.

It is not uncommon for a filmmaker to project two possible budget scenarios. For example, a filmmaker can approach investors with his or her legal documents (a PPM, etc.) and offer, for sale, interests in the limited liability company producing the film for a minimum amount of $150,000 and a maximum amount of $300,000. If the filmmaker raises $150,000, then he or she will produce a film at that level. However, the filmmaker in this scenario will continue to attempt to raise up to $300,000 after reaching $150,000. This may give rise to a question that will have to be answered by the filmmaker. If the filmmaker represents that he or she can successfully make the film for $150,000, then why is he or she trying to get *any* money above that amount? The answer to this question should be in the line-item budget. More often than not, the answer is found in the above-the-line cast salaries, that is, if the filmmaker can attach high profile talent, then the budget will increase by the amount necessary to secure such a "name" actor or actors. This expenditure is reasonable since it is calculated to bring more overall value to the final film, and will make sense to investors. There are many other aspects in a script which could enhance the value of the final film and would justify raising more money above the "minimum" amount. For example, certain locations, filming certain scenes in moving vehicles, certain action shots, certain special effects shots, etc. The explanation for these amounts will be found and explained in a properly created line-item budget.

THE MOTION PICTURE INDUSTRY

Whether or not a potential reader of your business plan already knows how the motion picture industry works, it should be written for an audience that *does not* know. Often individuals who have an interest in becoming involved, and do in fact become involved, are individuals who know nothing whatsoever about the motion picture industry, but they will be interested in obtaining an overview of the process through which the filmmaker intends to take the project. It will also assist them in formulating questions about the project for the filmmaker to answer, a process which often helps a potential investor to resolve many of their concerns. Sophisticated movie people will already know this information and will skip through it, but what they will want to see is that the *filmmaker* knows the information. This section of the business plan should satisfy both audiences, that is, to inform the novice and convince the initiated that the filmmaker is well versed in the operational aspects of the industry, has done his or her homework, and that he or she takes the process very seriously. By the way, the filmmaker should actually *do* his or her homework, and learn the information in these sections. If asked questions relating to what is presented without responding in a manner that exhibits confident knowledge, then the filmmaker has wasted his or her time, and will have lost credibility in the eyes of any inquisitor.

Since most people outside of the industry primarily define motion pictures by the major studio output with which they are primarily familiar, the difference between studio films and independent films should be outlined. Major studios such as Walt Disney Pictures, Paramount Pictures Corporation and Warner Brothers Pictures are large, diversified companies that are accountable to larger conglomerates and their shareholders. Major studios have the resources to finance a film, utilize its in-house marketing departments and generally exert disproportionate leverage in their relationships with creative talent (including recognizable actors), television broadcasters, Internet companies, movie theater owners and other key elements in the process of producing and distributing films around the world. An independent filmmaker has none of these resources at his or her disposal.

Independent film has its own history and is largely unknown to the general public except for the few instances when "indie" films have burst through to the mainstream—*sex, lies, and videotape*, *El Mariachi*, or *The Blair Witch Project* being some examples. It is important for the filmmaker to demonstrate to the sophisticated reader that he or she understands that the proposed film is not being produced in a vacuum, but is in fact a part of the history of independent film, and will be evaluated by the gatekeepers of distribution as such. It is also important to educate the uninitiated reader so that there will be no confusion or misunderstanding as to the process that the filmmaker's project will go through, and, therefore, no unrealistic expectations. It is essential to highlight a comparison of the studio budgets versus independent film budgets, and where the filmmaker's project lies in terms of the spectrum of budgets should also be made clear. Placing specific information in the plan will be very useful, especially for the uninitiated. For example, as mentioned in an earlier chapter, the Motion Picture Association of America reported that the average cost per film by the major studios in 2007 was $106 million, representing $70 million for negative costs and $36 million for marketing costs, and the average cost per film by subsidiaries and affiliates of the major studios in 2007 was $74 million consisting of $49 million for negative costs and $25 million for marketing costs. It is important that the business plan makes it clear that the film the filmmaker is trying to produce is not to be compared to the films made with these budgets.

The business plan should also identify where the revenue streams usually come from for a project. Investors cannot be assumed to know that most numbers generally reported by mainstream media, which track the financial record of a film, refer to the "United States Domestic Box Office" (or "United States/Canada Box Office") performance of a film. It should be highlighted that most films do not receive a theatrical release, and even those that are released theatrically generate most revenue from sources other than the United States Domestic Box Office. In 2012, the MPAA reported that total US/Canada gross box office receipts were approximately 30 percent of worldwide gross box office receipts amounting to $10.8 billion while the foreign theatrical gross box receipts represented approximately 70 percent. However, very few nonstudio (or studio affiliates/subsidiaries) films are released theatrically in either the domestic or foreign market. A glance at some independent films released theatrically between 2005 and 2012 will show the difficulty in gathering strong revenues through a theatrical release. The cost to theatrically release an independent film in three or four major cities for two weeks with little or no advertising money spent still costs between $100,000 and $500,000.

Until recently, home video (DVD/Blu-ray) has been the primary and most lucrative source of revenue for an independent film. However, changes in the distribution landscape have made it difficult for independent filmmakers to confidently rely on home video as a primary or lucrative source of revenue. Most importantly, the increase in the number of feature films made over the years due to the technological advances of digital video production and the leveling of consumer demand for purchases/rentals of home video should be cited. Traditionally a film has been released in the home video market four to six months after its domestic theatrical release. Most independent films are not released theatrically but are instead released directly to home video. Home video distribution consists of promotion and sales/revenue sharing of DVD and Blu-ray with local, regional, and national home video retailers who rent or sell them to consumers for home viewing. DVDs generally have a retail price of between $14 and $20 per unit for purchase, while Blu-rays, generally more expensive to produce, are usually offered to consumers at a price between $18 and $25 per unit for purchase. In addition, revenue sharing arrangements have significantly impacted the business because of the meager amount of the rental per DVD unit that flows back to the filmmaker. A revenue sharing arrangement could be one by which retail stores pay little or nothing for a DVD or Blu-ray unit, and instead share the revenue from the retail rental with the licensor.

Television rights for films that are initially released in theatres are generally licensed in the following order: a) first to video-on-demand and pay-per-view within six to nine months following its initial theatrical release; b) then to pay television approximately twelve to fifteen months after initial theatrical release; and c) thereafter to basic cable or free television. However, it should be noted that independent films often do not follow the traditional order of release, for example, an independent film may be released in theaters and on video-on-demand simultaneously.

Video-on-demand is a burgeoning source of revenue for films in general and especially for independent films. Satellite broadcasters do not presently employ the technology to offer video-on-demand, but cable and fiber optic providers can and do offer video-on-demand. There are very few cable television providers (Time Warner Cable, Comcast, Cox, Cablevision) and they offer between 125 to 250 movies at any one time through video-on-demand. Verizon fiber optic television service (FIOS) makes thousands of video-on-demand titles available, but as of the end of 2012, it had relatively few subscribers compared to the cable providers (Comcast alone has 22 million subscribers compared to FIOS' approximate 4.6 million subscribers). The business plan should outline these facts, and once again, the filmmaker should be prepared to discuss them in detail. Readers should be made aware that the chances of an independent film being offered through video-on-demand are slim, but for those that do get selected, the potential revenue generated can be relatively immense. When one considers that films are generally offered for $3.99 per order and the cable companies reach between 25 million and 40 million homes (and fiber optics are reaching about 2 million), the reason for this latter statement becomes obvious. A film only needs a small fraction of this market to generate substantial revenue, and unlike DVD and Blu-ray, there is little to no cost associated with delivering a film via video-on-demand.

Pay-per-view also generates revenue, but its revenue is more limited since it runs a film on preset intervals and it is less viewer convenient than video-on-demand which provides a subscriber the ability to watch a film within any twenty-four (or forty-eight) hour period whenever the subscriber decides to watch a film. Pay television allows subscribers to view movies via servers such as HBO/Cinemax, Showtime/The Movie Channel, Encore, etc. offered by cable and satellite providers for a monthly subscription. It has become very difficult, however, for independent filmmakers to obtain a licensing deal with the pay television servers and in the rare instances that a deal is completed, the licensing fees tend to be very small, even as low as $10,000 per year for a one or two year licensing period.

Other sources of revenue for independent films are either small or still developing, but they should be presented in the business plan and carefully examined to see if there are areas that the particular project being produced can exploit. These sources include airlines, schools, libraries, and military; novelization rights (including possible graphic novel and comic books); mobile/wireless platforms; and merchandising. Obviously an explanation of possible revenue streams will be quite important to anyone interested in the independent film business. By no means are the last several pages intended to be an exhaustive analysis but merely a sampler of what a filmmaker should know when producing an independent film. The filmmaker should expect some penetrating questions on this section of the plan and should be prepared to give informed answers.

THE MARKET AND MARKETING

One of the most important elements in the evaluation of a film project is the target audience for the film and how that target audience will be reached. Target audiences are determined according to the demographics of the movie-going public. Demographics are generally the age, gender, ethnic background, and income level of a person. Marketing is the means used to let the target know that the film is available. The formulation and fulfillment of a marketing plan is generally handled by the distribution company that acquires the right to exploit the film. However, these companies can only exploit elements in a film that already exist by the time it reaches them. It is important for the filmmaker to examine a particular target audience for the film and take steps to revise elements so that it will appeal to that audience for the film. The problem arises from the fact that creative individuals are not eager to make changes to their work based on the crass motive of marketing advantage. It should be noted here that, as put forth in the introduction, the filmmaker's faithfulness to his or her artistic vision for the film will be the most critical factor in achieving its success; however, if the filmmaker affects a rigid anti-business/marketing bias, then he or she should be neither surprised nor angry when he or she cannot find a distributor willing to distribute the film. Or further, finding a distributor willing to distribute the film, but who will commit little or no money to the marketing of the film. Neither should the filmmaker be upset if he or she fails to find an audience upon taking the initiative to self-distribute. The trick is to find a way to fuse artistic integrity and sound business judgment—difficult yes, impossible no.

The filmmaker should also take the opportunity in this section of the business plan to address the risks involved in producing his or her project, which includes the competition and marketing. The production and distribution of a film involves risks and it is better to identify some of those risks and to discuss possible implications and potential plans of dealing with these risks or minimizing their effects. A filmmaker is operating in a business that has numerous competitors, many of whom have substantially greater market presence, branding recognition, deep financial pockets, and other resources far greater than the filmmaker's. The filmmaker should recognize these disadvantages, and counter with facts that differentiate his or her project from the rest.

There are facts that support the view that the competition spends far more money than necessary in order to produce and release a film, thereby reducing their potential profit margin. Further, low-budget, independent films represent a niche neglected by the competition which is a strategic opportunity for the independent filmmaker. It is also a fact that the technology of digital production, such as 1080 resolution high definition, creates an opportunity for technically competitive films at drastically lower costs than those created using 35 millimeter film. The filmmaker should identify and provide facts about an audience who will enthusiastically respond to the filmmaker's independent film, an audience that is traditionally ignored by established film production and distribution companies. A sports movie concerning a particular sport such as rugby, or lacrosse or girls soccer, or a hobby such a stamp collecting, coin collecting, or bird watching, or a religious affiliation are just some examples. The only limit to the list is the imagination of the filmmaker.

DISTRIBUTION

The business plan must assume that the reader is generally not aware of how a film product gets from the manufacturer (i.e., filmmaker) to the final consumer (movie viewer). This section is intended to demystify the process, a process in which the filmmaker should be well versed. As in the case of film production, distributors and distribution systems are, in simplest terms, either major studios (and their subsidiaries and affiliates) or independents. Major studios have distribution divisions within which all marketing and other distribution decisions are made. This division formulates and executes the distribution and marketing strategies for each motion picture. Each studio releases between twenty and twenty-five films a year and also acquires a select number of independent films for distribution. Usually these films are produced with high-profile name talent and enormous budgets. Although stated previously, it is worth repeating that the Motion Picture Association of America reported that the average cost per film by the major studios in 2007 was $106 million, representing $70 million for negative costs and $36 million for marketing costs, and the average cost per film by subsidiaries and affiliates of the major studios in 2007 was $74 million with $49 million for negative costs and $25 million for marketing costs. *These amounts are spent on each film.*

Independent distributors operate in a manner similar to studios except they don't have the funds to spend on the marketing of their films and they most often do not have guaranteed distribution channels for all the mediums through which a film can be channeled. For example, one distributor may have a deal with a cable operator to release films via video-on-demand, while another independent distributor may not have such a deal, but will have one to release films on a certain cable channel, and vice versa. Although independent distributors have developed a reputation for handling films targeting niche markets that require special care in attracting a following, they nevertheless still want to distribute films that can reach the largest possible audience. Because of the leveling demand for independent films and the increase in the supply of independent films, even the independent distributors have begun to acquire and distribute only films that have recognizable name talent and are of a proven "genre," such as horror, thriller, action, and comedy. Most independent distributors only release films in the domestic market (i.e., basically North America) so an independent filmmaker will most often have to secure a second distributor to handle the foreign rights to the film. Most often, the filmmaker will contract with a foreign sales agent and get a percentage of the net receipts coming from licensing contracts that are obtained by the sales agent for each foreign territory (i.e., generally outside North America). The fee charged by the sales agent ranges between 15 and 60 percent, with the average fee at approximately 35 percent. In general, distributors and sales agents recoup any and all expenses they incur in the exploitation of a film. These expenses include costs for manufacturing home video devices (DVDs, etc.), advertising, marketing, promotional materials, shipping, delivery, and insurance. See Chapters 14 and 15.

The marketing of a film is primarily the responsibility of the distributor, and includes such actions as: decisions regarding the creation of posters, trailers, and other advertising materials; the placement of advertising in various media; the sales approach for the exhibitors, retailers and foreign buyers; and, the creation of interest and "hype" for a film through word of mouth, Internet, and other viral marketing campaigns, promotional activities, and alliance with special interest groups. Each of these activities plays a critical role in the process of exploiting a film, which is why a film must have a healthy marketing and release budget to begin to have an opportunity to penetrate the market. As a rule, studios theatrically release films as widely as possible in the first two weeks in order to reach as many viewers as possible. This strategy attempts to maximize up-front revenue with little regard to any decrease in revenue in the following weeks. Independent films do not have the budget to release films in this manner. In fact, just about all independent films are never released theatrically, and of those that are released in theaters, it is usually in one or two theaters in certain select cities. Even a limited release in one or two theaters in one or two cities with minimal advertising will cost between $50,000 and $250,000. These types of releases generally result in a total loss of the money spent because they do not generate enough box office receipts to even cover the costs associated with the release. As a result of such drastically limited theatrical release, they have minimal or no advertising impact on other distribution channels like DVD, video-on-demand, etc. There are exceptions where independent films have caught on with the audience and have garnered substantial box office receipts, but these are the exceptions to the rule. Chapters 13 and 14 will explore the topic of distribution in more detail.

In the context of what should be put in a business plan, briefly put, distribution is the process of selling or licensing the rights to various media outlets such as theatrical, home video, video-on-demand, pay-per-view, cable, free television, and other media outlets. A film must be distributed to earn revenues. In the independent film world the primary mediums in which the films are exploited are home video (DVD/Blu-ray), pay-per-view, video-on-demand, and cable television. However, there are other ancillary rights available, and certain independent films lend themselves to the exploitation of such rights. A traditional ancillary right that certain independent films have exploited are the merchandising rights, for example, t-shirts, hats, key chains, basically any item on which the film's logos or images can be reproduced. Other emerging areas which distributors have recently been asking filmmakers to license are mobile/wireless rights ("digital rights") and graphic novel/comic book rights. If any of these revenue outlets are applicable to a filmmaker's film they should be discussed in this section.

Finally, it is important to keep in mind that a business plan, although scrupulously truthful and straightforward, is a promotional document. It should be designed to promote the project to people who may have an interest in becoming involved with the film. The next chapter will examine the Private Placement Memorandum (PPM), which is a critical document that works in tandem with a well-drafted business plan. Unlike the business plan which is primarily promotional in function, the PPM primarily serves as a legal document to provide information to prospective investors in compliance with federal and state securities laws.

10

The Private Placement Memorandum

*"I know more about casino security than any man alive.
They got cameras, they got watchers, they got locks,
They got timers, and they got vaults....
That's why we need to be very careful, very precise.
Well funded..... Alright, who's in?"* —Ocean's 11

A "private placement" derives its name from the fact that the offer and sale of a company's stock (or other securities) will not be offered or sold to the general public. This is an important distinction since most of the popular media information concerning securities refer to companies whose stock is registered with the Securities and Exchange Commission (SEC), whose purpose is to approve securities before they are sold to the general public. Microsoft, Google, AT&T, GM, etc. are companies whose trading transactions receive high profile coverage in popular media, and which represent general popular conception of what a "stock" is. A private placement on the other hand occurs when a company proffers a limited offering and sale of its stock (or other securities) generally to "private" parties only (i.e., not offered or sold to the general public). These private placements utilize exemptions that exist under the securities laws (see Chapter 4) and which allow the securities to be offered and sold without the company having to first register the securities with and securing the approval of proper authorities. Although the company is being allowed to offer and sell the company stock (or other securities) without approval, the laws require that certain information must be presented to potential purchasers of the company's securities before they make a decision to purchase. The private placement memorandum (PPM) is the document that a filmmaker will provide to such investors which will contain all relevant and material information necessary for them to make an informed investment decision.

Naturally, each PPM is tailored to the facts and circumstances of each individual endeavor, including the types of investors the filmmaker will approach, the particular exemption the filmmaker is utilizing, the laws of the different states in which the filmmaker will approach investors, etc. Whether or not any particular exemption requires providing specific information to prospective investors, an issuer is always required to comply with the antifraud rules and other securities rules that require any issuer to provide information necessary to avoid misrepresentations or omissions of material facts regarding an investment. A recent lawsuit filed by investors against Paramount Pictures (and others) provides an example of how litigation attorneys can "cherry pick" and quote from PPMs when hired by disgruntled investors. In 2004 Allianz Risk Transfer and three other investors provided approximately $40 million in production funds to Melrose Investors LLC (the so-called Melrose Slate) which the investors claimed was entirely lost. The investors' amended complaint stated that "the plaintiffs (investors) read and relied on the accuracy and completeness of the statements contained in a private placement memorandum dated July 22, 2004 . . . statements that Paramount (Pictures) knew were incomplete and otherwise false and misleading." The investors' attorneys continued to quote liberally from the Melrose Slate PPM to support their claims that Paramount not only "misrepresented the actual financial risks associated with the investment but also omitted material facts necessary to make statements made in the PPM not misleading."

The quotes from the PPM by the investors' attorneys to support their claims filled numerous pages in their complaint (and amended complaints).

The following are just two examples of exact language quoted from the PPM which the investors' attorneys deemed misleading: 1) "...Paramount aims to achieve consistent slate profitability by managing capital commitments for each film project, opportunistically entering into output agreements and territory sales with third parties, and emphasizing cost mitigation programs...the purpose of these risk-management techniques is to reduce a film's net production cost..."; and 2) "The section entitled 'Risk Factors' contained the following statement: '...The costs of producing, marketing and distributing motion pictures have increased dramatically in the past decade...Paramount will control all decisions (i.e., business, creative or otherwise) relating to the development and production of each Covered Picture...'.'" It is not the purpose here to go into the logic employed by the attorneys leading them to contend that the statements in the PPM were misleading, but merely to illustrate how litigating attorneys carefully review these documents in search of language to support their claims of wrongdoing. Private placement memoranda are drafted by attorneys, and it is not recommended that a filmmaker attempt to draft this document or acquire a PPM from someone else (such as another filmmaker). Simply editing the information from another project's PPM is a dangerous endeavor, and will most probably end with a document that, however unwittingly, will provide the context for later claims that the information provided will be in violation of the securities laws.

In 1998 the SEC made changes that required the language used in a prospectus filed with the SEC to be in "plain English." Although these requirements do not technically apply to securities that will not be registered with the SEC, such as private placements, attorneys often follow the plain English guidelines as standard practice when drafting a PPM. These guidelines include requirements that drafters: use short sentences; use the active voice with definite, concrete, everyday language; use no legal jargon or technical terms; use lists and charts whenever possible; and avoid the use of double negatives. Generally, PPMs are between 25 and 75 pages in length, not including the exhibits which can bring them to 100 pages or more. The subscription agreement and the purchaser questionnaire would be such exhibits and will be described at the end of this chapter. Although the requirements for a prospectus, which is required with securities registered with the SEC, are not applicable to securities that will not be registered with the SEC (such as PPMs), the primary sections in a PPM will most often follow the guidelines for a prospectus. In consequence of the latter, a PPM will usually include: "The Summary of the Offering"; "Risk Factors"; "The Offering"; "Investor Suitability"; "Tax Considerations"; "The Company"; "The Management of the Company"; "Financing: Return of Capital and the Share of Profits"; "Conflicts of Interest"; "Financial Statements"; "The Project"; and "Additional Information."

THE SUMMARY OF THE OFFERING

The summary of the offering is a "snapshot" of the investment opportunity, and references the reader to a relevant corresponding section in the PPM for a more complete analysis of the topic. Included is the company that is offering its securities for purchase, a description of the securities that are being offered, the offering price for the securities, the intended use of the proceeds, risk factors, investor suitability, the project, and cash distribution/profit participation.

RISK FACTORS

A statement of "Risk Factors" is generally required to follow the summary of the offering in a prospectus (or the cover page), and this practice is usually employed in a PPM. This usually induces the filmmaker to question the reason for the extent of negativity articulated in the Risk Section. The goal of this section is to make sure that a potential investor understands that making an investment in a film is a highly speculative venture. From the filmmaker's position, listing factors that highlight the high risk of investment in the film helps protect him or her from potential claims of wrongdoing if the film is made and the investors lose their money. Protecting the filmmaker is never a bad thing. Even if a filmmaker is more tolerant of risk, he or she should remember that the parties the filmmaker will approach to invest would be parties with whom the filmmaker has a "pre-existing relationship" (i.e., parties the filmmaker already knows and will probably encounter again). It is because of the filmmaker's relationship with them that he or she will want to alert them as to the risks involved with investing in a film.

Usual risks that are highlighted in this section include, but are not limited to: the fact that the company is a start-up company with no track record; that there is an absence of audited and unaudited financial statements; that the company is relying on key personnel who may not be able to provide the necessary services to the project; that the film market is a highly competitive market; that there are restrictions on transferability of the securities; that there are no assurances that the film can or will be completed, including the fact that there will be no bond to insure completion of the film.

THE OFFERING

"The Offering" should describe the principal rights and responsibilities associated with the securities that are being offered for sale. The stated goal is to produce a film, and passive investors usually provide the money to the company (i.e., purchasing ownership in the company) that will produce the film. Having an entity is not an absolute requirement to raise money. There could be an investment contract or some other written document signed by the filmmaker and the investors, but such a document does not change the fact that the filmmaker is offering a "security" for sale under the securities laws. For the reasons stated in Chapters 7 and 8, filmmakers almost always choose to create an entity.

The description of the offering is not a detailed legal presentation, but rather presents the primary aspects of the securities such as: the name of the company that is offering the securities for sale; the type of company that the investors are purchasing (e.g., corporation, LLC); the total number of securities being offered; the purchase price for each security offered; the voting rights in the company that the purchaser will have attached to the security; the names of the parties involved in the formation and the operation of the company; restrictions on resales of the securities; and whether or not the money received from the purchase will be placed in an escrow account or will be immediately spent by the company.

As discussed in a previous chapter, the common entity for producing a film is an LLC that is managed solely by the filmmaker (or the filmmaker and one or two others) with no right of control over the company by the investors. The company seeks to raise a minimum amount of money (i.e., the amount necessary to produce the film), and the moneys that are received will be placed into an escrow account until that minimum amount is raised and/or a specified time limit is reached (usually one year). If and when the minimum amount of money is raised it will then be released from escrow to the company's bank account to be spent in producing the film. If the minimum amount is not raised within the specified time frame then the amounts that were placed in the escrow account will be returned to the investors. Because the securities are usually offered utilizing one of the exemptions from registration mentioned in a previous chapter (see Chapter 4), this section informs investors that the securities are subject to restrictions as to resale or transfer.

INVESTOR SUITABILITY

It is standard practice to describe the requirements that an investor must meet in order to be eligible to purchase the securities. This section again highlights the high level of risk associated with the investment and makes clear that it is only suitable for a party who can sustain a loss of their entire investment. Other investment requirements may include a potential purchaser signing representations that he, she, or it is an "accredited investor," that is to say, a party with high net worth (as defined by the securities laws, see Chapter 4). In order to rely on certain exemptions, other suitability standards may apply including assurance that the investor is a "sophisticated investor" or that the investor has "business and financial experience making him, her, or it capable of evaluating the merits and risks of the investment."

TAX CONSIDERATIONS

Often the disclaimer of any tax representations regarding investment for the film can be found in other sections of the PPM such as in the "Investor Suitability" or "Risk Factors" sections; however, it is prudent to segregate the disclaimer into its own section so it will not be overlooked by investors. A tax disclaimer basically states that the company makes no representations regarding the federal, state, or local income tax consequences resulting from the investment; that each prospective investor should consult their own tax advisor with respect to the federal, state, and local tax consequences resulting from an investment; and that no tax opinion has been requested or obtained from federal, state, or local tax authorities regarding the investment.

THE COMPANY

"The Company" section of a PPM generally provides facts about the development of the company and a detailed description of the company's business, including the products and/or services the company provides, as well as the market for the company's products and/or services and the sources for the materials necessary to provide the products and/or services. The history and development of a start-up company formed to produce one (or more) films is a very short story. The Company section for a start-up company in this situation focuses on the location of the company, a description of the company's plans of operation, including the story of the film to be produced, an overview of the motion picture industry, and the company's overall strategy for producing and bringing its film or films to the market. Sometimes the top sheet of the budget is provided in this section detailing what the company will spend to produce the film (with reference to the availability of the full line-item budget or the inclusion of the full line-item budget as an exhibit). The latter is sometimes segregated into a separate section entitled "Use of Proceeds," which is a section that describes the anticipated uses for the money the investors are providing. It may also be presented in a section entitled "The Project." Exactly where the top sheet of the budget is presented is less important than the fact that it is presented *somewhere* in the PPM.

MANAGEMENT OF THE COMPANY

This section identifies who are or will be the managers and executives of the company. Since there is no track record of activity for the company, this is very important information for a start-up company. In this section the name, title, and biography of each person managing the company or otherwise occupying an executive or similar position is presented. The length of the term for each person together with their backgrounds, experience, and their relationships with the people involved is also included. The same information is provided for all key people who are not managers, executives, or officers, but who have been engaged to provide key services to the company such as producers, financial consultants, or even foreign sales agents. Other issues covered in this section include the amount of fees, if any, that the manager(s), executives and other advisors will be paid from the money to be raised; any agreements that have been entered into to secure the services of the manager(s), executives, and other advisors; and any other special considerations that are material to the management of the company.

FINANCING: RETURN OF CAPITAL AND THE SHARE OF PROFITS

The financial plan represents one of the most important issues to potential investors. Investors generally want to know: What is the film about?; What is the budget?; and What is the "deal" if they put up money? And by "deal" they basically want to know how the money will flow back to them when the film is distributed. There is no "standard deal" but there is a general "return of capital contributions" (return of investment) and "division of net profits" that is often the basis of the "deal" offered by the company to investors regarding the making of an independent film. An example of a framework for a deal will include the items mentioned in Chapter 8 "Allocation of Gross Receipts" and may resemble the following:

1) The first revenues will be distributed to the investors until they have received a return of their original capital investment.
2) Subsequent revenues will be distributed to the investors until they have received a 10 percent cumulative preferred annual return for the two years following the date of the closing of the "offer."

3) After items 1 and 2 above have been satisfied, subsequent revenues will be distributed to any cast, crew, and vendors that have entered into deferred payment agreements with the company.

After the satisfaction of items 1, 2, and 3 above, all subsequent revenues will be distributed, 50 percent to the investors and 50 percent to [Name of Parties Inserted Here] (usually the producers of the film).

The revenue flow of 1 through 3 above is only the basic framework and filmmakers often revise the flow of revenue to meet their particular needs. For example, some filmmakers want to offer: no cumulative preferred return or a longer time period for the cumulative preferred return; no deferred payment agreements with cast, crew, or vendors or a limit on the total amount of deferred payment agreements; different distribution percentages of net profits (i.e., more for the filmmaker or a certain amount apportioned for key personnel such as actors, other producers, etc.); the ability to repay loans and advances as item number 1, thereby subordinating the subsequent obligations to be paid after loans and advances (i.e., return of the original capital investment would become item number 2, and so on). Since no two projects are the same, the above should not be considered as applicable to any specific case.

CONFLICTS OF INTEREST

Any actual and potential conflicts of interest involved in the operation and management of the company must be disclosed to potential investors. These conflicts of interest can include: the lack of arm's length negotiations regarding compensation to be provided to the filmmaker and other people who manage the company; any investments in the company by the filmmaker and other managers; the filmmaker or other company executives being designated as the "tax matter" person for the company. If it is a manager-run LLC then the investors are relying solely on the judgment of the managers and executives of the company concerning the resolution of any potential or actual conflicts of interest.

FINANCIAL STATEMENTS

Financial statements include audited and unaudited balance sheets of the company and company income and cash flow statements. For security law purposes, a statement of company equity and a statement of changes in financial condition are also defined as "financial statements." These types of disclosures of financial information are to be prepared by qualified accountants and presented to potential investors when documents are filed with the SEC. Since the issuer is using an exemption from registration, private placements are not documents to be filed with the SEC. As a practical matter, start-up companies such as companies formed to make a feature film do not have any business activity to report. At first glance it would seem that a filmmaker with a start-up company producing a film need not be concerned with providing any of these financial statements. However, it is important for a filmmaker to be cautious as to how he/she and his/her legal advisor approach this issue. When offering a security, each exemption from the necessity to register with the SEC has its own unique requirements.

The most common exemption that first-time filmmakers rely on is the exemption under Regulation D (see Chapter 4). Under Reg. D a company is not required to furnish any specific information (financial information or otherwise) to purchasers when it sells securities to an "accredited investor" (a person or company with substantial assets or income, as defined under the securities laws, see Chapter 4 for the definition) or when it is raising money under Rule 504 of Reg. D. (i.e., raising up to $1 million). The first-time filmmaker is most likely making a film for under $1 million (the low-budget filmmaker is definitely under $1 million) and/or approaching only "accredited investors," so the standard is that the filmmaker is required under the antifraud laws to provide all material information. It could be argued that under these two circumstances (i.e., approaching only "accredited investors" or raising money under Rule 504) a simple statement in the PPM that the company is recently formed and has no financial information to report will suffice to fulfill the requirement of providing "all" material information.

However, if the filmmaker is attempting to raise funds above $1 million and the offer goes out to any unaccredited investor then the requirements under the Reg. D exemption regarding what needs to be presented to potential investors is more extensive. For example, the company may be required to prepare audited balance sheets; or unaudited balance sheets; or audited statements of income and cash flows; or unaudited statements of income and cash flows; and other required financial disclosures. Preparing such information substantially increases the time and expense of compliance with the information requirements of applicable securities laws exemptions. In most circumstances, the filmmaker will be utilizing a newly formed entity that has no financial activity, so the decision to forgo the preparation of audited and unaudited financial statements is often what a filmmaker decides is the most efficient decision. Regardless, since the facts of making each film are never identical, the filmmaker should carefully weigh the possibility of losing the exemption against the cost of absolute compliance with requirements of such exemption, especially if the film will be produced through a company that has financial activity in prior tax years. Once again, it must be stated that the filmmaker should only make these decisions in consultation with an attorney experienced in these matters.

THE PROJECT

Sometimes a PPM will segregate certain information regarding the film to be produced into its own section. Such information might include the synopsis of the story, the top sheet of the budget, and a description of the key people involved in producing the film. It is perfectly acceptable to present this information under the "Company" section, a "Use of Proceeds" section, or elsewhere, but it may be most efficient to segregate such information into its own section. As mentioned above, the fact that the information is clearly presented *somewhere* in the PPM is the paramount issue.

ADDITIONAL INFORMATION

It is critical to remember that the basic requirements of private placement exemptions require that the potential purchaser be provided with "all material information." Even if certain information is not technically required to be provided to a potential investor under any specific exemption the company may be exposed to liability if it is later determined that certain information was "material" but not disclosed to the investor. "Material information" has been defined as information that a reasonable investor would consider when deciding to purchase the security. The determination of what should be included in a particular filmmaker's PPM will become apparent as the filmmaker works with his or her attorney reviewing the circumstances that are specific to the filmmaker in the development and production of his or her film. Further, if a filmmaker is utilizing a Reg. D exemption then the company is required to provide purchasers the opportunity to ask questions of and obtain answers from the company and to obtain any additional information to the extent the company has the information or can acquire it without unreasonable expense. A statement to this effect is also presented in the PPM.

SUBSCRIPTION AGREEMENT AND PURCHASER QUESTIONNAIRE

The subscription agreement and the purchaser questionnaire are two additional documents provided to prospective investors with the PPM and the LLC operating agreement (or limited partnership agreement, or corporate by-laws, etc.). A subscription agreement is effectively a purchaser's "offer" to purchase the securities of the entity. It is an "offer" because the acceptance of the offer to purchase is usually within the sole and absolute discretion of the company issuing the securities. The subscription agreement provides such information as the total number of securities being purchased and the total amount of money the investor is providing. The purchaser also provides representations and warranties that he, she or it has received and carefully reviewed the PPM and all other documents, and has such knowledge and experience in financial and business matters as to be capable of evaluating the merits and risks of the purchase of the particular securities. Entities such as LLCs and corporations also represent and warrant that they were not formed specifically to purchase the securities. Each subscription agreement is drafted to fit the facts and circumstances of the issuing entity and the specific securities exemption upon which the issuer is relying. The completed and signed subscription agreement is returned to the company with the funds for purchasing the securities.

The "purchaser questionnaire" is often included within the subscription agreement document but sometimes is a stand-alone document, especially if the issuer wants to discover the financial and business experience *before* providing an "offer" to a prospective purchaser. The purchaser questionnaire is completed and signed by the purchaser providing information such as the purchaser's investment experience, income, and other information such as whether the purchaser is a not-for-profit entity, a "broker" or "dealer" under the securities laws, an insurance company or an "investment company," each of which has an effect on the securities exemption upon which an issuer may be relying.

11

The Interaction of the Business Plan and the PPM

"Lotta ins, lotta outs, lotta what have you's." —The Big Lebowski

UNDERLYING PURPOSE OF SECURITIES LAWS

The securities laws are designed to protect investors when they are presented with "investment decisions." In general, if a party is presented with an investment decision the laws require that the potential investor receive sufficient information regarding the investment, the opportunity to review the information and to ask for further information. Sufficient information is provided by either registering the securities with the SEC (and providing the information required in such registration) or by providing the information required under an applicable exemption from registration. The bottom line is if a "security" is being "offered" for purchase then securities laws are triggered and must be complied with. Chapter 4 explored these issues in depth.

RELATIONSHIP BETWEEN A PPM AND A BUSINESS PLAN

This triggering of securities laws is important for a filmmaker who has a business plan and/or a PPM. If a filmmaker decides to raise money from passive investors for the film solely by virtue of a PPM, then the filmmaker is addressing this issue by acknowledging that a "security" is being "offered." The securities laws will be triggered and addressed by the information in the PPM. As was alluded to in the previous chapter, in this circumstance the PPM is a "stand-alone" document. If the business plan and PPM are combined into one document then the securities laws are triggered and covered by the combined document. If, however, the filmmaker provides a business plan independent of a PPM then the filmmaker needs to be careful that the information provided in the business plan does not fall under the securities laws' definitions of "offering" a "security" for "sale." In general, an offer of securities for sale includes attempts to dispose of a security or an interest in a security for value. Securities laws are applicable to the entire process that leads to an investment decision, therefore the business plan can and will be examined as a part of the process in which the filmmaker is engaged when he or she seeks funding for his or her film, that is, the business plan will be reviewed in determining whether or not it triggers the securities laws requirements either for registration or for using an exemption from registration.

The application of the securities laws to any particular situation will depend on what the filmmaker puts in his or her business plan, what the filmmaker says to investors, and the circumstances surrounding each. The bottom line is that the information presented in the business plan should be carefully reviewed by the filmmaker and an attorney experienced in securities law. Further, the filmmaker should be under clear instructions as to what he or she should say to others about what is in the business plan and its purpose. What to leave in and what to leave out does not always have clearly defined parameters, and each filmmaker will have a different comfort level regarding the amount of potential risk he or she will want to bear. Therefore the business plan should be drafted with these considerations in mind. There is, however, certain information, which, if included in a business plan, will have a greater tendency to support a conclusion that a security is being offered for sale.

First, any information that discusses a "security" will tend to support a conclusion that a security is involved. This information by itself may not absolutely constitute an "offer" under securities laws, but it may evidence that the filmmaker is *planning* to make an offer, and is language generally to be avoided if a filmmaker seeks to minimize his or her exposure to risk. This includes avoiding language such as: a) "*First-Time Filmmaker Productions* will raise the production financing from investors using a Limited Liability Company," or, "*Entity Producing Film, LLC* is a California Limited Liability Company that will serve as the investment vehicle for *First-Time Feature Film*"; b) "Production financing for *First-Time Feature Film* will be raised using a Private Placement Offering Memorandum subject to Rule 504 (or Rule 505 or Rule 506) of Regulation D" (the language in a and b may easily support the conclusion that the people involved are in the process of "offering" this "security" for sale); c) language such as "*First-Time Filmmaker Productions* is the manager of *Entity Producing Film, LLC,* and is appointed the manager for the life of the LLC," or, "The manager shall have the right to manage and control the business and affairs of the LLC, and make all decisions regarding the business of the LLC"; and d) "The investors shall not participate in the management of or have control over the LLC business nor shall any investor have the power to represent, act for, sign for, or bind the manager or the LLC." Any of the above type of language indicates the presence of a "security" in as much as the investors will not "actively" participate in the making of the film but will rely "on the efforts of others."

Second, any information that provides details regarding the financial investment in the production of the film or the terms of a "deal" is also to be avoided since this type of language can support the conclusion that an "offer" is being made. Examples would be such language as: a) "Investors receive a full 100% return of all funds invested before any net profits are disbursed. Net profits of *Entity Producing Film, LLC* are then divided with investors receiving 50%, the producers receiving 25%, the director receiving 10%, the writer receiving 5%, and 10% to be distributed to select parties involved in the production at the discretion of the manager"; or b) "The cost of the film is approximately fifty thousand dollars ($50,000). *Entity Producing Film, LLC* is seeking an investment of fifty thousand dollars ($50,000) for the production and distribution of the film. Investments are available in five thousand dollar ($5,000) increments for a total of ten (10) units. Investors shall recoup one hundred percent (100%) of their investment from all revenue generated worldwide from all sources. After the investors receive one hundred percent (100%) of the money invested then any and all deferred payment compensation to cast and crew, if any, is paid after which the investors and the manager shall divide all net profits fifty percent (50%) to each." Such wording in a business plan, or anything similar to it, can support a conclusion that a security offering is occurring thereby triggering the applicable securities laws. In addition, a disclaimer should be prominently displayed on the first page after the cover page and any other place in the business plan where language is used that could be construed to be an "offer to sell securities." This disclaimer should basically state in bold print:

> **This memorandum is a business plan. It is not an offering for sale of any securities nor a solicitation of an offer to buy securities. It is for your confidential use only and may not be reproduced, sold, or distributed without the prior, written approval of [Filmmaker's Name]. If interests in the company's project, [First Feature Film], are to be sold then it will be through a Private Placement Memorandum Offering at the discretion of the principals of First-Time Filmmaker Productions, LLC pursuant to all applicable securities laws.**

WHO WILL THE FILMMAKER APPROACH AS A POTENTIAL INVESTOR?

The parameters of an "active" and "passive" investor were explored in Chapter 4 and that analysis becomes the basis for a filmmaker's crafting of the business plan and the PPM. If a filmmaker will only approach parties for money who will "actively" participate in the making of the film, then the filmmaker will not trigger securities laws. In this type of situation a properly drafted business plan can be provided to those potentially "active" investors without the need of a PPM. A separate document will, however, need to be negotiated and drafted between the "active" investors to memorialize the rights and responsibilities of the participants.

In addition, any party who qualifies as an "active" investor will, by definition, also need to have "experience and knowledge" in the film industry, and most likely will not need to review a business plan in order to evaluate the prospect of working with the filmmaker on the project. Therefore, a simpler package of the script, the budget and any relevant attachments may be the extent of necessary information to begin negotiations with such an experienced ("active") investor. If a filmmaker is approaching any "passive" investors for money to produce the film then, for the reasons stated previously in this chapter and Chapter 4, the prudent action is to have a PPM drafted and presented to the potential investors. Depending on the filmmaker's goals, he or she, together with an attorney, will decide whether or not to augment the PPM with a business plan in the PPM package.

Independent filmmakers tend to minimize the importance of the ramifications associated with "passive" investors; this is because they are usually soliciting very few investors, and/or they have a close relationship with such investors, and/or they may be dealing with highly sophisticated investors. The importance of dotting all the i's and crossing all the t's when dealing with "passive" investors is best illustrated by the facts in the lawsuit filed in 2010 by independent filmmaker and star actor Jada Pinkett Smith. Ms. Pinkett Smith wrote, directed, and produced an independent film entitled *Human Contract*, which received domestic DVD distribution and foreign distribution in some mediums and some territories. Ms. Pinkett Smith met with a potential investor who eventually provided the financing for producing the film. The complaint filed by Ms. Pinkett Smith (and other parties) alleged that "while all parties were pleased with how the movie turned out, production and postproduction of the film, though on schedule, were completed during an extremely unfavorable market for independent film distribution [making it] extremely unlikely that it (*Human Contract*) will ever make a profit." Ms. Pinkett Smith's attorneys sought declaration by the court that Ms. Pinkett Smith did not fraudulently induce any investments and her attorneys quoted liberally from the documentation provided to the investor. Some examples of the wording included the following representations and warranties agreed to by the investor: a) the investor was an "accredited investor"; b) the investor had the ability to bear the substantial economic risk of investment and had knowledge and experience to evaluate the investment; and c) the investor understood that the movie business is very risky and there is no assurance that there would be any return on investment. The filmmakers eventually requested dismissal of the complaint and it is not a stretch to believe that the fact that the producers provided the investor with appropriate documentation explaining the risks involved with investing in independent films helped resolve any dispute more quickly and more favorably than if such documentation had been absent.

INCLUSION OF RETURN ON INVESTMENT ("ROI") ANALYSIS AND FINANCIAL PROJECTIONS

A major issue that arises in the drafting of business plans and PPMs is whether or not to include revenue projections which may proceed from producing the film. This includes whether or not to provide any financial information showing the money made for other investors from actual films that have been released in the past, in other words, revenue projections. There is also a question as to whether or not any type of "waterfall" with actual numbers should be provided describing how revenue flows back from the different markets and mediums (taken together I will reference financial projections, revenue projections, and "waterfall" presentations as "Financial Information").[2]

Financial Information about other films that have produced a substantial return on investment ("ROI") for investors is sometimes provided in

---

2. The following several pages will attempt to answer this question. However, if you have firmly resolved never to include Financial Information in any documents then you can skip the discussion that follows and move on to the next chapter. On the other hand, if you have any temptation to include Financial Information then you should read the next several pages.

the documentation and is compared to the film that the filmmaker is pro-posing to make. This comparison to the other financially successful films then becomes the basis for revenue projections for the film the filmmaker plans to produce. One often sees a business plan or PPM which includes a page that presents five to ten films as comparable films showing the year each film was made, the budget of each film, and the estimated revenue for each film. The following table is an illustration of such a comparative analysis appearing in some PPMs or Business Plans.

Return on Investment						
Film Title	Budget	Domestic Box Office	Domestic Ancillary Revenue	Foreign Box Office	Foreign Ancillary Revenue	Total Revenue
Film 1 (1994)	$50 K	$2,600 K	$1,300 K	0.00	$250 K	$4,150 K
Film 2 (2006)	$250 K	$1,300 K	$400 K	0.00	$850 K	$2,550 K
Film 3 (2001)	$400 K	$141,000 K	$70,000 K	$107,000 K	$37,000 K	$355,000 K
Film 4 (1999)	$1,000 K	$5,350 K	$2,800 K	$425 K	$1,2 K	$9,775 K
Film 5 (2004)	$125 K	$800 K	$500 K	0.00	$250 K	$1,55 K

*K denotes that this figure is multiplied by one thousand

This type of table is then often followed by a table similar to the one below that provides projections of possible financial performances of the filmmaker's proposed film.

"Title of Film to Be Produced" Financial Projections			
	Low/Worst Case Scenario	Medium/ Middle Case Scenario	High/Best Case Scenario
Domestic Box Office	$0.00	$0.00	$1,300,00
Domestic Ancillary Revenue	$0.00	$300,000	$650,000
Foreign Box Office	$0.00	$0.00	$0.00
Foreign Ancillary Revenue	$0.00	$490,000	$850,000
Total Revenue	$0.00	$770,000	$2,800,000
Budget of "Film To Be Produced"	$750,000	$750,000	$750,000
Profit/(Loss)	($750,000)	$20,000	$2,050,000

Because of a concern about the possibility that such numbers may expose the filmmaker to potential legal ramifications, *it is not advisable to include any information like this in a business plan, the PPM, or in any other paperwork regarding the film.* It is not a certainty that a filmmaker who provides such numbers will end up violating federal and state securities laws, but including financial projections when raising money through a private offering does create legal exposure. There are also practical reasons why financial information should be omitted from the filmmaker's paperwork because when combined with the meaningful cautionary disclosures required under the law, these projections do not help a filmmaker convince an investor to support his or her film, in fact, they may even do the opposite. These inclusions give rise to two dilemmas that require discussion: first, what are the parameters of this potential legal exposure, and second, how do projections with "disclaimers" potentially undercut investor confidence in a filmmaker's project? The starting point is to understand that financial information is broadly characterized under securities laws as "forward looking statements," which includes statements such as projections of revenue, income, losses, earnings, capital structure, and other financial items. It is easy to imagine that the actual results of an endeavor, such as making a low-budget independent feature film, will be much different than the numbers provided in any such projections of revenue, income, and so on. The difference between what a securities issuer (the film producer) "projected" and what actually occurs can easily be the basis of any potential claim by an unhappy investor (or the SEC). The question often arises as to whether or not providing language "disclaiming" the accuracy of "forward-looking statements" will negate, or at the least limit, the exposure from such projections. In fact, there are laws that protect an issuer from legal actions regarding "forward-looking statements." Two such potential shields from issuer liability may be mentioned. The first is a "safe harbor" that is applicable to any legal action by an investor based on an alleged untrue statement or omission of a material fact relating to a "forward-looking statement." The good news is that the safe harbor does in some measure protect an issuer against claims that it recklessly or in a grossly negligent manner provided untrue statements or omissions in connection with "forward-looking statements," but, the bad news is that the safe harbor does not apply to "non-reporting" companies. Start-up film companies raising money for a film under an exemption from the securities laws *are* "non-reporting" companies. Although this "safe harbor" protection will most likely not be available to a filmmaker producing a low-budget feature film, a second shield is potentially available to protect an issuer against claims that it provided untrue statements or omissions in connection with "forward-looking statements," that is, the "bespeaks caution" doctrine. This doctrine has been developed by courts with each circuit court having its own specific definition as to what it is. Generally, it states that if "forward-looking statements" are accompanied by language that identifies factors that could cause actual results to be different than the "forward-looking statements," then a lawsuit regarding such statements cannot be sustained. However, if a "forward-looking statement" is not accompanied by cautionary statements, or if such statements are not sufficient, then the "bespeaks caution" doctrine would not apply and will not stop a claim against the issuer.

If a filmmaker is going to provide "forward-looking statements" there are some basic precautions that the paperwork must contain. First, these statements must have a reasonable basis. Second, any appropriate statement should be identified as a "forward-looking statement." Third, the cautionary statements must "accompany" the "forward-looking statements," which generally means it appears in the document with such "forward-looking statements." To satisfy the latter, it is safest to place the cautionary language in a bold font next to the "forward-looking statement." Fourth, and the most difficult requirement to fulfill, is that the cautionary statements must *specifically* address the risk factors that can change the accuracy of the "forward-looking statements."

It is clear from the courts' decisions that boilerplate statements of risk are not sufficient for these purposes. For example, the comparative analysis and comparative film tables above would at the very least require *four areas* of "meaningful cautionary statements" to address specific risk factors. First, the specific details of the deals between the producers of a film and the distributors are almost always an unknown. Since it is not uncommon for the producer to get anywhere from 20 to 35 percent of each revenue stream, how much of the quoted numbers in these tables are actually returned to the filmmaker/producer cannot be known. Absent any "standard" distribution deal it is impossible to guess what the exact percentage will be for any distribution deal for any film. However, these presentations ordinarily use the gross numbers to present comparable films and then often use those gross numbers to calculate potential projections. Because the identified numbers are "gross" numbers, and what percentage the filmmaker/producer(s) and investor(s) received from the gross numbers is unknown, these variable factors should be expressed in a cautionary statement.

Second, it is matter of opinion as to what constitutes a "comparable film." There are many material elements which underlie why and how a film reaches distribution and performs well financially; for example, the cast is a crucial element that weighs heavily in determining whether a film receives distribution and generates revenue. Although the genre of a comparable film may be the same as that of the filmmaker's film, perhaps the year in which the comparable film was released was a year that such genre was in high demand and the market has since changed for such genre. Any filmmaker will verify that different budgets create different films; in fact, take the same script with the same people involved and a very different film will be made depending solely on the budget. The genre, the cast, and the budget are just three examples but it is possible to evaluate every element in a film and make a very plausible case that each such element is different from the filmmaker's proposed film thereby rendering the film identified as a "comparable" film not "comparable" at all. These variable factors should be specifically identified and explained in a cautionary statement.

Third, the information regarding a film's budget and revenue is most often not public, verifiable information. The only accurate way to verify a budget for a film is to review its bank statements and calculate the expenditures. Also, the only accurate way to verify the revenue for a film is to review the distribution contracts and the revenue received from distributors. This is nearly impossible for anyone to do (in fact, very often the reported budget of a film is inflated when provided by the producers of the film in the hope of acquiring a better distribution deal). These facts must be provided in a detailed cautionary statement by the filmmaker. In addition, the filmmaker should provide the sources for his or her numbers in any "forward-looking statements," and evaluate the accuracy of such sources.

Fourth, there are thousands of independent feature-length films produced every year, and it is generally understood that the great majority of these films do not get distributed by an established distributor let alone return the investors' money. For sake of space and time, the names of these films are omitted here but it would be quite a dramatic and sobering presentation to present thousands and thousands of independent films next to the five or ten "successful" comparable films. Exposing the budgets of these thousands of films and the fact that they have never been distributed let alone received any revenue, and resulted in a near or total loss to the investors, would be quite an eye opener to any potential investor (especially the novice). A cautionary statement should alert potential investors that the filmmaker has provided a limited number of "successful" films, but there are thousands of independent films produced each year that are never distrib-uted. Further, of the films that do generate revenue, it is widely believed that the overwhelming majority of them fail to recover more than a percentage of the budget itself—this possibility should be provided and addressed in a cautionary statement as well. Therefore, the presentation of the three pos-sibilities of losing the investment, recovering the investment, or making a profit should also include the information of what percentage of indepen-dent films falls within each of three categories, and if such information is omitted, the omission of this fact should be noted in a cautionary statement.

The basic goal of providing meaningful cautionary statements is that even if any of the "forward-looking statements" are misleading, when these statements are examined in total with the "forward-looking statements," then the meaningful cautionary statements make them not "material" statements, and they also render reliance by a potential investor on such "forward-looking statements" not reasonable. *In crude terms, if the filmmaker successfully provides meaningful cautionary statements with "forward-looking state-ments" then the filmmaker has successfully provided immaterial information that an investor should not rely upon.* The unavoidable conclusion to be drawn from providing information with explanations as to why such information is immaterial or not to be relied upon is that it will substantially undermine any investor's confidence in the filmmaker or the film project. Further, the filmmaker has shouldered more risk because even if the "bespeaks caution" doctrine applies, the "forward-looking statements" provide fertile ground for litigation from an unhappy investor, or the SEC, and the filmmaker's lawyer will have to prepare a legal argument countering any potential claims which will create anxiety and expense for the filmmaker.

With all of the former said, regardless of the potential risks associated with "forward-looking statements," many filmmakers still decide to include revenue projections from comparable films (and similar information) in their business plan and other documents and presumably I will see more of it in the future. From a practical perspective it should be understood that each filmmaker has a unique level of acceptable risk that he or she is willing to shoulder. Although it is usually wiser to be more conservative than aggressive regarding these issues (based not only upon a legal analysis, but also in terms of what seems to be more persuasive with potential investors, i.e., inducing them to provide the money), many filmmakers have deemed inclusion of these types of statements an acceptable risk. But regardless of the final decisions made by a filmmaker, a more informed decision-making process when deciding what to include and what to omit is always preferred to a complete lack of consideration of such information altogether.

12

Making the Film

*"So, first we went up the Amazon. And then up the Pachitea.
We are here right now. We are going to drag that ship over this
mountain."* —Fitzcarraldo

WHEN IS THE FILM READY TO BE MADE?

Put simply, the film is ready to be made when all of the money is acquired, but putting things simply can also be misleading. The private placement memorandum and limited liability company operating agreement should make it specifically clear as to when the money is to be considered "acquired." These documents should also clearly define how much money must be raised before the producers can begin spending it. In general, the money that is being raised is placed in an escrow account which the producers may not access unless and until a minimum amount of money is raised. When the minimum amount of money is raised, money may be released from escrow into an operating account which can be accessed by the filmmaker to produce the film. On rare occasions a filmmaker may insert language in the legal documentation that allows him or her to spend a certain amount of money before the full budget is ever raised. Because of the inherent risk of spending investor money that may never lead to a finished film, these types of arrangements make raising money much more difficult, and as a result, are not often used by filmmakers, especially by first-time filmmakers. As soon as the money is accessible it is standard to reimburse the producers for expenses they may have spent from their own money, such as legal fees, accounting fees, state fees to start the company, costs for preparation of the budget, and so on.

SETTING THE DATE FOR PRINCIPAL PHOTOGRAPHY

The filmmaker should set the date for commencing principal photography far enough in the future so as to have plenty of time to complete preproduction. At the very least, a first-time filmmaker should schedule the commencement of principal photography at least six months after receiving the PPM and operating agreement from his or her attorney. If possible, setting principal photography nine months to a year from that time would be even better. If the filmmaker plans to approach established production and distribution companies to see if the money and script the filmmaker has produced can be parlayed into a larger co-production, then the filmmaker should add an additional four to six months so as to be able to complete the process of dealing with these companies. Unfortunately, it is all too common for filmmakers, especially first-time filmmakers, to rush into preproduction and principal photography. It may be taken as an almost universal principle that the longer the filmmaker works on the film in the preproduction stage the better the final film will be. Rushing through preproduction usually leads to irredeemable mistakes that will ruin the possibility of either finishing the film or achieving distribution. The best counsel any filmmaker can follow is to be diligent and methodical in preproduction regardless of the time involved.

EXPANDING THE TEAM

The next order of business is to expand the "team" the filmmaker will need to help complete the physical production of the film (i.e., the preproduction, production, and postproduction).

Additional Producers. As discussed in Chapter 2, the filmmaker should have already secured a writer, a producer, and an attorney. Many films with a budget below $1 million have one individual, that is, the filmmaker, who assumes numerous key positions like writer, director, producer, actor, editor, and in some rare situations, other positions. I have often dealt with film-makers who are the "writer-director-producer," "director-producer-editor," "actor-director-producer," or "writer-director-producer-editor," etc. It is understood that the hyphenation is based more on necessity than ego, but there are still factors that need to be carefully weighed if a filmmaker plans to assume more than one position on the film. The talent level of the indi-vidual assuming such roles, the cost of acquiring the services of a replace-ment person to assume such roles, and the time frame in which the film is being produced are only a few of the questions which need to be answered.

There are no universal answers to these questions. The only thing that can be stated categorically is that an independent filmmaker is pursuing the production of an independent film from the compulsion to express a vision, and usually to create an opportunity for him or herself. Clearly the filmmaker should take a firm grip on *that* role, whether it is an actor who is creating a film to showcase acting skills, or an actor who wants to branch out into directing, or a writer who wants to direct his or her script, or a writer/director of commercials/short films who wants to take the next step to direct a feature film, or whatever the ambitions of the filmmaker might be. In addition to this primary role, it is important for the filmmaker to take on the responsibilities of "producer" of the film. For the script to be polished to its maximum level, for the money to be raised, for the film to be completed and distributed, the filmmaker will be the primary engine driving the process forward (i.e., "producing" the film). Beyond shouldering these two responsibilities the filmmaker should be very careful not to take on more responsibilities than necessary; making a film is a collaborative pro-cess and there is a certain amount of control that needs to be relinquished to other collaborators. Overall, once the money has been raised and is ready to be spent on production, the first-time filmmaker will be relying on a group of people who are much more experienced than he or she—a group of people who probably have been developing their own short films and feature-length scripts, or who harbor their own desire to be a first-time feature filmmaker, or who have already made one or more feature films. Although a collaborative process, wherein control over certain areas of activity has been relinquished, like any organization, the CEO must implement and monitor control systems. Certain terms and conditions giving the filmmaker control over the performance criteria for certain key personnel should be inserted in the contracts of these collaborators. The ability to remove any person working on the film with the obligation to pay the person only up to the day he or she has provided services to the film is a crucial provision. There are certain key personnel over whom maintaining extra control is especially important. Drafting and execution of the contracts for these certain key personnel should be approached by the filmmaker with the object of striking the perfect balance of extracting maximum performance from each individual while simultaneously retaining ultimate control over him or her. In the earliest stage, the key personnel to add are: one or more producers; the unit production manager/line producer, and a casting director. At this point all of the money has been raised and released from escrow— the time clock for completing the film has begun ticking and the money starts pouring out.

The selection process of an additional producer or producers is somewhat similar to the selection process that occurs when choosing the first producer (see Chapter 2), but the circumstances are vastly different at this point since the money is now in the bank and the film is *definitely* going to be made. At the beginning of the process the producer who committed to the film assumed great risk of time and energy since a very small fraction of people who undertake to raise money for an independent film are actually successful. Therefore, the reasoning goes, the terms of the deal for the additional producer or producers should be less favorable than the terms received by the first producer, who more than likely was the filmmaker.

It will behoove the filmmaker to remember that the people with whom he or she is negotiating are in the "business" of making films, so they are approaching the negotiation as a business transaction and so should the filmmaker. It is usually a "dream" to make an independent feature film, and when that "dream" starts to become reality it is important for the filmmaker to keep his or her feet firmly planted on terra firma, and approach each task in a business-like manner while at the same time never compromising his or her vision. A basic reality in filmmaking is that there are far more qualified people to do each job on a film than there are filmmakers who have the money to spend (as the filmmaker will learn when on the other side of the table), therefore the basic economic bargaining position weighs strongly in favor of the filmmaker at this point. Too often filmmakers, especially inexperienced filmmakers, allow the pressure of the perceived "limited time frame" of making the film force them to make decisions that are not in the filmmaker's best interest. Too often after being razzle-dazzled by a person experienced in the industry, a first-time filmmaker will find out that the chosen key person is not good for the film. By the time it is discovered it may be too far into the process, and the terms of the contract with the person may not favorably address the process of removing him or her from the film. This is a prescription for catastrophe. Learning is a painful and expensive process, and the filmmaker should take his or her time in making future selections of key personnel. If it takes longer than expected or desired it is well to remember that the lost time is better than allowing the wrong person to compromise critical aspects of the production of the film.

The skills the additional producer(s) need to possess are different from those of the producer who is secured in the early phase of the process (probably the filmmaker him or herself). The additional producer(s) need to be adept at spending the available money so that, as stated on several occasions in earlier chapters, each dollar spent looks on screen as if five dollars were spent. The skills that such a producer should bring to the film include: a) the talents to find and negotiate deals for the goods and services needed for the film; b) past contacts with vendors and crew; c) a person who will energetically accept responsibilities when delegated leaving more time for the filmmaker to concentrate on directing or acting or writing for the film; and d) the openness and self-confidence to bring ideas and feedback to the nuts and bolts decisions being made in production, including script notes, actor choices, and so on.

Often it is helpful to look beyond "experienced" independent film producers to see if the filmmaker can secure someone who can bring the same talents necessary to the film at a discounted price in exchange for a "producer" credit. Some of the most efficient deals made by certain filmmakers have been the ones where an experienced unit production manager/line producer or even casting director has accepted less money in salary in exchange for credit as "producer" on the film. Finding the right person who has an interest in developing producer credits in addition to being able to deliver the needed services to the film is not an easy task, so the filmmaker should be searching for these team members much earlier than when the money is released from escrow, even if unable before that point to make a firm offer. In any case, the filmmaker would do well to secure another producer for the project besides him or herself. If it is determined that the budget provides for the hiring of an experienced producer all is well and good; however, if the budget does not provide for a second or third producer, then the filmmaker will have to look to people who have less experience but who are eager to learn and build up their credits. Either way, the filmmaker has to have someone to whom he or she can delegate these tasks.

Unit Production Manager/Line Producer. A unit production manager/line producer should also be added to the team when the funds are available. *The importance of hiring the "right" person as the unit production manager/line producer can not be emphasized too strongly—especially for the first-time filmmaker.* This person will not only take on the task of finding the vendors and crew members needed to make the film, but also of creating the updated shooting schedule and budget, and basically overseeing the proper execution of all expenditures. Experienced producers and filmmakers usually know a number of these types of people, and have contacts to reach out to for a good unit production manager/line producer. The first-time filmmaker, on the other hand, will be establishing a first-time relationship, and will be relying on a person who is more knowledgeable and more experienced in making films than he or she is. Such a relationship will inevitably shift the leverage from the filmmaker to the unit production manager/line producer, which is what makes the selection process for this position so critical. It is particularly important that the experience of the unit production manager/ line producer should be with films that are on approximately the same budget level of the film to be produced by the filmmaker. There is a great difference in spending decisions for a $100,000 film as compared with decisions for a $500,000 film or a $2 million film. The independent filmmaker will find that it is difficult to find an experienced, competent unit production manager/line producer for a film with a budget under $1 million. One of the reasons for the latter is that the good ones usually graduate to larger budget films after working on a handful of films in this budget range, and once they have graduated they are not interested in "stepping down" to a lower budgeted film. On the other extreme, the unit production managers/line producers who do many films in the under $1 million budget range and do not "graduate up" become very skilled at finding their own ways of cutting corners and are very reluctant to abandon them whether or not they best serve the film-maker's vision for the film they may be working on. This is completely understandable because it is very difficult to secure high quality goods and services in this budget range, and better quality is usually outside of the budget constraints. Therefore, the filmmaker should be alert to the fact that many experienced unit production managers/line producers at this level adopt an attitude of "getting the job done, *period*," with little creative thinking and with little or no discussion with the filmmaker. It may not be completely fair to characterize this attitude as universal, and it is only fair to say that, after all, the job must get done, but what a film needs, especially at this budget level, is an inspired unit produc-tion manager/line producer who is responsive to the particular film and filmmaking team that is assembled around the filmmaker and can think outside of the box. A strategy for increasing communication can be to hire an additional producer who meets the same four criteria above, so the unit production manager/line producer can have a liaison who is involved in daily decision making and can report back daily to the film-maker, keeping him/her abreast. It is virtually impossible to determine whether the person who is hired will be an inspired and responsive unit production manager/line producer. The position is so critical for completing the film that it is recommended that the contract entered into with the unit production manager/line producer be a "step deal." A "step deal" is one in which objective criteria are established for the unit production manager/line producer to meet at various stages, with the filmmaker retaining the ability to decide whether the unit production manager/line producer will be allowed to continue to the next stage. A clause should also be included stating that *all* services must be provided under the contract in order for the unit production manager/line producer to receive his or her credit on the film.

It has been my experience that the first-time filmmaker resists negotiating and executing a contract with the unit production manager/line producer that includes these types of provisions, and there is also resistance by the potential unit production manager/line producer to agree to such terms. But the more control the filmmaker retains over this person, the smoother the process will be for the filmmaker. Period. The more this person becomes uninspired and/or nonresponsive to the needs of the filmmaker and film, the greater the chance the film will never get completed, and if it does get completed, it will be at much greater cost and probably of inferior quality. In addition, the scope of authority the unit production manager/line producer will have to bind the company must be strictly determined. Certain items should be especially placed outside of his or her scope of authority, such as no access to the bank account, credit cards, or petty cash. Any person who resists the addition of these terms to the contract is probably not the right unit production manager/line producer for the film. This is not a question of honesty, but one of quality control and cost control, and will compel consultation on all but minor purchases.

Casting Director. The next key position to fill is a casting director. Most independent films with a budget less than $1 million cast the film without the services of a casting director—this is a mistake. A good casting director can generate ideas for potential actors for each role, has relationships with working actors and agents and managers in the business, and will help in the administrative process of making offers and securing their acceptance by actors. As mentioned earlier, the talent that is secured for the film is a variable which can make a significant difference as to whether or not the film achieves distribution, and if considered for distribution, will have dramatic impact on what a distributor offers. Although the filmmaker and the producers will be very involved in the process, and often an attorney's services will be engaged to assist in the negotiation and drafting of certain actors' contracts, the casting director will be the key person in the process of securing talent. Of course, having the funds necessary to engage a casting director's services is a primary factor in determining whether or not an independent filmmaker can secure such services.

Foreign Sales Representative. In addition, if the budget is above $300,000, then the filmmaker should also consider engaging the services of a reputable foreign sales representative. A foreign sales representative can assist by providing his or her opinion as to which potential actors will be most valuable for selling the film in international markets. Foreign sales agents can, and do, represent films while they are in the script stage with actors attached. They present the package to foreign buyers in the hope of securing their assent to a "presale" agreement in the foreign territory. Unfortunately, these types of arrangements are extremely difficult for a first-time independent filmmaker to secure because of the limited budgets involved. Foreign sales agents want name actors legally bound to the film; however, this is usually not feasible at the script stage for a low-budget independent film. Foreign sales agents need enough time to go to major film sales markets (such as Cannes, American Film Market, National Association of Television Program Executives Market & Conference, MIPCOM, etc.) to gauge the potential interest in a finished film with specific actors bound to the film. See Chapter 6. Since no two projects are the same, however, for certain projects the extra time and expense may be worth the investment, so it is an area the filmmaker should be aware of and should investigate to determine its applicability to his or her project. In any case, the foreign sales agent who is engaged to render an opinion regarding the potential value of certain actors must be currently active in selling films to the foreign market, and must have attended and have had sales/licenses at each of the previous major markets (Cannes, American Film Market, National Association of Television Program Executives Market & Conference, MIPCOM, etc.). It should be pointed out that since the market is constantly shifting, an opinion is only valuable if it is "fresh."

GUILDS: SCREEN ACTORS GUILD–AMERICAN FEDERATION OF TELEVISION AND RADIO ARTISTS; WRITERS GUILD OF AMERICA; DIRECTORS GUILD OF AMERICA

The filmmaker will need to decide whether or not the film will be a signatory to any of the applicable guilds like the Screen Actors Guild-American Federation of Television and Radio Artists, which is the union with the greatest impact on most films. A film does not need to sign with SAG-AFTRA or comply with any SAG-AFTRA rules whether or not the film uses the services of any actors who are SAG-AFTRA members. However, any actor who is already a member of SAG-AFTRA will be in violation of SAG-AFTRA rules if such member provides acting services to a film that is not a SAG-AFTRA signatory. So if a filmmaker decides that he or she will not sign with SAG-AFTRA then there is the possibility that certain actors that the filmmaker would want and could get for the film will decline to participate if it is not a "SAG-AFTRA film." In 2005 SAG (before the merger with AFTRA) unveiled new guidelines for low-budget films (i.e., films with budgets less than $2,500,000).

There are currently three basic SAG-AFTRA low-budget agreements for feature films: the Ultra Low-Budget Agreement, the Modified Low Budget Agreement, and the Low Budget Agreement. If the filmmaker decides to participate, one of the producers or the unit production manager/line producer or the production attorney can complete the paperwork and file for the company to become a signatory to SAG-AFTRA. The total budget for the film will determine which agreement the film will fall under. The Ultra Low-Budget Agreement applies to films with a budget of less than $200,000, while the Modified Low Budget Agreement applies to budgets less than $625,000, and the Low Budget Agreement applies to budgets less than $2,500,000. There are certain restrictions and requirements that apply to each agreement, and filmmakers should review them with the person filing the paperwork on their behalf. In addition to the salaries to be paid to each actor, the filmmaker is required to make payments to the SAG-AFTRA Pension and Health Plans, which is currently an additional 16.8 percent to be paid on all gross compensation paid to each actor. The producer is also required to make the payments for social security, disability, and all other state and federal tax obligations, as well as purchasing workers' compensation insurance for the film.

Although being a SAG-AFTRA film increases the costs paid for the actors' services, a filmmaker may find it a necessary expense in order to sign a certain actor or actors to the film whose services would, in the long run, more than offset the extra costs. On the other hand, it is possible that such costs will not be offset by the SAG-AFTRA actors' services, so this decision should be carefully considered by the filmmaker and his or her advisors. Becoming a signatory to the Writers Guild of America (WGA) and the Directors Guild of America (DGA) will also be required if the filmmaker wishes to engage the services of any writer or director who is a member of these organizations. For budgets at $1 million and below it is rare for the filmmaker to engage a writer who is a member of the WGA, and it's even rarer still for a filmmaker to engage a director who is a member of the DGA. However, if the filmmaker wants to engage the services of a writer or director who is a member of the union and the member will not provide the services unless it's a union film, then the filmmaker must complete the paperwork and become a signatory to the appropriate guild. Like SAG-AFTRA, becoming a signatory to the WGA or the DGA adds an extra cost to the budget, but unlike SAG-AFTRA, these unions are almost always avoided by filmmakers in this budget range.

HIRING A LAWYER

The lawyer is another key person on the team, and should be engaged at the very beginning of the process. At the earliest moment possible the attorney should be available to provide legal advice on everything from the financing and production all the way through to distribution of the film. This is not always the case. First of all, filmmakers sometimes engage different attorneys to service different aspects of production based upon their immediate needs, the available budget, and/or specialty of a particular attorney. Not only is this cost ineffective, but there will be an absence of synergy throughout the process. It is preferable to find an attorney who has experience in all aspects of producing a low-budget film and is competent to provide all necessary services from the beginning of the process through final distribution. This is complicated by a couple of things, specifically location and cost. Most often these attorneys are concentrated in major cities, particularly in Los Angeles and New York. With regard to cost, the filmmaker should be aware of the multiple possible arrangements for securing legal representation. Many attorneys will provide a flat rate deal to provide all the legal services needed. Although varying widely, a general range of cost that a filmmaker can expect is between $7,500 and $20,000 depending on the complexity of the work involved and the type of services provided by the attorney. Production attorneys usually provide a retainer agreement to a potential client with an "addendum" that lists the services required for the production of the feature film. On each page of the addendum three columns will be provided naming the law firm, the client's name, and "other." In consultation with the filmmaker-client, the attorney will then check either the box of the law firm, the client, or "other" next to each legal service listed in the addendum indicating who will be responsible for each item. The filmmaker should review this document carefully and discuss each line item with the attorney to determine what services the filmmaker can expect to receive for the flat rate quoted by the attorney. Most attorneys are open to providing only the particular services the filmmaker wishes to access, with a quoted fee (i.e., from $7,500 to $20,000 depending on the number and nature of the services the filmmaker has selected to secure).

Some filmmakers obtain template contracts either from another film or by purchasing them from a store or from the Internet. The forms that can be purchased are better than not having any contracts at all, but these forms are intended to serve as educational material so that when the filmmaker does work with the attorney he or she will have sufficient background to be able to ask the right questions as well as being able to make a reasonable comparison between what is being suggested and some general industry standards. Solely utilizing template contracts by a filmmaker for the many service agreements necessary in producing a film is not only wrought with peril, but in fact detracts from the time the filmmaker should be devoting to the creative aspects of making a movie. In addition, as will be brought out in the chapter on distribution, distributors won't touch a film unless it is legally "clean." Although drafting and executing contracts is a service included when experienced legal counsel is secured (and oftentimes template contracts are provided by such legal counsel to defray costs), the filmmaker should not think about the relationship in terms of "buying contracts" when an attorney is engaged. Filmmakers are engaging an attorney for his or her expertise and advice regarding the scores of legal decisions that arise in making a feature film. Most experienced film attorneys bring not only legal expertise and contract drafting to the relationship, but an insightful perspective on the many tangential issues that arise in the making of a film that are intertwined with the legal issues. In a word, hire an experienced production attorney for your film.

ACTORS, CREW, AND VENDORS

The negotiations and contract signings with actors, crew, and vendors have their own peculiarities and it would be wise to involve a lawyer in this process as well. There are a number of specific terms that are found in each of these types of contracts, but the contracts within each of these primary groups have certain similarities with all the contracts the filmmaker enters into for services. If the film is a SAG-AFTRA film, there are usually three different contracts that are executed with each actor. The first contract is usually a one- or two-page "deal memo" that the casting director (or producer) forwards to the actor, or if the actor has an agent or manager, to his or her representation. Terms may vary but the basic terms usually covered in this deal memo include: a) the name of the film; b) the production company making the film; c) the director; d) the actor; e) the role the actor will play; f) the name of the loan-out company (if there is one); g) the address of the actor; h) telephone number and email of actor; i) the name and contact information for any agent involved; j) the schedule (i.e., the start date and the number of work days); k) compensation; l) credit/billing; m) paid ads credit/billing; n) profit participation, if any; and o) miscellaneous, including transportation, no nudity, photo approval, dressing room, looping days, recitation of the fact that it is a SAG-AFTRA signatory film. This contract will go out from the casting director (or the producer) and may or may not come back to the filmmaker signed. This is not a problem as long as the filmmaker is diligent in following up with subsequent paperwork, and is diligent in getting the subsequent contracts signed; such subsequent contracts should encompass the terms in the "Deal Memo." If applicable, a SAG-AFTRA employment contract should also be sent to the actor or his or her representative. This is a one-page employment contract which covers some of the administrative information found in the deal memo in addition to information stating that the actor has been advised of the particular SAG-AFTRA contract that the film is utilizing, certain attestations regarding such contract, and certain terms from the SAG-AFTRA contract. This contract must be signed and received back from the actor in accordance with SAG-AFTRA requirements. In addition to the "Deal Memo" and SAG-AFTRA agreement, an actor's contract will be sent to the actor or the actor's representative. This contract can vary in length from four to thirty pages depending on who is generating the contract (and who the actor is). On average, actor's contracts for an independent film run about six to ten pages in length. These contracts will contain the terms found in the deal memo in addition to legal language regarding work-for-hire terms, transfer of rights, promotional film rights, assignment rights, representations and warranties, etc. Often the agent or attorney for the actor will request changes and revisions to the terms offered; although some are cosmetic in nature, some are substantive changes that materially affect the scope of the language in the contract. This is where sound judgment must prevail. If the filmmaker wants the actor and doesn't want to go through the process of replacing the actor, unless it's a major deal-breaking change, most changes requested by the actor or the actor's representatives are accepted by the filmmaker. *Sound negotiations should be focused on "interests" and not "positions."*

Crew agreements are similar to actor agreements in that they each contain basic terms such as the services to be provided, the engagement duration, compensation, work-for-hire terms, transfer of rights, applicable guild and union exclusions, workers' compensation language, meals, transportation, travel, responsibility for bringing equipment, and any additional rental for such "kit" and insurance to cover loss or damage, publicity, assignment rights, etc. In the drafting of each of these contracts tailoring the definition of "services" to be provided by each crew member should be as explicit as possible. As mentioned earlier, it is wisest to draft a "step deal" agreement wherein the satisfactory fulfillment of one step is necessary for the crew member to move to a subsequent step, especially for certain "key" crew members such as the unit production manager. In any case, all of these contracts should be "at-will" engagements so a crew member can be released at any time with remuneration up to the time of separation.

MISCELLANEOUS CONTRACTS

Following is a brief listing of other contracts typically required in making a movie:

1) vendor agreements which review and comment on the equipment rental agreements, any special effects, etc;
2) product placement contracts and releases;
3) location agreements;
4) merchandising agreements;
5) film clip license agreements;
6) artwork license agreements;
7) composer agreement(s);
8) music synchronization/public performance agreements for each song;
9) music master use agreements for each song;
10) distribution contract(s);
11) errors and omissions insurance application and policy; and
12) delivery requirements with a distributor.

Whether or not the attorney will be responsible for drafting and/or reviewing these contracts should be stipulated in the retainer agreement as stated in the attorney section of this chapter.

ACCOUNTING, BOOKKEEPING, AND PAYROLL SERVICES

There are other personnel that a filmmaker should seriously consider engaging at this point. The first is an accountant and/or bookkeeper. If one of the producers has the necessary skills to be responsible for writing all checks and utilizing any credit cards in the production of the film, then he or she can assume the responsibility of keeping track of every expenditure, acquiring and retaining every receipt, and maintaining control over the petty cash expenditures—in other words the bookkeeping. If this is not the case, and it usually is not, then the filmmaker should hire someone whose job it is to do this work. One of the primary reasons a film fails to reach completion is the producer's failure to maintain strict control over money expenditures. There are production accountants who can be hired to do this work. In any event, the filmmaker eventually will need an accountant to formalize the process and file the applicable federal and state tax forms. Hiring a production accountant to control expenditures is expensive; as a result it is not usually an economical expenditure until the budget is at $1 million or more. Hiring the accountant to file tax forms can usually be left until the end of the year in which money was spent in producing the film, but he or she will need to receive diligently kept records from the filmmaker to be able to do this.

Although an extra expense, the filmmaker would be wise to hire a payroll service company to handle wage payments to employees. A payroll company will complete much of the necessary paperwork in connection with salaries and wages. However, even if the filmmaker utilizes a payroll company, he or she must still be diligent in having each actor complete a federal Form W-9, "Request for Taxpayer Identification Form and Certification," a Federal Form I-9, "Employment Eligibility Verification" form (with photocopies of the relevant proof of identification, e.g., driver's license and social security card). If the actor has a loan-out company, then the filmmaker is also responsible for securing copies of the loan-out company's paperwork that verifies that the loan-out company exists and pays taxes (i.e., the certificate of incorporation for a corporation or articles of organization for a limited liability company, etc.), and the loan-out company's employer identification number (EIN). These papers are usually handled by the unit production manager/line producer, but the unit production manager/line producer usually delegates these tasks so it is incumbent on one of the additional producers to supervise these tasks and ensure they are completed.

INDEPENDENT CONTRACTOR OR EMPLOYEE?

It is important to note here that there is a difference between paying for services provided by an employee and paying for services provided by an independent contractor. The primary difference is that payments to an employee require the filmmaker to withhold federal and state taxes (and for some taxes to make a matching payment) and remit those payments to the proper federal and state authorities on a monthly or quarterly basis. In addition, the filmmaker is required to cover unemployment payments for employees and secure worker's compensation insurance for them. Under SAG-AFTRA, actors are to be considered as employees, so the filmmaker will be required to treat the actors as employees and incur the added expenses generated by the above responsibilities. For other crew members it is not as clear as to whether they are independent contractors or employees because such determination is based on specific facts and circumstances, which are different for the services provided by each crew member. A twenty-factor test has emerged from case law over the years and has been adopted by the Internal Revenue Service (Revenue Ruling 87-41) to help guide in the determination as to whether an individual is an employee or independent contractor. A detailed analysis of the issues involved in such a determination is beyond the scope of this book, but a general guideline is that there is an employee/employer relationship when the filmmaker has the right to control and direct the person's work. The IRS has also issued internal audit guidelines to help ensure more accurate and consistent determinations of the employee/independent contractor evaluation in the "Television Commercial Production and Professional Video Communication Industries." The filmmaker should not try to make the determination by him or herself, but should consult an accountant or tax attorney to help guide any decisions in this area.

PART III

Distributing the Film

13

Distributors

*"As far back as I can remember,
I always wanted to be a gangster."* —Goodfellas

Obviously, the ultimate goal of any producer is to achieve distribution of the film. At what point in the project should a distributor become involved in the process of bringing a film to the market? The short answer is as soon as any can be found to be interested in becoming involved. This doesn't mean that the filmmaker should give away any rights to the film in the "packaging" stage (i.e., before full financing for the budget is obtained or before commencement of principal photography) unless the deal offered by a distributor is a very strong one. This is less of a "dilemma" than it may seem, because distributors are generally not interested in committing to a film until after the film has been completed. There is more uncertainty in determining what markets (if any) may exist for a film when it is in script form as opposed to seeing the final product that a distributor will actually be trying to sell to consumers. Since the supply of completed films far outweighs the demand for completed films, distributors will not usually commit to acquiring/licensing a film until after they have the opportunity to view the final product.

WHEN SHOULD A FILMMAKER APPROACH DISTRIBUTORS?

Even though distributors are not inclined to commit to acquiring/ licensing a film in the early stages of development, it is still a worthwhile endeavor for the filmmaker to target a select number of nonstudio distributors and solicit their involvement in the project. Which distributors should be approached will become clear as the filmmaker works with the script (see Chapter 3). Ideally, the distributor would like the filmmaker to approach it with some aspects of the "packaging" already secured, that is, some (preferably all) of the funds for the budget already in escrow, and ideally with two or three "name talent" cast members legally attached to the project. The likelihood of the latter occurring for a low-budget film is very rare, and even if it does occur, approaching distributors at that point is not always advantageous. Although rare for a first-time filmmaker producing a film in the under $1 million budget range, distributors have been known to provide funds in exchange for certain rights to a film at this stage. They will, however, usually be receptive to reviewing a filmmaker's film package to see if it might have promise; that is if there are elements legally committed to the project (funding, talent, etc.). The reality is that it could take forever for a script with no funds or firm attachments to obtain a response from a distributor, if at all.

However, none of the above should deter a filmmaker from exposing the project to distributors at an early stage; the aim would be to obtain free feedback from the distributors regarding the project. More often than not, when pressed, a distributor will provide the company's market perspective on the film package. This is extremely valuable information to a filmmaker since the information is coming from people who are in the business of *selling* films. No single opinion should be considered the be-all and end-all opinion, but if more than one distributor provides similar feedback regarding the potential market for the film, it would be prudent for the filmmaker to take the information into consideration. At this stage (i.e., before principal photography is started), there are project adjustments still available to the filmmaker which can be made without doing violence to the filmmaker's original vision, including making minor adjustments to the script. Once the film is shot and completed there is very little a filmmaker can do to change the film without incurring financial expenditures generally prohibitive to an independent filmmaker. As was discussed in a previous chapter, film distribution is not a simple matter and it behooves a wise filmmaker to acquire a profound understanding of the process at the earliest stage of project development.

CLASSIFICATION OF DISTRIBUTORS

Classified By Market. Distribution channels can be divided between the "domestic" market and the "international" market. The domestic market primarily includes North America (Canada and the United States and United States Territories and Possessions), whereas the international market is simply the rest of the world. The major studios and their affiliates/subsidiaries (and certain select other distributors, such as Lionsgate) have the infrastructure to exploit both the domestic and international markets for a film. However, most distributors market films to either the domestic market or the international market.

Classified By Rights. Another primary distinction between distributors is based upon the type of rights that they tend to demand from a filmmaker. In general, it is very rare for distributors to accept a contract that limits the types of rights they will be allowed to exploit, even if it can be shown that the distributor has never generated revenue from a particular right they are demanding. The fact is that each distributor generally generates revenue from a specific market which it has become adept at exploiting. For most distributors it is primarily home video rights. The reality is that a filmmaker will be forced into a position of granting a distributor all of the customary distribution rights to the film regardless of the distributor's ability to exploit all of those rights; that is unless the filmmaker has the leverage to split the rights among different distributors thereby taking advantage of the particular strengths of each distributor.

Although new channels of distribution are evolving as this is being written, the primary rights of a film that are presently available for exploitation are: a) Theatrical; b) Home video (DVD, Blu-ray, any other device devised for home use); c) Free television; d) Pay television; e) Pay-Per-View;

223

f) Video-on-Demand; g) Satellite television; h) Download-on-Demand serviced through the Internet (both rental and download to own); and i) Mobile/wireless. For many years the goal of the independent filmmaker was to land a deal with a distributor that exchanged all of the distribution rights to the film for a large advance of money (usually referred to as a "minimum guarantee"). Seeking these types of deals today is illusionary, since they have become practically extinct. It is more common for an independent filmmaker, when lucky enough to strike any deal at all, to receive no advance sum of money, or a very small sum of money (relative to the production budget of the film) in exchange for giving up all of the distribution rights for a particular market(s). Further, the landscape for the distribution of independent films (and studio films for that matter) is changing very quickly with the introduction of new mediums and new channels of distribution. So it can be very difficult to analyze the cost/benefit of turning the rights of a film over to a particular distributor, or turning them over to any distributor at all (see "Self-Distribution" in this chapter). However, despite the changes, there is one constant that guides the decision-making process. The object in making a film is to gain distribution that will reach paying customers. This sounds like a simple objective, but the process of achieving it is anything but simple. Major studios (and their affiliates/subsidiaries) do acquire or license some independent films and can utilize their comprehensive pipeline of distribution. The major studios (and affiliates/subsidiaries) have direct relationships, and in some cases, output deals, with companies that directly reach the consumer in each specified medium in the domestic market. The breakdown of the mediums and the companies that directly reach consumers in such mediums can be summarized in the following chart:

Distribution Medium	Companies That Directly Reach Consumers
Cable, Satellite, Internet Protocol TV (IPTV), Fiber Optic	Comcast, Time Warner Cable, Cox Communications, Cablevision, DirecTV, DishNetwork, AT&T, Verizon (FIOS)
Retail Home Video (DVD, Blu-ray, etc.) Sales	Wal-Mart, Blockbuster, Target, Best Buy, Amazon.com
Retail Home Video (DVD, Blu-ray, etc.) Rentals	Redbox (Kiosks), Netflix, Blockbuster, Moxie Gallery, Family Video, Holly-wood Video, Hastings Entertainment, Trans World Entertainment, Independently Owned ("Mom & Pop") Video Rental Stores
Internet Providers	Apple itunes, Netflix, Amazon, Cin-emaNow, Walmart/Vudu, Hulu, Sony Playstation, Microsoft Xbox, Hastings Entertainment, YouTube/Google, Samsung, Time Warner Cable and Comcast Cable

STUDIO DISTRIBUTION

The major studios (and affiliates/subsidiaries) generate the majority of their revenue for their films through international sales by utilizing their own foreign sales force/office and/or through strategic alliances with sales companies in various nations throughout the world. Their films move through these distribution pipelines in an efficient manner maximizing the exploitation of each film through both the domestic and international markets. The Motion Picture Association of America reported that in 2007 the affiliates/ subsidiaries of the major studios spent an average of $25 million per film on marketing costs on such films as: *The Darjeeling Limited* (Fox Searchlight); *Juno* (Fox Searchlight); *Walk Hard: The Dewey Cox Story* (Columbia); *Across the Universe* (Columbia); *Superbad* (Columbia); *Dan In Real Life* (Focus Features); *Into the Wild* (Focus Features); *There Will Be Blood* (Miramax); *Gone Baby Gone* (Miramax); *The Brothers Solomon* (TriStar); *Feel the Noise* (TriStar); *White Noise 2* (Rogue); and *Hot Fuzz* (Rogue). More recent examples include: *For A Good Time Call* (Focus Features); *Jeff Who Lives At Home* (Paramount Vantage); *Ruby Sparks* (Fox Searchlight); and *Robot and Frank* (Sony Pictures Worldwide Acquisitions). These are not the "independent films" that are the subject of this book.

Studios (and their affiliates/subsidiaries) are generally not interested in directly acquiring independent films because of the cost to support a theatrical release, and the fact that the films will each generate sales of less than 35,000 DVD/Blu-ray units in home video sales. Rarely will an independent film achieve sales of 35,000 DVD/Blu-ray units, and when it does reach those levels it usually engenders lawsuits. *Napoleon Dynamite* (2004) is an example of a film that was a low-budget film with a reported budget of $400,000. It was acquired and distributed by a studio subsidiary (Fox Searchlight) and returned large amounts of gross receipts. After auditing the distributor's books, the producer of the film filed a lawsuit against the distributor in 2011. In the lawsuit the producer claimed that its audit revealed that the distributor paid only approximately 9 percent of net profits instead of the agreed upon 25 percent for home video rights as well as underreported pay television payments. The suit also claimed that the distributor didn't report electronic sell-through revenue and overcharged residuals on home video sales. The producer claimed that payment of its 25 percent of net profits alone would equal approximately $10 million.

Although the studios do acquire or license some independent films (usually through an affiliate/subsidiary or from a separate sub-distributor, see "Sub-Distributors" in this chapter), an independent film most likely will not be acquired/licensed by a major studio or its affiliate/subsidiary. So, as can readily be seen, the filmmaker will need to explore avenues with other distributors. That is why an understanding of how a film reaches the consumer in each medium will help the independent filmmaker make intelligent choices regarding how to best distribute his or her independent film.

When an independent film is licensed to a distributor (whether domestic or international), a distributor will commonly expect all of the previously mentioned rights to be licensed to it for exploitation (i.e., theatrical, home video, pay television, etc.). It is understandable for a major studio or affiliate/subsidiary to demand all of the mediums for exploitation when acquiring/licensing a film because the major studios and their affiliates/subsidiaries clearly have the means to reach all these consumers through their relationships with all the companies that directly reach the consumers. However, when moving away from the studios, it becomes imperative that the filmmaker investigate exactly how, and if, a particular distributor being considered for licensing may be equipped to reach each consumer segment. Overall, as a filmmaker moves away from the studios, he or she will generally come in contact with distributors who, at best, reach consumers in only one or two market segments (usually home video and/or television), and with varying degrees of success. Even within the one or two mediums, companies are generally stronger in either home-video sales or home-video rentals and premium cable channels as opposed to pay-per-view/video-on-demand. A diligent investigation into each particular distributor will reveal the strengths and weaknesses of each.

The Hollywood Distribution Directory (www.HCDonline.com, since discontinued) listed approximately 575 companies that *identified themselves* as "distributors." The major studios and their affiliates/subsidiaries represent only about twenty on the list, which still left approximately 555 remaining companies. Of these, there are approximately 200 to 250 companies that are in the business of acquiring/licensing independent films. However, no two distributors are the same or equally valuable to an independent filmmaker with a specific film. The process described in Chapter 3 will help the filmmaker determine which distributors may become interested in the particular type of film the filmmaker intends to produce; what is being examined here is whether it would be in a filmmaker's interests to license his or her film to *anyone* who may express interest. Any "distributor" can "release" a film in home video (DVD/Blu-ray) with no financial or other support, but the filmmaker needs to investigate the commitment that each distributor will or will not make to his or her film. The rule of thumb is that to properly support a home video release for an independent film with a budget below $1,000,000 it will take between $50,000 and $100,000 in marketing expenditures to yield home video sales of 25,000 to 50,000 units. These costs are primarily incurred by strategically placed print advertising for the film. However, very few, if any, distributors commit a sufficient amount (or any amount) of marketing dollars, so the filmmaker would be wise to find out exactly how much a distributor will commit to spend on marketing for the release of the film in order to better evaluate any potential market success. A careful review of the general categories of independent film distributors will be helpful in better evaluating their potential penetration into the market.

SUB-DISTRIBUTORS

The first *type* of distributor is one that is one step removed from the studios but has an "output agreement" or "servicing" agreement with a major studio. MGM, which releases its DVDs through Fox, and Lionsgate, which utilizes Fox's DVD physical distribution services are examples of these so-called sub-distributors. Other examples of "sub-distributors" include Anchor Bay Entertainment which utilizes Fox's DVD physical distribution services, ThinkFilm, which has utilized Lionsgate's deal with Fox, and Vivendi Entertainment (a division of Gaiam), which services DVD distribution for companies such as Code Black, Palm Pictures, Blowtorch Entertainment, and The Shout Factory. These are not the only sub-distributors that exist, there are also a few other sub-distributors that have somehow obtained distribution deals through a major studio. A major advantage of sub-distributors is that they have penetration into the market and the ability to reach consumers because of their affiliation with major studios, that is to say, these companies can get the films they distribute on the shelves of Wal-Mart, Target, and other major video retailers and available for VOD through Comcast, Time Warner, Verizon FIOS, etc. A major disadvantage is that they also add an extra level of cost; this is because the studios allow these sub-distributors to utilize their established distribution for a fee. Fees can range between 10 percent and 25 percent, which is usually in addition to the fee the sub-distributor charges the filmmaker. So the "gross" that comes down from the studio to the sub-distributor has already been reduced by the studio's fee and often other distribution costs as well, such as physical fulfillment of the product and administrative, so-called, back office functions. These types of arrangements most often have a lack of "transparency," and give rise to the question as to whether the studio or the sub-distributor controls the process, which can be frustrating for the filmmaker. The filmmaker is entering into a distribution agreement with a sub-distributor who then outsources much of the process to a major studio. When the filmmaker has concerns or questions it is not uncommon for there to be a long delay in response, and it is common for the sub-distributor to say that there is nothing they can do since the decision-making process has been delegated to the studio by virtue of the sub-distributor's output deal with the studio. Further, since these types of sub-distributors are utilizing the major studio's distribution channels, and are therefore competing with the films that normally are released through those channels, these types of sub-distributors are reluctant to commit advertising money to a film unless the film has, in their estimation, the ability to sell many thousands of units in home video. A review of the films that some of the above companies (sub-distributors) have distributed shows that a very small percentage of the total films released by those companies qualify for that level of financial commitment. More likely, a film is packaged and released with the hope that the intrinsic features of the film (i.e., name cast, genre, great reviews, festival screenings, etc.) will generate revenue on that basis alone. What do all these considerations mean to the independent filmmaker? These types of distributors generally have access to consumers, but it is very difficult for the independent filmmaker to attract their interest, and even if his or her film is released by one of them, it is very easy for a lower budgeted independent film, with no advertising budget, to get lost among the other releases in the market, always being mindful that there is an added layer of cost associated with these types of arrangements.

It is important for the filmmaker to keep up with the rapid developments in distribution. Being ahead of the curve can be the "outsider's" ticket to success. For example, in 2009 certain studios began aggressively pursuing output deals with content providers for the video-on-demand and digital platforms alone. Warner Brothers Digital Entertainment has entered into deals with First Look Studios, Full Moon Entertainment, Mar-Vista Entertainment, Gravitas Ventures, Image Entertainment, Wolfe Video and Oscilloscope Laboratories to release films from these companies on video-on-demand and digital platforms. In turn Gravitas Ventures entered into sub-distribution deals with ten other companies including Liberation Entertainment, Submarine Entertainment, the Film Sales Company, and Traction Media. It is in the interest of an independent filmmaker to be aware of the fact that if one of these "sub-distributors" is interested in licensing his or her film, there is a chance that the independent filmmaker would have the opportunity to take advantage of the sub-distributor's deal with the studio and thus gain access to the burgeoning video-on-demand revenue. However, it would be wise for the filmmaker to specifically determine whether or not any such sub-distributor will actually wind up distributing his or her film through such studio output deal. The honest answer most often is that the sub-distributor can't accurately answer the question because the studio will most likely have the right to choose which films it wants from the sub-distributor's catalog based on which films the studio believes will generate the most revenue. This is another example of the confusion in the process when a filmmaker decides to license his or her film with a sub-distributor. Further, when dealing with companies that are effectively "sub-sub-distributors" (such as Liberation Entertainment and Submarine Entertainment), the filmmaker should be alert to the additional level of cost and loss of control over the process.

INDEPENDENT DISTRIBUTORS

Another type of distributor of independent films is one that has developed its own relationships with companies that directly reach consumers. Independent distributors have grown their own catalog of films, and have groomed their own sales force proficient in selling their catalogs to companies that are directly reaching consumers. There are few examples of these types of distributors simply because it is very difficult to develop and grow a distribution company that can achieve these goals. And even those companies that have achieved them find it hard to sustain them. It is not uncommon to see these types of distributors end in bankruptcy, or be merged with or acquired by another company, or to discontinue acquiring and releasing new films altogether, relying instead on exploiting their vast library of films. Cinedigm/New Video, Wolfe Video, First Look Entertainment, MPI Media Group, Peace Arch Entertainment, Koch Lorber Films, Echo Bridge Entertainment, E1 Entertainment, and Arts Alliance America are some examples of these types of independent distributors. This category of company primarily specializes in domestic DVD retail sales and rentals (although they may expand into other mediums), and they are widely considered to be very good at reaching consumers with their product. However, they rarely spend the marketing dollars necessary to garner public awareness and increased sales and rentals for each film. These types of companies also demand all rights to all mediums when they acquire/license a film.

The filmmaker must carefully ascertain in which particular mediums each company is successfully promoting its films. For example, in 2012 Wolfe Video launched its own worldwide video-on-demand service at www.wolfeondemand.com. A filmmaker licensing his or her film to this company should receive clarification regarding whether the video-on-demand right is exclusive to Wolfe Video thereby shutting out the film's access to the millions of subscribers that would otherwise be available if the film was licensed to an established company, for example, Comcast Cable or Verizon FIOS. In 2008 Echo Bridge hired a former studio employee to open a new division dedicated to online and subscription video-on-demand and other emerging platforms. Also in 2008 Anchor Bay announced the launching of a theatrical division set to roll out eight to ten projects annually in addition to engaging Sony Pictures Home Entertainment to exclusively distribute Anchor Bay's content outside of the United States, Canada, Australia, and the United Kingdom. However, it is unknown if or when these new platforms will generate revenue for the distributor (and hence the filmmaker). There are also a number of distributors that utilize these independent distribution companies for DVD distribution. For example, as of 2012 New Video is the exclusive DVD distributor for titles from Tribeca Film and distributes titles from Arthouse Films and Plexifilm; Independent Film Channel (a distributor) utilizes MPI Media Group; the Sundance Channel utilizes Arts Alliance America to distribute DVDs; E1 Entertainment has distributed United States DVD and Blu-ray discs for Palisades Tartan and Disinformation Company; and in 2006 MarVista agreed to a multi-year pact to release numerous films on DVD through Echo Bridge Home Entertainment (a contract that was reportedly terminated—the commencement of the agreement was reported in the press, but its termination was not). The more the independent filmmaker "without connections" knows about distribution at the very beginning of the process, the better his or her chances of a career breakthrough.

"OTHER" DISTRIBUTORS

Eliminating the studios, sub-distributors and major independent distributors from the list of distributors leaves about 180 to 230 other self-identified distributors who could possibly release a filmmaker's film. The questions a filmmaker wants answered are the same as those for the other distributors thus far mentioned. What rights do they want to acquire from the filmmaker? What process do they have in place to reach the consumers? What films have they released recently, in what mediums and how much was earned on these films? What financial commitment will the distributor make to market the film in order to raise consumer awareness? How much input will the filmmaker have in the process of formulating marketing strategies? There are a handful of excellent distributors within this miscellaneous group. A diligent filmmaker should ferret out distributors that: have experience releasing independent films, understand the marketplace and how to bring a film to the marketplace, *and* commit a certain amount of money to a film so it can compete in the market. The filmmaker's work is to separate the proverbial wheat from the chaff, and be resolute in the policy not to give his or her film to any distributor who is not both an "excellent" distributor and committed to a successful release of the film. It is very difficult to walk away from a "wrong" distributor at this point in the process even when the cost/benefit analysis clearly demands such an action, because, as stated above, distribution is the ultimate goal of a producer. The changing landscape of film distribution has included an increasing number of filmmakers who refuse to clutch at any straw and are deciding that the cost/benefit analysis leads them to the conclusion that it would be more beneficial to self-distribute a film rather than turn the film over to a questionable distributor.

SELF-DISTRIBUTION

Although self-distribution has been growing in popularity among independent filmmakers, choosing this route of distribution is a commitment that is as intense, if not more intense, than the process of making the film. Frequently independent filmmakers decide to self-distribute their film after they have tried unsuccessfully to obtain distribution through established distributors. However, an increasing number of independent filmmakers are beginning to include funds in the original film budget expressly for self-distribution, and are attempting to secure these funds during the beginning of the fund-raising process. In addition to approaching distributors to utilize established channels for reaching consumers, filmmakers are also making the commitment to theatrically release their own film. Sometimes, the filmmaker even decides to self-distribute the film through home video, television, video-on-demand, etc. By personally approaching the companies that directly reach consumers they are able to side-step established distributors. It is, however, virtually impossible to approach the large retailers such as Wal-Mart, Target, TW Cable, Cox, Verizon, etc. with an independent film under one's arm. It is not cost effective for these large companies to deal directly with thousands of independent producers worldwide. Large retailers only work with large distributors of films since they can demand a large volume of sales/rentals and choose from the largest budget and highest profile films available in the market. These large retailers want to put films that are instantly recognizable in front of consumers so as to maximize the potential of reaching a mass market. This does not mean that independent films never get into these large retail channels, only that it is extremely unlikely for an independent filmmaker to pull it off outside established distributors.

There has been and continues to be a fluid distribution environment which means that film rights do not have to be automatically licensed/sold to established distributors; however, the self-distribution route to reach consumers is becoming more challenging. The Digital Entertainment Group reports that in 2011 there were $8.9 billion in DVD sales and $5.6 billion in DVD rentals, a decrease of 40 percent and 25 percent respectively from 2008. Further, according to Rentrak Data in 2011, 3,600 brick-and-mortar home video rental stores closed and were replaced by more than twice as many "kiosks" where consumers can rent DVDs for as low as $1.20 per night. These kiosks accounted for 41 percent of the consumer spending on DVD rentals in 2011, with the major chains *and* the independents accounting for only 21 percent of consumer spending and Netflix (subscription) accounting for the remaining 38 percent. Therefore, the independent filmmaker is finding even less access to the home video rental consumer dollars because there is less money spent on DVD sales and rentals; there are fewer independent video stores offering independent films; the kiosks that have replaced traditional stores offer few titles and the titles that are offered are predominantly major distributors' product; and Netflix will not license one film directly from a filmmaker, requiring independent filmmakers to use an "aggregator" instead. In addition, Rentrak reports that 55 percent of digital online rental revenue is obtained by one company, Netflix, and 100 percent of traditional video-on-demand belongs to the cable, satellite, IPTV and fiber optic companies. In spite of these hurdles there are still rights and avenues that can provide revenue for an independent film. So after carefully considering all factors, it might be more beneficial for some or all of a film's ancillary rights to be distributed independently by a filmmaker rather than through an established distributor. If a filmmaker distributes some of a film's rights without an established distributor and some of the rights using an established distributor then the process has been termed a "hybrid model" of self-distribution, for example, utilizing established distributors for traditional video-on-demand and/or digital, but self-distributing other rights such as theatrical and home video sales (i.e., DVD and Blu-ray).

Regardless of whether it is full self-distribution or the so-called hybrid distribution, the first step is for the filmmaker to become completely familiar with the distribution landscape before engaging in self-distribution, and the earlier in the process this occurs, the better. There are new avenues emerging that the filmmaker may be able to exploit for self-distribution so that the process can be specifically tailored to the filmmaker's film. Needless to say, the costs and benefits of each new company must be carefully considered. For example, Flicklaunch, a 2011 online start-up company, offers tools for a filmmaker to launch his or her film through Facebook. Topspin Media is a company that provides marketing software and services for content creators to reach consumers. However, it should be noted that new companies like Flicklaunch and Topsin Media provide their assistance in exchange for fees and/or a percentage of revenue generated by each film. In addition to the latter, if the filmmaker has raised the funds to travel with the theatrical release of the film, sell copies of the DVD directly to consumers and seek out independent "mom and pop" video stores across the nation who might be open to putting an independent film on their shelves, the prospects for self-distribution become even more favorable. As stated earlier, providing for these expenses in the original budget is an excellent strategy. By eliminating the established distributor, the independent filmmaker is also eliminating the percentage that is taken by an established distributor. Established distributors take between 50 percent and 75 percent of the revenue from the gross receipts received, leaving the filmmaker with 25 percent to 50 percent of the revenue. By eliminating the established distributor and approaching the companies that directly reach consumers the filmmaker is doubling or tripling his or her potential gross receipts, not to mention returns on investors' dollars. With self-distribution, a filmmaker only needs to sell a small fraction of the units in order to acquire a dollar inflow equal to the dollar amount generated by unit sales through "established" distribution channels.

As a rule, distributors no longer provide funds to support a theatrical release for independent films with a production budget between $50,000 and $1 million. Not that there aren't occasions when a distributor has expended funds for a theatrical release for such a film, but those few exceptions only prove the current rule. In general, whether an established distributor theatrically distributes a film or an independent filmmaker does, a theatrical release of an independent film has extremely long odds of breaking even, not to mention making a profit. There are, nevertheless, good reasons for attempting a theatrical release including the fact that it is a way to increase awareness of a film and may potentially create a larger revenue stream from rights other than theatrical rights (i.e., home video sales and rentals, television, video-on-demand, etc.). It was reported on the panel "Distribution X," at the 2012 Sundance Film Festival, that industry experts continue to confirm the benefits of this strategy. Further evidence of the distribution industry's belief in a theatrical release is the reported joint venture in 2012 between video-on-demand distributor Gravitas Ventures and theatrical distributor Variance Films whereby they agreed to annually release seven or eight films in theaters and on video-on-demand simultaneously.

In exploring the distribution possibilities for a film the filmmaker should be asking him or herself the same questions that an established distributor would ask, that is, who is the audience for the film and how can they be reached? As mentioned earlier, from a business perspective, the independent filmmaker should have asked and answered these two questions in the script stage of developing the film. Is the audience a general audience or is there a specific niche audience that would want to see the film? An independent film targeted at a general audience will have a slim chance for success unless backed by a large sum of money supporting its release; however, films like *I Am Not A Hipster* (2012), *Ballast* (2008), *Disappearances* (2006), *Four Eyed Monsters* (2005), *What the Bleep Do We Know!?* (2004), and *The Debut* (2002) have demonstrated that a film targeting a narrow niche market accompanied by a well-planned and executed theatrical release can succeed. Specialized, niche audiences, also called the "core audiences," are usually based on ethnicity, religion, sexual orientation, or on subject matters like sports, politics, or hobbies. Success for the independent filmmaker will be predicated upon figuring out how to reach such audiences.

Recognizing the fact that the independent filmmaker is constrained by severely limited cash, reaching even a niche audience will take thinking outside of the box. Self-distribution will take some money; the trick is to spend the least amount of money while generating the greatest amount of ticket sales. The first step in the process is usually to submit the film to as many festivals as possible, and *personally attending* the screenings of the film. Depending on the film festival, films screened are often reviewed in the local papers and in online publications, and good reviews are a very important (and cost-effective) marketing tool for the self-distributing filmmaker. The emergence of the Internet has provided a powerful tool for filmmakers to use in the marketing of a film. Websites that cater to specialized audiences with discussion communities and blogs represent a rich opportunity for reaching niche audiences. Filmmakers can use websites like Facebook to spread the word about their film in a more "personal" way. The use of a traditional website to generate interest and awareness for a film, in addition to more cutting edge technology such as video and audio podcasts, were not available to the independent filmmaker even a few years ago, but now have revolutionary potential. Filmmakers are also reporting that in the process of interacting with people online and in person they are generating email lists of from 5,000 to 50,000 names of people interested in their film. This grassroots virtual marketing is relatively inexpensive in terms of cash expenditures and is becoming the vital backbone of self-distributing independent filmmaking—inexpensive in terms of cash, not time and effort.

A "successful" theatrical self-distribution will take between twelve and twenty-four months after film festival screenings. A traditional way that filmmakers theatrically self-distribute their films is to travel with the film to the cities in which the film will be screened, which incurs hard travel and lodging costs. Filmmakers who decide to go this route in the distribution of a film are committing to being involved on a full-time basis. There are filmmakers who scale down their physical travel and involvement in the theatrical release of their film by signing a theatrical service deal with a theatrical release company, such as Freestyle Releasing, Balcony Booking and Releasing, Roadside Attractions, and Slowhand Cinema Releasing. The downside (and usually prohibitive) aspect of this strategy is that these types of companies charge an up-front fee (generally between $25,000 and $100,000) in addition to a percentage of the revenues generated from the release. In exchange, they provide theatrical service for the release of the film which includes such services as: guidance on the release date(s) of the film, drafting the press kit and other marketing materials, booking of theaters, shipping film prints and collecting revenues, hiring and supervising publicist(s), and formulating and developing the advertising campaign, which includes consultation on the creation of posters, television, radio, and print advertisements. Of course, each self-distribution route is unique and filmmakers would be wise to choose the specific services, if any, they believe are necessary to delegate to a professional theatrical releasing company. As in so many other instances, it is a matter of how deep the filmmaker's pockets are (or if he or she has *any* pockets).

Whether a filmmaker decides to enter a service deal or personally undertakes all of the work to be done in a theatrical release, there are other cash expenditures required for a traditional self-release, including: theater rental; advertising; film prints and trailers; payroll for support staff; insurance; merchandise expenses; and DVD creation. Theater rental is secured by what is referred to as "four walling" the movie. Basically the filmmaker must convince a theater owner to allow the film to be shown for a week or two in the theater. This is a limited "platform release," whereby the filmmaker targets an area, chooses one or more theaters and screens the film for one or two weeks. If the film has a good box office return (i.e., a large dollar per screen average), then the platform release will continue, either remaining in the original theater(s), adding new theater(s), or both. The cost of renting a theater depends upon the city in which the theater is located, the type of theater (i.e., art house, multiplex, or nontraditional theater such as libraries and schools) and the number of seats available. Generally, the cost of renting a theater for one week will be between $5,000 and $10,000. Large studios are in a position to avoid paying an up-front fee for the use of theaters, and instead to negotiate a split of the gross box-office receipts. Theater owners are very reluctant to accept this arrangement from an independent filmmaker. The studio's product and advertising budget supporting the product is a guarantee equivalent to an up-front payment, and in the event of any unforeseen anomalies in the box office receipts, theater owners are satisfied that they will be able to address them with the studios in the long run because of the large number of studio releases. These factors are not applicable to an independent filmmaker screening his or her film.

Advertising costs include design and multiple prints of posters, design of traditional print advertising and the cost of placing print advertising in local newspapers and publications, creation of television commercials and the cost of placing the television commercials, and hiring a publicist in each city where the film is released. Aggregately, these costs can add up to astronomical numbers. A one-week release in a major city (Los Angeles, New York, Chicago, San Francisco, etc.) generally costs approximately $100,000 for advertising, excluding television advertising. Television advertising costs approximately $500 for local cable, and of course, into the millions for primetime network broadcasting. Conventional wisdom states that for television advertising to be effective it must run between fifty and one hundred times in the few weeks preceding the theatrical release. Most self-distributed films do not utilize television advertising unless it is public access outside of major cities where it can be cost-effective.

Even if the filmmaker travels with the film, it is virtually impossible to complete every task personally. Ideally tasks such as helping with the grassroots publicity, distributing posters and flyers regarding screenings, helping during screenings, staffing merchandise tables during screenings, and generally being available as support staff could be performed by volunteers, and should be pursued. But even if successful, while the filmmaker may be able to get by with a volunteer staff during the first theater release (especially if it is in the filmmaker's home city), as the theatrical release travels, it will become increasingly difficult to find volunteers in advance and count on them once the release begins. The bottom line is that some people will have to be paid to support a theatrical release. Errors and Omissions insurance is also a necessity for a release, and, depending on the potential liability of a particular film, it runs between $7,000 and $16,000. Merchandise sales, which can generate between 25 percent and 50 percent of the gross box office receipts, also requires expenditures. Typical items include t-shirts, hats, CDs of the soundtrack, behind-the-scenes "making of" DVDs and books and posters. All of these items involve manufacturing and shipping costs. In addition to merchandise sales, theatrical screenings are a perfect opportunity to sell DVD copies of the film. Creating the DVD (authoring, packaging, etc.) can cost between $5,000 and $20,000 after which each DVD can be mass reproduced for as little as $0.80 to $1.00 each. For example, $10,000 to create and author a DVD and $1.00 a DVD for 20,000 DVDs is a total of $30,000, or $1.50 cost per DVD. Selling each unit for $11.50 means the filmmaker needs to sell only 3,000 DVDs to cover the costs. Compare these numbers to a traditional distribution deal in which the film is sold for $19.99, the retailer (e.g., Wal-Mart) traditionally takes 50 percent, or $10.00, the distributor then covers its costs (broadly defined in most distribution contracts) and then retains 50 percent to 75 percent, leaving the filmmaker with approximately $2.50 to $4.00 from each sale.

All the numbers provided so far are a best guesstimate, since it is generally difficult to find reliable numbers regarding the costs incurred by the relatively few independent films that have been self-distributed. *Filmmaker Magazine* did publish a useful article in its Summer 2002 and Spring 2003 issues in which it examined the self-distribution of the independent film entitled *The Debut*. The 2002 article is "Debut Performance" written by Justin Lowe and the 2003 follow-up article is "Self-Distribution Success." The filmmakers of *The Debut* engaged in a twenty-month, fifteen-city release of the film, which was described as a coming-of-age film of an eighteen-year-old Filipino American. It is reported that the production cost of the film was $1.2 million and the self-distribution approximately broke even, spending approximately $2.4 million in distribution costs and collecting approximately $2.4 million in revenue. Although the film began its theatrical run with weak home video offers from distributors, by the end of the theatrical run the filmmakers had accepted an offer for the home video rights from Columbia TriStar Home Entertainment, which reportedly eclipsed the other home video offers and reportedly offered a six figure minimum guarantee with additional 15 percent to 30 percent participation in net sales.

In an industry still ambivalent about its status as an artform or a business, the only fail-safe to a total dominance of business over art lies with new innovative and successful avenues of distribution for nonstudio films. The truly independent entrepreneurial filmmaker's path to success no longer stops with the completion of the film but includes personally running the gauntlet of distribution to reach an audience through traditional mediums such as a theatrical release and cutting-edge, new media outlets such as mobile devices and the Internet.

A more recent example of this path is the experience of the filmmakers of *Four Eyed Monsters*. This low-budget independent film (a reported budget of $100,000) debuted at Slamdance Film Festival in 2005. In spite of its positive critical and audience response, the filmmakers failed to receive any distribution offers for the film. They screened their film in over thirty film festivals over nine months, and they decided after the debut festival to begin a video blog depicting their experiences on the festival circuit. With the emergence of DVD, this "extra" footage is usually edited into a short "special feature" provided on the DVD of the film, or the basis of a "filmmaker's commentary" track on the DVD. The filmmakers of *Four Eyed Monsters*, however, decided to immediately edit the footage and post episodes on the Internet as "video podcasts." As is common for low-budget independent filmmakers, the *Four Eyed Monsters* team received feedback from the distributors who commented that they did not know how to market and sell the film because the film had no recognizable name actors and "no production value." The filmmakers decided to stop trying to prove to distributors that there was an audience for their film, and instead focused on creating an audience to whom they could directly sell it.

This is where their innovative, DIY (do-it-yourself) approach was fully implemented. They utilized their video blogs to quickly gather thousands of "fans" of their episodes, which led to press coverage from established media outlets, which in turn helped expose their film to more "fans." They also began to get audio and video responses to the video podcasts, including requests from people who wanted to see the film. Most shrewdly, the filmmakers collected the contact information from these people (e.g., zip codes, emails), and utilized this information to determine where their audience was geographically located. They then seized an opportunity to include their film in a traveling film festival; based on the contact information they gathered from the podcast fans, they emailed advance invitations to people in the areas of each screening. Their screenings were met with an overwhelming audience turnout and response. From this experience the filmmakers determined that they had an audience for their film, so, with no hard resources, they decided to theatrically self-distribute their film. As mentioned above, traditional theaters expect a "four-walling" producer to advance between $5,000 and $10,000 per week for the space, so the theater owners were naturally not excited about "going into business" with the filmmakers by agreeing to a split of the theatrical revenue, regardless of the positive "audience data" the filmmakers provided (from their Internet efforts and the film festival run). Through persistence, the filmmakers convinced some operators to work with them, and they scheduled screenings on four consecutive Thursdays at 8 p.m. in six theaters—New York, Los Angeles, Boston, Chicago, Seattle, and San Francisco. According to the filmmakers, their theatrical self-distribution essentially broke even, but it also attracted the Sundance Channel, which led to a reported "$100,000 broadcast and DVD deal." They also parlayed their experiences into an opportunity to release their film online via YouTube. They released the entire film for free on YouTube and partnered with Spout.com for sponsorship revenue; for every person who joined spout.com (referencing their film), the filmmakers received one dollar. The sponsorship model reportedly generated multiple thousands of dollars for the filmmakers through the end of 2007, and the attention boosted healthy DVD and merchandising sales.

The makers of the film *I Am Not A Hipster* (2012) also decided to self-release their film after a successful screening in the "Next" section of the 2012 Sundance Film Festival. After Sundance the film screened at several film festivals around the country, after which they then decided to launch a Kickstarter campaign to release the film on their own. The Kickstarter campaign successfully closed in June 2012 after raising over $30,000, which was more than the stated goal amount. The filmmaker's distribution plan entailed an independent release of the film through select theaters, video-on-demand, and digital platforms, such as iTunes and others. The funds raised were allocated for local promotion of the film while it was screening in each city and for other delivery costs such as insurance, DVD and Blu-ray mastering and duplication, as well as for the creation of required digital masters. Any funds remaining were allocated for marketing and promotion. It is interesting to note that they raised approximately $5,500 from pledge amounts of $250 or more (one pledge of $1,000, four pledges of $500 and ten pledges of $250), but the remaining $25,000 was raised from pledges of $100 or less from approximately 700 backers.

Since the film depicts the independent art and music world of San Diego, the filmmakers reached out to many of the people involved in that community to contribute art, music, and talents to the film, in addition to the crowdfunding, marketing, and promotion of the film. For example, musical performances were offered as rewards in the crowdfunding campaign and were also provided at many of the live screenings of the film. The fictional band in the movie, Canines, also created a "real" album that was sold individually. The band also contributed songs to the soundtrack of the film and contributed live performances at screenings and other events for the film.

The experiences of the makers of *Four Eyed Monsters* and *I Am Not A Hipster* are just two examples of what the dynamic and fluid nature of filmmaking and film marketing in the international digital world provides every filmmaker: the opportunity to exploit communication tools in ways limited only by the filmmaker's imagination. It is never an easy process, but control over that process and the ultimate ownership of the filmmaker's work are rewards previously unavailable to independent filmmakers. The balance of power is clearly shifting away from studios, conglomerates, and established distributors and to the independent filmmaker.

14

Distribution Contracts

"How terrible is wisdom if it brings no profit to the wise, Johnny."
—Angel Heart

There are a wide variety of "distribution contracts" that producers will encounter, but the most common type of distribution contracts that impact first-time filmmakers are standard license agreements which are entered into *after* the film has been completed. In the simplest terms, these contracts grant a distributor the right to exploit certain rights to a film for a limited period of time within a certain territory. As a point of reference, some of the other types of distribution agreements that exist include: a negative pick-up deal; a co-production deal with a distributor; licensing agreements for certain territories entered before preproduction and principal photography (presale agreements); production/finance/distribution agreements (usually entered with studios); and output agreements (agreements wherein a distributor guarantees to distribute a fixed number of the producer's films). Having little relevance for the first-time low-budget filmmaker, a detailed discussion of these contracts is outside of the parameters of this book. Books and articles dedicated solely to the legal aspects of film distribution agreements exist, and these resources can provide the filmmaker with supplemental information on independent film distribution contracts. These sources can assist the curious filmmaker in gaining a deeper understanding of the complex terminology used in these more esoteric contracts. These sources can give *understanding*, not *competence*. The single biggest error that any filmmaker can make is to attempt to negotiate and draft a distribution agreement with a distributor without the assistance of an attorney. These books and other resources provide valuable information for educating filmmakers and helping the filmmaker to better understand the issues, thereby enabling him or her to make more informed decisions about the terms of the distribution agreement *in consultation with* his or her attorney. However, the negotiation and redrafting of the language is best accomplished by an attorney experienced in film and television distribution contracts. This chapter is designed to provide independent filmmakers a basic understanding of the most relevant elements of film distribution agreements as they apply to their endeavor.

On the most basic level, the terms of standard film distribution agreements include: a) the name of the film; b) the term of the distribution agreement; c) the territory in which the distributor is authorized to distribute the film; d) the rights granted; e) any advance consideration or minimum guarantees to be paid the filmmaker; f) the distribution fee; g) the expenses to be deducted by the distributor; h) marketing and distribution obligations of the distributor and the filmmaker's rights to be involved in the process; i) right of the filmmaker to receive accounting statements and right to audit the distributor; j) representations and warranties of the filmmaker and the distributor; k) termination rights of the filmmaker (if any); and l) miscellaneous provisions including, but not limited to, where notices to be forwarded and the location where any disputes will be filed (i.e., court system or arbitration, what city, what state law will be applicable, etc.). These are broad categories that also have additional subsections covering many ancillary issues. What follows is a brief survey of some of the issues related to the terms of a distribution contract, of which the independent filmmaker should be aware.

TERM

The term distributors generally ask for ranges from between ten years and twenty-five years. A filmmaker would ideally like to limit the term to five years and often the distributor and filmmaker compromise on a term of seven years.

RIGHTS

Distributors generally ask for every conceivable right to exploit. The filmmaker should carefully examine the sales history of the distributor and offer the distributor only those license rights for which it has a successful track record of exploiting. For example, a distributor may have a very strong track record of DVD distribution while very few of its titles have been offered on video-on-demand or pay-per-view. The filmmaker should request to withhold these latter rights from that distributor; however, if the distributor insists on these rights then the filmmaker should be able to demand a higher percentage of the revenue from such rights. Although very few distributors have a track record of making money from digital delivery rights/new media rights, they will nevertheless demand them. The digital/new media rights include viewing on personal computers, wireless devices, mobile phones, personal digital assistants (PDAs), and similar devices. In addition to the digital/new media rights, the filmmaker should seek to retain other rights such as theatrical rights, music publishing rights, soundtrack album rights, sequel, prequel, remake rights, and all other derivative production rights (e.g., television programming) and merchandising rights (including video games and comic books). For a couple of reasons distributors are very reluctant to forgo any rights whatsoever. First, being unsure as to how the market will receive each film, the distributor will want to be prepared to exploit every possible avenue. Second, and perhaps more importantly, distributors gather all the rights to as many films as possible to create a library that it can exploit for many years into the future. Once the distributor creates a library it can then approach banks to obtain credit using the library as collateral, or as is sometimes the case, the distributor may become an acquisition target of a larger distributor enabling it to sell its holdings at a profit. The filmmaker's leverage becomes an important element in determining the outcome of the negotiation regarding these rights (i.e., the more in demand any one film is the more leverage the filmmaker of that film has and vice-versa).

ADVANCES AND MINIMUM GUARANTEES

For films that have a budget below $1 million it has become more difficult to secure an advance or minimum guarantee from a distributor, and even when the distributor will agree to an advance or minimum guarantee, the amounts offered have been declining. An advance or minimum guarantee is simply a sum of money the distributor gives to the filmmaker before the film generates revenue. Often these payments are made upon certain events. For example, if the minimum guarantee is $75,000, $7,500 might be payable upon execution of the distribution contract, $22,500 upon "full delivery" of the film, and $45,000 upon the initial release of the film. Filmmakers should insist on some amount of advance or minimum guarantee upon the execution of the agreement, even if it's a token amount of $10,000 or $20,000. The reason for this is that the advance money (or guarantee) very often is the only revenue the filmmaker will ever receive from the distributor. As a note, it is not uncommon for distributors to charge interest on these advances (usually 2 percent to 3 percent above the prime rate), charged from the time the money is advanced until it is repaid in full (that is from any revenue generated). The distributor will recoup these advances plus interest as expenses deducted from revenue payments due the filmmaker.

DISTRIBUTION FEE

The amount of the distributor's fee generally varies according to the specific circumstances of the filmmaker. Does the filmmaker have more than one offer for the film? What is the level of desire by the distributor? Has the film been screened at any film festivals? Which ones? Has it won any awards? What is the commitment (if any) of the distributor to support the release of the film with a guaranteed amount of advertising funds? Is the filmmaker providing any funds to support the release? In which type of media will the film be released (i.e., different fee for theatrical, home video, video-on-demand, etc.)? In which territory will the film be released? For example, a theatrical distributor will usually take a 30 to 40 percent distribution fee but if the filmmaker is also providing funds for the prints and advertising to support the release of the film, then the distributors fee would be negotiated down, perhaps as low as 20 percent.

Although not to be taken as applicable to a specific deal, the fees for the following rights are not uncommon in a distribution deal between a filmmaker and a single distributor: Home Video (Net Deal), 50 percent distribution fee; Video-On-Demand, Pay-Per-View and Digital Delivery, 70 percent distribution fee (Royalty Deal); Free Television, 80 percent distribution fee (Royalty Deal). Distribution fees are subject to either "net deals" or "royalty" deals. The distribution fee as a royalty fee is generally higher for the distributor, as much as 75–80 percent. The difference between a net deal and a royalty deal is that under a net deal the distributor deducts all expenses incurred by the distributor related to the distribution of a film, and then the filmmaker and distributor split the amount remaining after the deduction of such costs (usually on a 50/50 basis or a 60/40 basis with the distributor taking the larger amount). On the other hand if the filmmaker receives a "royalty" deal then the filmmaker receives a percentage of the "gross" receipts from the film regardless of the expenses. Naturally, whether a net deal or a royalty deal is better for the filmmaker generally depends on the performance of the film in the market, which is obviously an unknown at the time of the negotiation and signing of the distribution deal. An experienced independent film entertainment attorney or an experienced producer's representative can help guide the filmmaker in exploring a more "educated guess" as to which type of deal would be better for which types of media.

A rule of thumb for home video (DVD/Blu-ray) is that if the film is projected to sell many units and/or generate a large amount of rentals then it is better to have a net deal, and vice versa. It is generally believed that a film would need to sell more than 50,000 to 75,000 DVD/Blu-ray units for a net deal to be more advantageous than a royalty deal. Because distributors receive a much smaller share of the DVD/Blu-ray rental pie, the film must be an even better performer in rentals for a net deal to be better than a royalty deal. Some distributors take the model one step further and hybrid the net deal and royalty deal by offering the filmmaker a royalty deal (with its lower filmmaker percentage of gross receipts) and then, as in a net deal, deducting many, if not all, of the costs from the amount the filmmaker is to receive. This is clearly not a preferred deal but it is often contemplated by the filmmaker as a last resort after all of the other distributors have declined to distribute the film and self-distribution is not a realistic option. Even so, some filmmakers decide to shelve their film rather than "give away" the film to a distributor under these terms. Not an easy decision to make.

EXPENSES

In either a net deal or a hybrid royalty deal the distributor deducts all third party, out-of-pocket expenses incurred in the distribution of the film. Caps on the aggregate amount of expenses that a distributor can expend to distribute the film should be negotiated and included in any distribution agreement, if possible. This cap can be stated as a total, "all-in" amount, that is, a sum certain for all costs or it can be limited by specific categories of expenses. For example: the expenses for the DVD authoring can be no less than $7,500 and no more than $15,000; the expenses for the DVD packaging design and printing can be no less than $10,000 and no more than $15,000; the publicity expenses can be no more than $20,000; and so on. It is also standard for the distributors to claim the express right to "cross-collateralize" all rights with all territories. What this means, for example, is if the distribution of the home video rights in the United States incurs unusually large expenses, then some part (usually all) of these expenses can be deducted against revenues generated in Canada for video-on-demand; and so on across all of the rights and all of the territories. One of the biggest deductions that a distributor deducts from a filmmaker's gross receipts is costs incurred when DVDs are returned from retailers because the DVDs did not sell. It is a good idea for the filmmaker to have the distributor agree to language that would require the distributor to secure orders in such a manner so as to minimize the possibility of returned DVDs. This can be accomplished by agreeing to a maximum number of DVD units that will be shipped in the first six months after the release of the film with a provision for more to be shipped if requested by retailers, or some other similar provisions.

MARKETING AND DISTRIBUTION OBLIGATIONS

Marketing and distribution obligations of the distributor vary from film to film. At the very least the filmmaker should obtain a written guarantee in the contract that the distributor will release the film within a certain period of time, such as within nine months from the date the filmmaker completes delivery of the film. The contract should provide for termination of the contract and the return of the film to the filmmaker if the distributor fails to abide by the release requirement. However, the filmmaker should remain aware that the contract will usually provide that all advance money or minimum guarantee money the distributor has provided the filmmaker would have to be returned if such a step were to be taken. In addition, it is common for all of the expenses incurred for the film as of the date of the distributor's failure to distribute the film might have to be reimbursed to the distributor. Of course, depending on the filmmaker's leverage in the deal, these provisions can be negotiated to the filmmaker's better advantage. In reality, it is very rare for a distributor to commit to expending money in the distribution of a film, especially if it is a nontheatrical release. The film-maker should at least have the distributor agree to exert its "best efforts" in the marketing and distribution of the film.

THE FILMMAKER'S RIGHT TO BE INVOLVED IN THE PROCESS

Any rights the filmmaker may have to be involved in the process are generally very minimal.

It is true that it is common for the filmmaker to be granted "meaningful consultation" regarding the marketing, distribution, or other exploitations of the rights of the film, but the distributor usually retains absolute control over the marketing, distribution, or other exploitations of the film's rights. The "meaningful consultation" language can be very difficult to enforce, and in practice the distributor's decisions regarding any such matters are usually conclusive and binding upon the filmmaker.

ACCOUNTING STATEMENTS AND THE RIGHT TO AUDIT

Distributors usually include a standard provision in the contract giving the filmmaker the right to receive regular accounting statements as well as the right to an audit of the distributor's books. This language hardly ever produces the fail-safe protection it promises, and it is hard not to be cynical about these "rights." The statements that filmmakers receive usually reveal very little information about the financial exploitation of the film. From a realistic standpoint, the audit rights the filmmaker gets to exercise are very expensive in time and money and rarely produce tangible results. However, they become useful in the case of a legal proceeding; having these rights and exercising them can be important in demonstrating to a judge or arbitrator that the filmmaker is a reasonable person who exercised reasonable judgment and had no choice but to ultimately file an arbitration claim or file a lawsuit.

TERMINATION

The right to terminate a contract under certain circumstances is a very powerful tool a filmmaker can use to protect his or her film, which is by the way the very reason that distributors are very reluctant to agree to such clauses. Distributing a film is a two-way risk—a risk for the distributor because the distributor expends money in the process of getting a film to market, and a risk for the filmmaker who is surrendering the rights of his or her film for a period of five to twenty-five years. It is a fact that most independent films do not make a profit or even cover distribution costs. That is why, as mentioned above in the section concerning the rights to a film, distributors gather the rights to as many films as possible to create a library that may be exploited for years. As also mentioned above, a library increases borrowing potential for a distributor as well as the potential of being bought out. From the filmmaker's point of view it is not unreasonable to include a termination provision in the distribution contract based upon a minimum amount of money the filmmaker must receive from the distributor from the exploitation of the film. For example, the contract can state that if the filmmaker has not received more than an agreed upon amount of revenue from the distributor within two years of release (for example, $20,000, or $100,000 or $500,000, depending on the film), then the distribution agreement is terminated and all rights revert to the filmmaker. Distributors generally never agree to such a provision, but a rejection of such a provision by a distributor should make the filmmaker wary as to whether to give his or her film to a distributor who does not have confidence that the film will meet even a low revenue benchmark.

There are other provisions that can lead to termination that may be more acceptable to distributors, including: if the distributor defaults on any obligation in the distribution contract and the distributor doesn't cure such default within a certain time period after the filmmaker alerts the distributor to such default; or if the distributor becomes insolvent or fails to pay its debts when due; or if the distributor commits any act of insolvency; or if the distributor or any third party files for bankruptcy, reorganization, or insolvency; or if the distributor fails to carry on business for any reason. An example of the usefulness of the latter provisions is evident in a producer's lawsuit that was filed against the distributor of the film *The Pearl*. The lawsuit alleged that the distributor, Maya Entertainment Group, Inc., advised the producer of Maya's inability to pay its debts as they came due. The producer thereby sought to terminate the distribution agreement and regain all of the rights to the film based on agreed terms that the "Licensor (producer) shall be entitled to terminate the contract in the event the distributor (Maya Entertainment Group) shall become insolvent howsoever evidenced, or admit in writing its inability to pay its debt as they become due." The latter is in contrast to the experiences of independent filmmaker Vincent Rocca, which are chronicled in his blog regarding the making of his independent film, *Kisses and Caroms*. He chronicles his struggle to receive money that his film had earned and to regain the rights to his film when his distributor declared bankruptcy. All of the distributor's assets (including Mr. Rocca's film) became tied up in bankruptcy court and out of the reach of Mr. Rocca, the independent filmmaker.

In the final analysis, the first-time low-budget independent filmmaker will have to face the reality that his or her bargaining leverage is not very substantial, which is why self-distribution should be recognized as a potential in the original budget of any independent feature film project. Finally, although not desirable, the filmmaker may decide to just keep the film on the shelf, hoping that, although unlikely, an opportunity for its release may arise sometime in the future.

15

Preparing for Distribution

"There is a fine line between winning and losing.
Yeah, the finish line." —Let It Ride

THE CHALLENGE TO ACHIEVE DISTRIBUTION

Every independent filmmaker should enter the filmmaking process with the clear understanding that there are far more films made each year than there are opportunities available for distribution through established distributors, a truth which makes the chance of achieving distribution very slim. There are no accurate numbers as to how many independent films are completed and seeking distribution each year. But to put the number in perspective it should be noted that Sundance receives roughly 3,700 to 4,000 domestic feature films each year under the proviso that re-application is prohibited. Add to that number all the films that never apply to Sundance, and one begins to get the picture. The competition is even tougher for films with a budget of $1 million and below because these films are competing for distribution with films that cost much more money, which, therefore, are more attractive to distributors. More money buys name talent, action scenes, special effects and other production values considered indispensable to traditional distributors.

Making an independent film is always risky and the best advice when it comes to distribution is to avoid becoming emotional about the process. Instead, the filmmaker should set an agenda, follow the agenda methodically, and hope for the best. Each film will have its own unique path to distribution, but every film must clear the same exact obstacles. Perhaps the biggest misstep a filmmaker can make is to show the film to anyone before the film is fully completed. This is a key step in successful distribution so I will repeat it: don't show the film to anyone until it is as much of a polished product as possible. This may appear to be an obvious observation, but the truth is that most first-time filmmakers rush the postproduction of their film. There are several common reasons for this, such as the desire to meet film festival deadlines, or to get the film to a distributor before the commencement of a major market such as AFM or Cannes, or because they simply run out of money, or because the filmmaker becomes exhausted toward the end of a very long process which may have taken several years of very difficult work. It is better for the film's prospects of screening at a festival or obtaining distribution that it be as polished as it can possibly be, with all flaws smoothed out as much as possible.

For example, it is always best to wait for the composer to finish scoring the movie—avoid using temporary music tracks; it is also always best to have the post-house do a full color correction—not done by eye with the editor at the computer upon which the film was edited; and it is always best to clean up all of the dialogue completely and have all of the tracks properly mixed by a professional sound person. It is even a good idea to wait until more money can be raised in order to reshoot scenes that might be killing the film, or even to shoot new scenes that the film might need to make it work. Some reject this philosophy, arguing that it increases the risk of the film never reaching "completion." This is all too true, waiting does increase the risk of not finishing the film. But the goal is to not merely "complete" a feature film; the goal is to maximize the impact of the finished film. In the balance of risks and rewards it is better to maximize the possibility of having a film that can lead to rewards such as festival screenings, distribution and revenue, than to maximize the probability of merely finishing a flawed film. Of course, the lack of funds often dictates the path an independent film will follow at this point in the process. The point here is that filmmakers should not be anxious to get through postproduction in order to get the film to the market. There are voices in the process (producer's representatives, sales agents, festivals, the filmmaker's friends and family) who will tell the filmmaker that the film will be "stale" if it is not brought to the market immediately. Of course, the determination of whether that is true or not depends on the circumstances, but if getting the film out means it is not the best film you could possibly present, then it would be a mistake to rush.

FILM FESTIVALS

Once the film is completed the filmmaker must decide whether to apply to film festivals or go directly to distributors in search of a distribution deal. The answer depends on the type of film that the filmmaker has created, how much money the filmmaker has at his or her disposal, how much time the filmmaker has to devote to the process, and the specific goals of the filmmaker. It is recommended that the filmmaker, especially the first-time low-budget filmmaker, plan to have enough funds to fully explore the film festival circuit—*such funding should be a line item in the original budget.* The filmmaker should apply to as many festivals as his or her finances allow (the application fee for each festival is approximately $25 and higher), and should attend every festival into which it is accepted, regardless of whether his or her film is the type of film that is traditionally screened at a particular festival, or what the filmmaker believes are his or her goals with the film, or the time the filmmaker believes he or she has to devote to the film festival circuit, or the so-called prestige of the film festival.

Two primary advantages are gained by methodically applying and attending film festivals. First, films that screen at festivals and win awards are looked upon more favorably by distributors. This is because the film has gained an additional marketing "hook" from third-party validation (the festival screenings). This "hook" is enhanced further if the film is fortunate enough to also win awards at the festivals. Second, and more importantly, the filmmaker will meet other people at the festivals, those will be the relationships upon which the filmmaker will depend in the process of developing his or her career. The filmmaker should not operate under the illusion of "get into Sundance, sell my film, fly directly past 'Go,' and acquire fortune and fame." Does this happen? Not so much anymore. Are some films acquired at the top two or three film festivals? Yes, some are acquired, but the percentage of films this happens to is approximately equal to the percentage chance of winning the lottery, so if instant fame and fortune are the goals, then buying lottery tickets is a better bet than making an independent film. This should not lead to an attitude of "why bother?" Filmmakers definitely should submit their film to the top festivals like Sundance, Toronto, Cannes, Berlin, SXSW, Slamdance, Cinequest, and others.

Low-budget independent filmmakers should note that the 2010 Sundance Film Festival featured the addition of a new "Next" section dedicated to screening six to eight low-budget and "no budget" films. From 2010 to 2012 twenty-five low-budget and no budget films have screened in this section of the festival and it has been reported that approximately half of the films have utilized an established distributor for distribution, one self-distributed, and the remaining did not reach formal distribution. There are hundreds of film festivals in the United States and it is worth repeating that it is recommended to apply to as many as possible and to *attend them* if your film is screening. If resources are limited, it is best to research the festivals that the filmmaker believes will be most receptive to the film, such as festivals in his or her home state or festivals that cater to particular types of films.

PRODUCER REPRESENTATION

The question frequently arises as to whether or not the filmmaker should engage the services of a producer's representative. A "producer's rep" is a person who represents the film for sale or license by approaching distributors who might be seeking acquisition of the rights to the film. Does a film need a producer's rep? No. Many films have been licensed to distributors directly by the producers of the film, even by first-time filmmakers. However, filmmakers may want to engage the services of a producer's rep depending on their circumstances and goals. Producer's reps generally approach domestic distributors for sale or license of the domestic rights of the film. Resources such as the last edition of the Hollywood Distribution Directory and other directories found on the Internet that provide the companies that are in the business of distributing films are available to facilitate a filmmaker's direct approach to a distributor without the services of a producer's rep; however, producer's reps make the case that their relationships with distributors will have a positive effect on the way in which distributors will view the film he or she is representing. There is some truth in this view; however, the reality is that the process of distribution is a business, and established distributors do not knowingly make decisions that will cause them to lose the opportunity to make money. Their distribution decisions (such as which film to acquire, how much to acquire it for, how much financial support to place behind a film, etc.) are based upon the facts associated with each film, that is, what is the genre of the film, what is the "production value" on screen, who are the "name" actors in the film, who is the target audience, will they be able to reach the target audience in a cost-effective manner, etc. These facts will be evident from the film itself and it won't matter whether the filmmaker presents the film to the distributor or a producer's rep presents it or if the filmmaker's Mom presents it to distributors for that matter. Producer's reps also make the case that they will guarantee that the film will actually be viewed, implying that if the filmmaker or anyone else submits the film the distributor won't even view it. Again this is a questionable assumption. It has been my experience that distributors will generally watch a film regardless of who submits it. However, what *will* induce a distributor to immediately watch a film, or drop it on a whole pile of films already seeking distribution, will be the answers to the same questions: What is the genre of the film? What is its perceived "production value"? Who are the "name" actors in the film? etc. There are situations where a producer's rep could be extremely useful, such as when a film has been accepted to screen at the Sundance Film Festival or the Toronto Film Festival or other similar high-profile festivals. If a particular film is already determined to be commercially marketable, then an experienced producer's rep can help guide the screening and marketing of the film as well as facilitate the interaction between the filmmaker and the potential distributors at these film festivals. Generally speaking, it will become apparent if a film is determined to be marketable by virtue of the fact that producer's reps will approach the filmmaker almost immediately after it is announced that the film will be screening at one of these festivals.

Producer's reps generally require a signed contract engaging their services. These agreements generally state that the producer's rep will have the *exclusive* right to provide representation for a certain period of time, usually between one and two years. Exclusive means exclusive. If it turns out that the filmmaker is not happy with the rep chosen, he or she will be stuck with that person until the expiration date of the agreement, which simply means that someone else cannot legally be hired to bring the film to distributors during the term of the agreement. Most producer's rep contracts will provide that they receive a percentage of any and all gross sale or license fees received from the distribution of the film. Many of these agreements also state that the producer's rep is entitled to his or her fee if the filmmaker *ever* makes a future deal with any company, entity, or person that the original producer's rep may have contacted regarding the film, even if such deal is made after the contract expiration date. This provision can be limited by reducing the time frame (i.e., less than *forever*) so that the filmmaker will only be responsible for the original producer's rep's fee if that original rep makes a deal during the term of the agreement, and not if the filmmaker (or a subsequent producer's rep) makes a deal after the expiration of the agreement with the original producer rep. Of course, a filmmaker should be prepared to discover that a producer's rep will have contacted every relevant distributor regarding the film whether by mail, email, or phone during the exclusive period of representation. So that, in all probability, even if a subsequent rep produces a sale or license, thereby earning a fee, the first rep will be on line to collect his or her fee as well. The same would also hold true even if the filmmaker makes a deal directly with a distributor. Each producer's rep may also expect reimbursement of certain expenses incurred in the process of representing the film to distributors. These expenses include phone calls, messenger costs, mailing costs, copying costs, film festival expenses, screening expenses, etc. However, such expenses can be kept to a minimum if a clause is placed in the contract requiring the rep to secure prior written approval from the filmmaker for any expenditure in excess of fifty dollars.

Some producer's reps are attorneys, but many are not. If a distributor is interested in acquiring the film, then either the producer's rep or the filmmaker's lawyer will need to negotiate and redraft any distribution contract. An entertainment lawyer experienced with film distribution contracts can easily provide these services. Although they are generally not lawyers, producer's reps will often engage in the negotiation and redrafting of distribution contracts, usually because they have had years of experience with these contracts. If the filmmaker has chosen a producer's rep who is not an attorney, then the filmmaker will need to decide whether to incur the extra cost of hiring an attorney to provide this legal work or whether the filmmaker is comfortable with a nonlawyer producer's rep negotiating and redrafting the contract. Given the myriad of complex issues that could arise, as well as the potential for conflict of interests, it is wisest for the filmmaker to hire an attorney who has experience with distribution contracts.

FOREIGN SALES AGENTS

A foreign sales agent (or "sales agent") is a person or entity that represents the nondomestic rights of a film (i.e., generally all rights except North America). Some producer's reps described in the section above may also act as foreign sales agents and therefore represent the "worldwide rights" to a film. However, more commonly producer's reps focus on the domestic sales or licenses and a foreign sales agent focuses on sales or licenses to the rest of the world. One of the reasons for this division is the demand for extensive travel and increased expense involved in international marketing. Selling the foreign rights to a film requires attending the major festivals and markets throughout the world each year. Foreign sales agents must meet with film buyers around the world in order to remain current with market expectations, that is, what the world buyers are looking to acquire. Since each nation, region, or culture has its own unique view of film content, the sales agent must create personal relationships with buyers from around the world in order to maintain access to these markets. Personal relationships are based on face-to-face contact, so a minimum physical presence is required in these markets to make sales.

Foreign sales agents representing independent films will sign on and represent numerous films of many varieties because sales agents must be in the position to meet a buyer's needs immediately no matter how esoteric.

If the foreign sales agent waits to find out what the buyer wants, then tries to locate and acquire the proper film, and then return to the buyer to make the sale, the buyer will have had their needs met by some other seller or may have already moved on to seek a different type of film. Another reason why foreign sales agents handle many films at one time is because of the necessity for extensive travel and attendance at major film festivals and markets, which produces significant fixed costs and thus motivates agents to maximize potential revenue generated in relation to such fixed costs. Put another way, a foreign sales agent could be selling pretty much any product, rugs for example, it just so happens they are selling films. When film buyers walk in to a sales agent's "store" at festivals and markets around the world, the sales agent wants to be able to pull out a "green and red shag, size eleven by thirteen" rug if that is what the buyer is looking for, or a different color, texture, or size rug if requested by a buyer, and so on. This requires a substantial inventory.

Independent filmmakers understandably view the process of film sales in the worldwide market from a negative perspective. However, whether or not the licensing or selling of independent films in the international market is "fair" or "equitable" for individual producers and filmmakers is irrelevant, since it is highly unlikely that any one producer or filmmaker will be in a position to circumvent the current system. It is simply not cost effective or practical for an individual producer or filmmaker to personally license or sell his or her film in the international market. The skills and the inordinate amount of time, energy, and money required are beyond the realm of possibility for the independent filmmaker. There are stories of individual producers and filmmakers who buck these odds, set up "shop" at the Cannes Film Festival (or other such festival/market), and end up licensing his or her individual film. These stories are great to hear and they help sell movie periodicals, but they can be more appropriately characterized as the exceptions to the rule.

If a filmmaker should decide to utilize the services of a foreign sales agent there are a few standard aspects of the relationship with which the filmmaker should be aware. These aspects include: the "packaging" of films when licensing/selling to the foreign market; the apportionment of fixed costs among the many films the foreign sales agent represents; the cost prohibitive nature of utilizing foreign legal systems to collect money owed to the filmmaker; and the length of the term of the foreign licensing agreements (which is not the same thing as the term of the filmmaker's agreement with the foreign sales agent). There are some common aspects between foreign sales agency licensing agreements and domestic licensing agreements which will be addressed later in this chapter.

A closer look at the "aspects" mentioned above can be very instructive. To begin, as previously mentioned, foreign sales agents gather many films for representation to foreign buyers. As a result, the practice of licensing a "package" of films to each buyer in each territory has evolved. Each "package" contains a collection of various types of films for each territory, and each "package" is accompanied by one lump sum license fee for the territory. Like the sorting function of any wholesale distribution system, the foreign sales agent assigns a license fee to each individual film within the "package." From the point of view of the producers/filmmakers, the license fee assigned to their film seems arbitrary—and by and large it is arbitrary. The filmmaker could demand that the foreign sales agency agreement include a "nonpackaging" clause, but the result will most likely be that the foreign sales agent will simply decline to represent the film in the international market. The producers/filmmakers perceive the foreign sales agent's refusal to represent a film that won't be "packaged" as proof that the foreign sales agent entertains dishonorable business intentions. This is understandable, and mimics the view of the general public of wholesalers and intermediaries in general. But the point of view of the foreign sales agent is that since foreign buyers want to license a "package" of films, any individual film outside a "package" will not be licensed and a waste of everyone's time and money. It should be pointed out that higher budget, higher profile films may be an exception to this rule (i.e., may be licensed or sold individually to each territory), but most first-time filmmakers are not producing higher budgeted, higher profile films so they should not expect that they will be in a position to find an experienced, successful foreign sales agent willing to peddle their film on an individual basis.

The issue of "packaging" is often addressed in the sales agent agreement by the inclusion of certain language. This can be accomplished in a couple of ways. First, the filmmaker and the sales agent can agree that the film will be licensed for no less than a certain percentage of the total licensing fee obtained for the entire "package" in a given territory. Second, and more often, it can be dealt with by attaching a schedule of "minimums" to the sales agency agreement, which basically creates a floor for the amount that the filmmaker will accept for each territory to which his or her film is licensed. The schedule of minimums would be similar to the one below (Note: these numbers are not to be relied upon but are for demonstration purposes only):

TERRITORY	LOW	HIGH
	USD	USD
EUROPE		
France	$25,000	$75,000
Germany/Austria	$25,000	$80,000
Greece	$5,000	$10,000
Italy	$25,000	$60,000
Benelux (Belgium, Netherlands, Luxembourg)	$15,000	$50,000
Portugal	$5,000	$15,000
Scandinavia	$15,000	$35,000
Spain	$20,000	$75,000
United Kingdom	$25,000	$60,000
TOTAL	**$160,000**	**$460,000**
ASIA/PACIFIC RIM		
Australia/New Zealand	$10,000	$25,000
Hong Kong	$8,000	$15,000
Indonesia	$5,000	$10,000
Japan	$15,000	$45,000
Malaysia	$5,000	$10,000
Philippines	$5,000	$15,000
Singapore	$5,000	$15,000

South Korea	$10,000	$30,000
Taiwan	$15,000	$40,000
TOTAL	**$78,000**	**$205,000**
LATIN AMERICA		
Argentina/Paraguay/Uruguay	$2,000	$5,000
Bolivia/Ecuador/Peru	$1,000	$5,000
Brazil	$10,000	$15,000
Chile	$2,000	$5,000
Columbia	$2,000	$5,000
Mexico	$15,000	$25,000
Venezuela	$2,000	$4,000
TOTAL	**$34,000**	**$64,000**
EASTERN EUROPE & OTHER TERRITORIES		
Czech Republic/Slovakia	$5,000	$10,000
Former Yugoslavia	$2,000	$4,000
Hungary	$5,000	$15,000
Poland	$5,000	$10,000
Russia	$5,000	$15,000
China	$8,000	$15,000
India	$5,000	$12,500
Israel	$5,000	$15,000
Middle East	$5,000	$12,500
South Africa	$8,000	$15,000
Turkey	$10,000	$20,000
TOTAL	**$63,000**	**$144,000**
TOTALS ALL TERRITORIES	**$335,000**	**$873,000**

According to the above table if a filmmaker's film is packaged with other films in Italy, and the agency agreement has the "schedule of minimums," then the least amount that the filmmaker can receive from the licensing fee paid for the whole package is $25,000. Foreign sales agents will often add language to the contract stipulating that the foreign sales agent will first seek the filmmaker's approval if there is to be a license or sale below the "low" price on the schedule of minimums for any territory, with the further proviso that the filmmaker's approval of all such "low" offers is not to be unreasonably withheld. At some point in the process, maybe even on the first deal, the foreign sales agent will contact the filmmaker and inform him or her that a particular territory is offering below the "low" amount stipulated for that territory in the above schedule. This places the filmmaker in a difficult position since if he or she rejects the offer the foreign sales agent may either inform the filmmaker that they have no deal at all or invoke the "unreasonably withheld" clause and argue a breach of contract. On the other hand, if the filmmaker accepts the lower offer, then a precedent has been set implying that the filmmaker will accept less money than the minimum in future deals in any other territory. As one may expect, the filmmaker will receive frequent future contacts from the foreign sales agent with lower offers from the other territories in which the film is being marketed. These are always difficult decisions and can only be resolved in the context of each individual circumstance. The numbers set down in any schedule of minimums should not be viewed as those that will be attained by the agent; in fact, there is usually language in the sales agency contract specifically disclaiming any such conclusions or guarantees. The numbers should only be viewed as a formal way of dealing with the "packaging" of independent films for licensing in the international market.

In addition to being concerned about losing potential licensing revenue, filmmakers need to keep a close grasp on the expenses. The apportionment of ancillary cost incurred by the foreign sales agent is another complex, negotiable issue for a filmmaker to comprehend. On its surface, this would seem to be a fairly straightforward issue since foreign sales agents should only charge a filmmaker the actual, verifiable third-party costs incurred in the course of their licensing activities. However, the issue is more complicated because the foreign sales agent represents many films at the same time, and travels to festivals all over the world in marketing those films. Agents can be expected to put money out of pocket for such things as festival and film market costs (booth rentals, market entry fees, shipping, air travel, ground transportation, meals, lodging, etc.), as well as corporate advertising, posters, brochures, public relations, market screenings, legal costs associated with the licensing/sales of films, staff costs, overhead costs, costs associated with the administration of sales/licensing agreements, etc. The problem is that it is virtually impossible for the agent to accurately apportion each of these costs to each specific film in the package, and can only approximate the apportionment of the costs to each film. Unless a third party has access to all of the books and records of a distributor, it is impossible to determine whether the apportionment was accurate and fair, or even if the total amount of costs apportioned to all of the films was equal to or greater than the actual dollars spent by the agent. Of course, it is clear that these costs are generally fixed costs whether the sales agent is representing 20, 30, 40, or 100 films in the foreign market. (As a note, the only real limitation on the number of films a distributor can carry at one time is the number of filmmakers who can provide all of the "Delivery Items" required to sell or license films. "Delivery Items" will be addressed below). To address this situation it is often more cost effective to have the foreign sales agent agree to a flat fee deduction for any and all costs incurred for the entire term of the agreement. This so-called all-in number will vary from film to film; so the filmmaker would be wise to rely on the advice of his or her legal counsel and/or his or her domestic producer's rep in determining this amount. These team members should have enough experience to know what the norms might be for a particular film in the international market.

Another issue that frequently arises regarding foreign sales agents is the extreme difficulty in tracking and collecting money that might be owed to the filmmaker from the sales or licensing of a film. It is well worth the protection if a filmmaker can get a foreign sales agent to agree to utilize a collection account—most agents will resist these agreements because of the associated administrative efforts and costs. A collection account is a bank account that is established and governed by a separate agreement signed by the filmmaker and the sales agent creating a distinct bank account solely for the collection and disbursement of funds relating to a specific film. No other funds are allowed to be commingled with the monies deposited in a separate collection account, and monies are disbursed from the collection account solely in accordance with the terms of a collection account agreement, which must be consistent with the terms of the separate distribution agreement entered into between the filmmaker and the sales agent. The parties designate a neutral third-party company as the sole party authorized to manage the collection account and disburse funds. The neutral third-party company will of course charge a fee for these services. There is usually an up-front fee of between $5,000 and $15,000 in addition to a percentage of the gross receipts from the film—usually 1 or 2 percent.

The length of the term of a foreign sales agent agreement, and the length of the term that the foreign sales agent is authorized to license the film to distributors in different territories throughout the world are further items subject to explicit agreement. The length of agreement with a foreign sales agent is between five and ten years. The term of licensing authorization is stipulated by separate language within the sales agency contract and allows the foreign sales agent to enter into sale/licensing agreements with third parties in each territory for a period that can be as long as twenty-five years, well beyond the term for the agency agreement itself. This is another reason why it is important to have a collection account established which would require any third-party foreign buyers or licensees to send payments directly to the collection account. In the absence of a special collection account, any funds generated past the five to ten year term become very difficult to collect once they are pocketed by the foreign sales agent. It is also not uncommon for the foreign sales agent company to go out of business leaving third party distributors with no place to send any funds owed to the filmmaker. For all of these reasons, the filmmaker or his or her representative should make every possible effort to overcome an agent's resistance to the establishment of a special collection account.

SUMMARY OF DELIVERY ITEMS

Delivery of the items required by a distributor in order to receive and accept a distribution offer is as challenging, if not more challenging, than the process of making the movie itself. Any of the issues that were not addressed or were addressed incorrectly during the formation, preproduction, production, and postproduction phases must be addressed before a film will be accepted and released by a distributor. One of the primary reasons it is so important to engage the services of an experienced unit production manager, a producer, and an entertainment attorney early in the process is that your "team" will know what each member must actively acquire and document throughout the process, so that when the filmmaker reaches the phase of acceptance of the distribution offer, providing the delivery requirements for the film will not be insurmountable.

There are many stories of films that received distribution offers but were unable to meet the delivery requirements with the result that the films were never released. Many independent filmmakers neither address delivery issues at each step in making the film nor provide funding for such issues in the original budget for the film. As a result, at the end of the process of making a film no money is available to secure the delivery items required in a distribution contract if one is offered. Even if there is money, the process of securing delivery items after the film has been completed is much more expensive than if the work had been properly completed during the making of the film. More often than not the people who were involved in making the film have moved on to other jobs, and perhaps the filmmaker cannot track down a certain person who appeared in a small role in the film or as an extra in the film. Or, for example, the owner of the rights to a picture that appears in the film cannot be reached, which leaves the filmmaker in the position of not being able to secure the necessary rights at all. Sometimes parties are tracked down, but recognizing their increased position of leverage over the film and the filmmaker, demand payment or other compensation in amounts greater than what would otherwise have been paid if the rights were secured at an earlier, appropriate time. There are numerous items which, when neglected, can leave a completed film on the shelf indefinitely. Delivery items can be categorized in five major groups: a) Video/Film Elements; b) Ancillary Items; c) Legal Documentation; d) Insurance Documentation; and e) Other Documents.

Video/Film Elements. A movie shot on film is more expensive to deliver because there are additional elements the filmmaker will have to provide to a distributor. For a film these elements include: a composite 35 millimeter positive print; distributor access to the original 35 millimeter picture negative; optical soundtrack negative; access to the digital data files for main and end titles; and access to the original DAT digital audio files, with separate tracks for dialogue, music, and effects. Whether a movie is shot on film or video, the filmmaker will have to provide: one or two 16 x 9 High Definition video masters; one or two 4 x 3 High Definition video masters; one or two 1080i/29.97 High Definition video masters; Dolby 5.1 mixed audio master on DA 88; Dolby 5.1 music and effects audio master on DA 88; stereo mixed audio master on DA 88; stereo music and effects audio master on DA 88; music used in film on disc or hard drive; music cue sheet in PDF format; and a dialogue list with the timecode, the character, and dialogue.

Ancillary Items. There are ancillary items the filmmaker needs to provide to the distributor which are necessary in order to promote and distribute the film/video. These include: unit still photography (photography on the set and any special photos, in digital format); any photos that were rejected by talent who may have contractual rights to reject photos; all logos that are contractually required to be placed in the credits and/or billing; the electronic press kit; any and all DVD extras, including, but not limited to, interviews, behind the scenes featurettes, commentaries, music videos, and behind the scenes footage; final billing block for DVDs, posters, paid advertising, trailers (the billing block is the list of names of participants in the film and the job they did on the film); a full cast and crew list; summary of any and all obligations regarding credits, photos, dubbing, or editing; a synopsis; production notes; and press coverage.

Legal Documentation. Most of the legal items to be delivered should have already been completed by the time the distribution phase is reached. The items that will be required include: copies of all fully executed contracts regarding the services provided by all above-the-line and below-the-line persons (this is covered by the production legal attorney during preproduction, production, and postproduction); copies of all fully executed SAG-AFTRA contracts; copies of all fully executed agreements regarding the use of any product, copyrighted, trademarked, or any other material used in the production or exhibition of the film; copies of all fully executed agreements regarding any and all services provided in the making of bonus material for the film and any and all material incorporated in such bonus material; copies of all fully executed agreements regarding stock footage, photographs, or other material used in the film; chain of title documents including copies of all fully executed agreements regarding the acquisition of the underlying rights upon which the film is based (screenplay, literary, option/purchase, writer employment, etc.); a copy of the Copyright Registration for the screenplay and the completed motion picture; all transfer documents filed with the US Copyright Office regarding the underlying rights; a copyright report and title report (usually from a company such as Thompson & Thompson); a copy of the fully executed Dolby license (if applicable); copies of all music agreements; copy of certificate of authorship; and five to ten original, notarized certificates of origin (if required for the film).

Insurance Documentation. The filmmaker is required to provide an errors and omissions insurance policy usually covering not less than $1,000,000 for each claim and $3,000,000 aggregate for all claims, with a deductible no greater than $25,000, for a term of at least three years. In addition, the filmmaker is required to provide "additional insureds" certificates for the distributor, its affiliates, and subsidiaries.

Not every distributor requires all of the aforementioned delivery items. Each distributor has a unique set of requirements for delivery, but generally demands a core of elements which it deems necessary to bring a film to market with a sufficient level of confidence that the filmmaker has the rights to the product and the distributor is not exposed to an unacceptable level of potential litigation and judgments. Generally speaking, the specific elements to be delivered are not open to negotiation, but, depending on the distributor and the specific film, some items may be negotiable. A filmmaker should nevertheless be prepared to deliver just about every item covered in this chapter. Some items that may be negotiable include the number of still images to be delivered, the copyright research report, the MPAA rating, the final cost report, production files, accounting files, closed caption files and copies of all of the numerous signed legal contracts. Filmmakers also should not count on the distributor paying for the costs of delivery of the necessary items. It does happen on occasion that a distributor will provide an advance or "minimum guarantee" that will cover some or all of the costs of the items to be delivered, but this is more the exception than the rule. In the event that a distributor does provide an advance or minimum guarantee, it should be noted that the payment of these amounts is often deferred until the occurrence of certain events. As an example, 20 percent may be paid upon signing the distribution contract, 30 percent upon "complete delivery" of all delivery items and 50 percent upon the initial theatrical release (or for a straight to DVD release, upon the street date of the DVD). The bottom line is that even though the distributor may cover some of the costs, this is when credit cards become the facilitator with the plan to pay off balances upon the initial release of the film (see Chapter 5).

Other Documents. There are many other primary or supporting documents that distributors require for delivery which include: music cue sheets; final cast and crew list; MPAA rating; production documents (such as camera reports, call sheets, wrap reports, cast and crew contact lists); a dialogue, continuity and spotting list; final shooting script; a quality control (QC) report; laboratory access letter to any and all labs where work was done on the film; close captioning file; and all residual requirements for any and all applicable guilds such as SAG-AFTRA, DGA, WGA, IATSE.

COST OF DELIVERY

What the actual cost for delivery will be is a question filmmakers obviously need to know. It is best if the costs associated with delivery are included in the original budget so that this amount should be projected early in the process and accounted for in the funds initially raised to produce the film. The actual costs should be determined by the unit production manager/

line producer who creates the budget for the film. It is important to note that not only is each film different, but the costs of any item in the delivery list will fluctuate over time. Just as a point of reference, a movie shot on High Definition Video with 5.1 audio mix can cost between $20,000 and $50,000 just to deliver the video and audio elements. Films shot on 16 millimeter or 35 millimeter film can add an additional $15,000 to $35,000 to the latter numbers, raising the ante to $35,000 to $85,000. Other large expenditures include: the MPAA rating (approximately $7,000 to $10,000) and the quality control reports ($2,000 to $3,000 per tape) from the "Other Documents" category; copyright report ($500 to $1,500), title report ($750 to $1,500), and attorney fees to draft and deliver documents ($500 to $7,500) from the "Legal Documentation" category; and Errors and Omissions insurance ranging from $6,000 to $25,000 depending on the coverage terms and the risks associated with each individual film from the "Insurance Documentation" category. Viewed from any perspective the filmmaker should include between $30,000 and $100,000 in the initial budget to cover these delivery requirements.

CAREFUL REVIEW OF THE DELIVERY LANGUAGE

The delivery language in any distribution contract should also be carefully reviewed by the filmmaker and his/her legal representative. Any advance payment amounts or guaranteed minimums agreed to by the distributor are usually predicated upon "full delivery" of the delivery items. For example, it is standard that a filmmaker will need to deliver the "copyright certificates of registration with the United States Copyright Office" for the script and the film. Since the return of these certificates of registration usually takes six to nine months once the initial forms are filed with the United States Copyright Office, the filmmaker is forced into a situation where the film will not be considered "fully delivered" until the certificates are returned from the Copyright Office. This means that payment of any advances or minimum guarantees will not be turned over until the date of receipt of the certificates—this is just another of the catch-22 dilemmas that filmmakers face. However, a revision of this language could state, "For purposes of full delivery hereunder, any copyright certificate that has not yet been returned to the filmmaker may be satisfied by delivery of a copy of the completed copyright registration form, the cover letter to the appropriate copyright office, the registered mail receipt, and proof of payment of the required fees. Filmmaker agrees to deliver one copy of each and every certificate of registration when received by filmmaker."

Epilogue

It is not realistic to approach producing an independent feature film, low-budget or otherwise, with the view that it is possible to master and control all of the hundreds of issues that need to be addressed in the process. The best a filmmaker can hope to achieve is a basic understanding of the major issues which will enable him or her to have meaningful discussions with the project's team members, each of whom will have the detailed knowledge and experience in their respective profession. It is my hope that this book has contributed to this basic understanding by providing a framework for the major issues encountered in producing a low-budget feature film—at the least it should enable you to ask the right questions of attorneys and producers and anyone else you will need. As I mentioned at the outset, producing a low-budget feature film defies basic logic; however, history supports the conclusion that society's ability to embrace *that* logic is sustained by the individuals who challenge it. Make your movie, all the best.

Paul Battista

Appendix A

*List of Recommended Low-Budget Films to Watch
(Please Refer to Chapter 1, "Very Brief History of the
Independent Film")*

Aguirre, The Wrath of God (1972) (Director: Werner Herzog) (93 minutes)

The Bicycle Thief (1948) (Director: Vittorio De Sica) (93 minutes)

The Blair Witch Project (1999) (Dirs.: Daniel Myrick and Eduardo Sánchez) (86 minutes)

Blood, Guts, Bullets & Octane (1999) (Director: Joe Carnahan) (87 minutes)

Breathless (1960) (Director: Jean-Luc Goddard) (90 minutes)

Brothers McMullen (1994) (Director: Edward Burns) (98 minutes)

ChungKing Express (1995) (Director: Kar Wai Wong) (102 minutes)

Clerks (1994) (Director: Kevin Smith) (89 minutes)

Cube (1997) (Director: Vincenzo Natali) (90 minutes)

David Holzman's Diary (1967) (Director: Jim McBride) (74 minutes)

Detour (1946) (Director: Edgar G. Ulmer) (67 minutes)

The Driller Killer (1979) (Director: Abel Ferrara) (96 minutes)

El Mariachi (1993) (Director: Robert Rodriguez) (81 minutes)

Eraserhead (1977) (Director: David Lynch) (89 minutes)

The Evil Dead (1981) (Director: Sam Raimi) (85 minutes)

Four Eyed Monsters (2005) (Dirs.: Susan Buice and Arin Crumley) (85 minutes)

The 400 Blows (1959) (Director: François Truffaut) (97 minutes)

Go Fish (1994) (Director: Rose Trochet) (83 minutes)

Great Wall of Sound (2007) (Director: Craig Zobel) (106 minutes)

Hollywood Shuffle (1987) (Director: Robert Townsend) (78 minutes)

Hurricane Streets (1996) (Director: Morgan J. Freeman) (89 minutes)

Laws of Gravity (1992) (Director: Nick Gomez) (100 minutes)

Little Fugitive (1953) (Dirs.: Ray Ashley, Morris Engel and Ruth Orkin) (80 minutes)

The Natural History of Parking Lots (1990) (Director: Everett Lewis) (89 minutes)

Pi (1998) (Director: Darren Aronofsky) (85 minutes)

Pink Flamingos (1972) (Director: John Waters) (93 minutes)

Quiet City (2007) (Director: Aaron Katz) (78 minutes)

Return of the Secaucus Seven (1980) (Director: John Sayles) (110 minutes)

Rhythm Thief (1994) (Director: Matthew Harrison) (88 minutes)

Rome, Open City (1945) (Director: Roberto Rossellini) (100 minutes)

Shadows (1959) (Director: John Cassavetes) (81 minutes)

She's Gotta Have It (1986) (Director: Spike Lee) (84 minutes)

Slacker (1991) (Director: Richard Linklater) (97 minutes)

Spanking the Monkey (1994) (Director: David O. Russell) (99 minutes)

Stranger Than Paradise (1984) (Director: Jim Jarmusch) (90 minutes)

*Totally F***ed Up* (1993) (Director: Gregg Araki) (78 minutes)

The Unbelievable Truth (1990) (Director: Hal Hartley) (100 minutes)

Appendix B

Low-Budget Feature Film Sample Budget Top Sheet

Director: Name	Shoot:	18 days/6 day weeks	
Writers: Names	Location:	California	
Producers: Names	Union:	SAG-AFTRA, Non-DGA, Non-WGA	

Account #	Category		Total
3100	STORY RIGHTS		$ --
3200	WRITERS		$ --
3300	PRODUCERS		$ --
3400	DIRECTOR		$ --
3500	CAST		$ 39,000
3600	SUPPORTING CAST & STUNTS		$ 12,500
3900	SCENARIO MISCELLANEOUS		$ 1,400
4100	TRAVEL & LIVING		$ 1,500
	TOTAL ABOVE-THE-LINE		$ 54,400

4200	EXTRAS & STAND-INS	$ --
4300	PRODUCTION STAFF	$ 3,750
4400	WARDROBE	$ 16,750
4500	MAKE-UP & HAIRDRESSING	$ 6,300
4700	CAMERA	$ 22,500
4900	SET DRESSING	$ 2,500
5000	ACTION PROPS	$ 2,000
5100	ACTION PROPS-VEHICLES	$ 500
5300	SET DESIGNING	$ 4,350
5400	SET CONSTRUCTION	$ 4,000
5700	PRODUCTION SOUND	$ 6,900
5800	SET LIGHTING	$ 11,480
5900	SET OPERATION	$ 6,038
6300	LOCATIONS	$ 12,000
6400	TRANSPORTATION	$ 500
6500	CATERING	$ 7,000
6800	BELOW-THE-LINE LIVING & TRAVEL	$ 1,000
	TOTAL SHOOTING PERIOD	$ 107,568

7200	EDITING	$ 27,500
7300	TITLES	$ 2,500
7400	MUSIC	$ 7,565
7600	POSTPRODUCTION SOUND	$ 5,000
7700	DVD AUTHORING AND DUPLICATION	$ 3,500
	TOTAL POSTPRODUCTION PERIOD	$ 46,065

8500	INSURANCE/MEDICAL	$ 6,000
8700	PUBLICITY	$ 7,500
8800	PRODUCER'S REP	$ 2,500
	TOTAL OTHER	$ 16,000

9000	Organization and offering costs	$ 2,500
9100	Legal	$ 5,000
9200	Accounting	$ 2,500
	TOTAL ORGANIZATION COSTS, LEGAL & ACCT.	$ 10,000
	TOTAL CONTINGENCY	$ 8,482
	TOTAL BUDGET	$ 242,514
	TOTAL ABOVE-THE-LINE	$ 54,400
	TOTAL BELOW-THE-LINE	$ 169,633
	TOTAL ORGANIZATION COSTS, LEGAL & ACCT.	$ 10,000
	CONTINGENCY	$ 8,482
	TOTAL BUDGET	$ 242,514

Index

 **Books from Allworth Press**

Allworth Press is an imprint of Skyhorse Publishing, Inc. Selected titles are listed below.

Hollywood Dealmaking
By *Dina Appleton and Daniel Yankelevits* (6 x 9, 320 pages, paperback, $24.95)

The Filmmaker's Guide to Production Design
By *Vincent LoBrutto* (6 x 9, 240 pages, paperback, $19.95)

The Perfect Stage Crew
By *John Kaluta* (6 x 9, 256 pages, paperback, $19.95)

The Health and Safety Guide for Film, TV, and Theater, Second Edition
By *Monona Rossol* (6 x 9, 288 pages, paperback, $27.50)

Get the Picture? The Movie Lover's Guide to Watching Films, Second Edition
By *Jim Piper* (6 x 9, 336 pages, paperback, $24.95)

Fundamentals of Theatrical Design
By *Karen Brewster and Melissa Shafer* (6 x 9, 256 pages, paperback, $27.50)

Documentary Filmmakers Speak
By *Liz Stubbs* (6 x 9, 256 pages, paperback, $19.95)

Documentary Superstars
By *Marsha McCreadie* (6 x 9, 256 pages, paperback, $19.95)

The Directors: Take Four
By *Robert J. Emery* (6 x 9, 256 pages, paperback, $22.95)

Directing for Film and Television
By *Christopher Lukas* (6 x 9, 256 pages, paperback, $24.95)

The Art of Motion Picture Editing
By *Vincent LoBrutto* (6 x 9, 280 pages, paperback, $24.95)

Technical Film and TV for Nontechnical People
By *Drew Campbell* (6 x 9, 256 pages, paperback, $24.95)

The Screenwriter's Legal Guide
By *Stephen Breimer* (6 x 9, 336 pages, paperback, $19.95)

To see our complete catalog or to order online, please visit www.allworth.com.